DATE DUE

			PRINTED IN U.S.A.

GREAT ARTISTS OF THE WESTERN WORLD

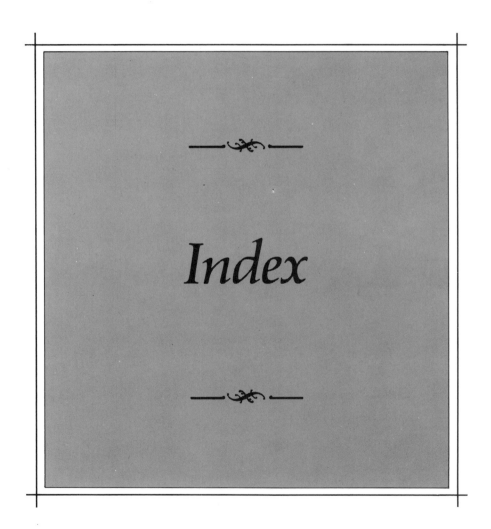

Index

GREAT ARTISTS OF THE WESTERN WORLD II

Thirty-six of the great Masters of Western art in nine
thematic volumes:

1 The Early Renaissance
Giotto di Bondone Fra Angelico
Giovanni Bellini Sandro Botticelli

2 The Northern Renaissance
Albrecht Dürer Lucas Cranach
Hans Holbein Pieter Bruegel

3 The Baroque Tradition
Caravaggio Diego Velázquez
Anthony Van Dyck Jacob van Ruisdael

4 Romanticism
Francisco de Goya William Blake
Caspar David Friedrich Eugène Delacroix

5 Post-Impressionism
Paul Cézanne Paul Gauguin
Vincent van Gogh Georges Seurat

6 Fantasy and Surrealism
Henri Rousseau Paul Klee
Marc Chagall Salvador Dalí

7 Abstract Artists
Wassily Kandinsky Kasimir Malevich
Joan Miró Bridget Riley

8 Social Commentators
William Hogarth Gustave Courbet
Henri de Toulouse-Lautrec Diego Rivera

9 Symbolism
Dante Gabriel Rossetti Odilon Redon
Gustav Klimt Edvard Munch

GREAT ARTISTS OF THE WESTERN WORLD

Index

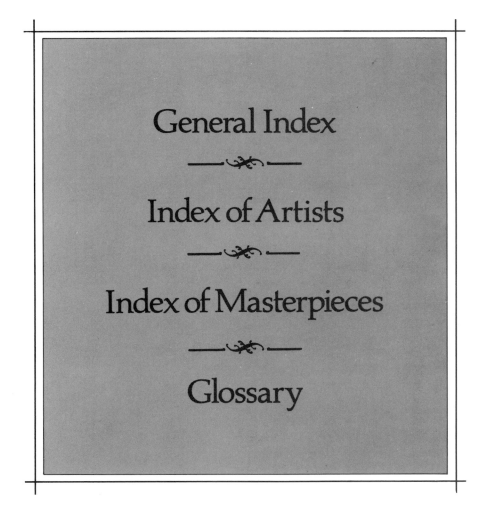

General Index

Index of Artists

Index of Masterpieces

Glossary

MARSHALL CAVENDISH·LONDON·NEW YORK·SYDNEY

Staff Credits

Editors	Clive Gregory LLB Sue Lyon BA (Honours)	**Picture Researchers**	Vanessa Fletcher BA (Honours) Flavia Howard BA (Honours) Jessica Johnson BA
Art Editors	Chris Legee BFA Kate Sprawson BA (Honours) Keith Vollans LSIAD	**Production Controllers**	Tom Helsby Alan Stewart BSc
Deputy Editor	John Kirkwood BSc (Honours)	**Secretary**	Lynn Smail
Sub-editors	Caroline Bugler BA (Honours), MA Sue Churchill BA (Honours) Alison Cole BA, MPhil Jenny Mohammadi Nigel Rodgers BA (Honours), MA Penny Smith Will Steeds BA (Honours), MA	**Editorial Director**	Maggi McCormick
		Publishing Manager	Robert Paulley BSc
		Managing Editor	Alan Ross BA (Honours)
Designers	Stuart John Julie Stanniland	**Consultant and Authenticator**	Sharon Fermor BA (Honours) Lecturer in the Extra-Mural Department of London University and Lecturer in Art History at Sussex University

Reference Edition Published 1988

Published by Marshall Cavendish Corporation
147 West Merrick Road
Freeport, Long Island
N.Y. 11520

Typeset by Litho Link Ltd., Welshpool
Printed and Bound by Dai Nippon
Printing Co., Hong Kong Ltd.

Library of Congress Cataloging-in-Publication Data

Main entry under title:

Great Artists of the Western World II.

Includes index.
1. Artists – Biography. I. Marshall Cavendish Corporation
N40. G774 1988   709'.2'2 [B]   88–4317
ISBN 0–86307–900–8 (set)

ISBN 0–86307–900–8 (set)
0–86307–754–4 (vol)

Contents

How to use the index ——————————— 6

General Index ———————————————— 7

Index of Artists ———————————————— 26

A Glossary in Pictures ——————————— 49

THE PLATES

The Madonna and Child with St Anne (Masaccio) ——————— 49

Portrait of Anne of Cleves (Holbein) ———————— 50

A Woman, known as Mrs Holland (Hilliard) ——————— 51

The Discovery of the Body of St Mark (Tintoretto) ——————— 52

Bacchus and his Companions (Caravaggio) ——————— 53

The Avenue at Middelharnis (Hobbema) ——————— 54

The Horses of San Marco in the Piazzetta (Canaletto) ——————— 55

The Bathers (Fragonard) ———————————— 56

The Sleeping Spinner (Courbet) ——————— 57

The Great Oak (Ruisdael) ——————— 58

The Bathing Posts (Whistler) ——————— 59

The Rehearsal (Degas) ——————— 60

Riders on the Beach (Gauguin) ——————— 61

Argenteuil (Manet) ——————————— 62

Elasticity (Boccioni) ——————————— 63

Madonna (Munch) ——————————— 64

Index of Masterpieces ———————————— 65

Glossary ——————————————————— 74

How To Use
The Index

The following pages are a complete index to volumes 1 to 9 of **Great Artists of the Western World II.** The index is divided into three sections: a General Index, an Index of Artists, and an Index of Masterpieces. This volume also contains a Glossary of art terms, illustrated by sixteen colour plates.

The General Index
This index includes entries on all topics – people, countries, technical terms and historical events, as well, of course, as art and artists – that appear in **Great Artists of the Western World II.** Where possible, people are indexed under surnames; where this is inappropriate (for example, Louis XIV, King of France), the person is listed under his or her most familiar name. Works of art such as books, plays and movies are also listed in this index. Portraits and self-portraits are indexed under the sitter's name as appropriate, though other paintings and sculptures are listed in the Index of Masterpieces. Famous names in other fields of art are also listed in this index, but for painters and sculptors, turn immediately to the Index of Artists.

The Index of Artists
In this section, all fine artists (painters and sculptors) appearing in the nine volumes are listed; other artists – writers, architects, etc. – are not included here, but in the General Index. Fine artists are indexed under their main surname – for example: Botticelli, Sandro; Klee, Paul; Gogh, Vincent van – but where this does not apply, the artists are indexed under their best-known names – for example: Raphael Sanzio; Giotto di Bondone. Each entry is followed by detailed subentries on the artist's life and works; the works themselves are listed alphabetically at the end of the subentries.

The Index of Masterpieces
This index lists paintings and sculptures alphabetically from Abbey in the Oakwoods (Friedrich) to Zing I (Riley); other works of art can be found in the General Index. Portraits and self-portraits are listed alphabetically by sitter under the entries, 'Portraits' and 'Self-portraits'. Each work of art is followed by the artist's name in parentheses.

The Glossary
In this section there are definitions of nearly two hundred terms used in the art world, including explanations of movements in, or Schools of, art, definitions of technical terms, and descriptions of specialist equipment. Sixteen of the Glossary entries are explained in greater detail and are illustrated on pages 49 to 64 by colour plates of the works of some of the great Masters of Western art.

Using the Index
The number immediately following an entry is the number of the relevant volume. This is followed by a colon and then the page numbers on which the entry appears. If an entry can also be found in other volumes, these volume and page numbers are printed in numerical order and are separated by a semi-colon. Page numbers which refer to illustrations are printed in italics in all three indexes, as are titles of works of art. The thirty-six artists who are featured in **Great Artists of the Western World II** are printed in **bold type,** both in the General Index and in the Index of Artists.

General Index

A

Aachen 2:*16-17*
Abraham, Karl 6:71
abstract art 7:18-20
 comparisons of 7:116, *116*
 emergence of 9:71
 first artist *see* Kandinsky, Wassily
Abstract Expressionist Exhibition, London: Riley and 7:109
abstraction, experiments with 7:52, *52*
Abul Hassan 1:138
Académie des Beaux-Arts: Delacroix and 4:113
 Manet and 5:98
Académie Française, recognition of 3:*104, 106*
academy of art, Antwerp, Van Gogh and 5:78
Academy of Art, Madrid, Goya and 4:12
Academy of San Carlos, Rivera at 8:108, 119
Academy of St Luke, Rome *see* Accademia di San Luca
Accademia di San Luca 3:13
 and Velázquez 3:49
Act in Restraint of Appeals (1533) 2:105
ADLAN *see Amics de l'Art Nou*
Adler, Alfred 6:71
 theories 6:71
Afghanistan: Russian invasion of 5:137
 capture of Kabul 2:72
Africa: Herero uprising (1904) 9:74, *74*
Agnese, Battista, map by 2:*41*

'AICA Critics' Prize', Riley and 7:111
Aix-la-Chapelle, Peace of (1748) 8:40-41, *40-41*
Akbar the Great, Mogul Emperor of India 2:*137*
Alba, Duchess of 4:*15*
 and Goya 4:14, 15
Albania, revolt in (1910) 6:41
Albert, Archduke 3:*41*
 and Battle of Nieuwpoort (1600) 3:*41*
Albert, Prince Consort 4:72
Albert, Josef *see Artists' Index*
Alberti, Leon Battista *see Artists' Index*
Alenza, Leonardo *see Artists' Index*
Alexander I, Tsar of Russia, and Napoleon 4:42
Alexander III, Tsar of Russia 8:103
Alexander VI, Pope: and alliance with Naples 1:105-106
 and Savonarola 1:112-13, 135
 denunciation by 1:104
Alexandra, Empress of Russia 7:69
 Rasputin and 7:*68*, 69
Alexis, Paul, by Cézanne 5:*14*
Alfonso of Naples, marriage of 1:106
Ali Pasha 4:*133*
Alighieri, Dante *see* Dante Alighieri
All Souls College, Oxford University 1:74
allotments 4:*73*
Almagro, Diego de 2:105
Alphonso XIII, King of Spain, exile of 7:100

Alps, effect on Bruegel 2:110, *110-11*
altarpieces: by Gozzoli 1:49
 influences on 14th-century Italian 1:17, *17*
 see also individual names
Altdorfer, Albrecht *see Artists's Index*
Alva, Duke of: atrocities 2:113
 invades the Low Countries 2:113, *136*, 136-7
America: anti-war protests 7:137
 Apollo 8 7:*136*
 'Atlantic Charter' (1941) 6:105
 Black Power 7:138
 and Niagara Falls: bridge 8:*71*
 buys 5:*136-7*
 circus in 5:133
 and Cuba 6:74
 detente in space 6:*136*, 138
 end of prohibition (1933) 6:*73*
 Flower Children 7: *135*
 and Germany 7:104
 Gold Rush (1848) 8:*70*
 golf in 5:*135*
 and Latin/South America 4:136-7; 6:74
 and Mexican Revolution 8:34-5
 Lend Lease Act 6:105
 'Monkey Trial' 7:106
 Oklahoma settled 5:*72-3*
 and overthrow of the Tsar 7:70
 and the Panama Canal 9:*104-105*
 Pearl Harbor attacked (1941) 6:*104-105*, 106
 Pueblo incident 7:138
 Revolution, in (1775) 4:*66*, 66-7
 slavery laws 4:39
 Spiritualism in 9:*40-41*

Statue of Liberty presented to 5:*137*, 138
 student riots 7:137
 war in Vietnam 7:137
 withdrawal from 6:136-7, *137*
 Washington monument 5:138
 Watergate 6:138, *138*
Amics de l'Art Nou 6:135, *135*
Amigoni, Jacopo *see Artists' Index*
anarchy, growth of 8:68-9, *69*
Anarchy, Malevich and 7:47
anatomy: 17th-century study of 3:*132-3*, 134
 Botticelli and 1:113
Anatomy of the Universe 3:134
anecdotes, moralizing, Bruegel's use of 2:115
Andreewsky, Nina de 7:16
Anguissola, Sofonista, by Van Dyck 3:*80*
'animalcules' 3:134
animals in art 6:36-9
 the Unicorn 6:*36-7*, 38
Anjou, Philip Duc d' 3:*138*
'Anna O' 6:69
Annah the Javanese, Gauguin and 5:49, *49*
Anne of Austria 3:137, 138
Anne of Cleves 2:81, *83*
 by Holbein 2:*83*; 10:*50*
Annual Register, on 1808 4:39
Annunciations, comparisons in painting 1:53
Anquetin, Louis *see Artists' Index*
Apollinaire, Guillaume 6:101
 by his mistress (Laurencin) 6:*103*
 Chagall and 6:79
 Rousseau and 6:16-17, *17*
 on working method 6:18

Apollo/Soyuz link-up 6:*136*
  details 5:*22, 23*
apprenticeships:
  Blake's 4:45, *45,* 50
  Botticelli's 1:109, *109*
  Bruegel's 2:108-109
  Caravaggio's 3:12
  Chagall's 6:76, 77
  Dürer's 2:12, 37, 39
  Giotto's 1:12-13
  Goya's 4:12
  Hogarth's 8:12
  Holbein the Younger's 2:76
  Van Dyck's 3:76
  Velázquez' 3:44-5
aquatint, Goya and 4:21
Aragon, Louis, Miró and 7:77
Aratori, Lucia 3:12
Archbishop of Florence, post of 1:48
archetypes/symbols, comparisons of 6:52, *52*
Archipenko, Alexander *see Artists' Index*
architecton (Malevich) 7:*51*
architecture: Gothic Revival 4:98, 99
  Strawberry Hill 4:*99*
  Venetian 1:*100*
Arena Chapel, Padua 1:14-15, *15, 24*
  architect of? 1:17
  decorative plan 1:*25*
  frescoes in 1:22-3
    details 1:*18, 24-5*
Ariosto, Ludovico: on Giovanni Bellini 1:79
  Orlando Furioso 2:105
Aramana Prouvencau, L' 5:36
Arosa, Gustave, Gauguin and 5:45
Arp, Jean (Hans) *see Artists' Index*
Arpino, Cavaliere d', and Caravaggio 3:*12,* 13
Art Academy, Besançon, Courbet at 8:45
Art Academy, Frankfurt, Courbet at 8:48
Art Academy of Parma competition 4:13
Art Brut, Miró and 7:84
Art Deco, launching of 7:106
art movements, 20th-century, foundations of 5:20
  see also Dada; Surrealism etc.
Art Nouveau: German name for *see* 'Jugendstil'
  Kandinsky and 7:19
  waning of Viennese 9:*80-81,* 81
art theory, Dürer and 2:21
Artaud, Antonin, Miró and 7:77
Arthur, Prince of Wales 1:*104*
Artigas, Joseph Llorens *see Artists' Index*

Artistes Indépendants *see* Société des Artistes Indépendants
artists: as propagandists 2:80
  status in medieval society 1:44
  Dürer and 2:14, 16
Arts and Crafts, Klimt and 9:84
Arundel, Earl and Countess of, and Van Dyck 3:77
astronomy, in the 17th century 3:*132-3,* 134
assistants: Botticelli's 1:110
  Fra Angelico's use of 1:47
  Giotto's use of 1:16
Aubert, Anne Elizabeth 5:12
Australia: Commonwealth of 5:*40*
  crossing of the outback 9:*41*
Austria: and the Balkans (1910) 6:41
  concessions to Hungary 8:72
  dissolution of the Nazi Party 6:73
  and Greek revolt (1824) 4:135-6
  Mayerling scandal 5:*70*
  and Peace of Aix-la-Chapelle (1748) 8:40-41
  terrorism in 6:137-8
  Vienna: artistic groups in 9:100-101
    cultural life of 9:82
    storming the barricades 8:*70-71*
  War of the Austrian Succession (1740-48) 8:41
  war with Serbia (1914) 9:105
  and World War I 9:105-106
auto da fé 4:*36,* 36-7, *37*
avant-garde: in Barcelona 6:135
  Courbet and 8:45
  Kandinsky and 7:19
  Miró and 7:77
  and Phalanx group 7:15
  and Rousseau's works 6:15, 19
  Russian 7:16
    clampdown on 7:16
  Seurat and 5:110, *110*
Avanti, editor of 7:73
Avril, Jane 8:101
  by Toulouse-Lautrec 8:*90*
Azbe, Anton, Kandinsky and 7:14
Aztec Empire, fall of (1519) 2:42, 72

B

Baader-Meinhof gang, West Germany 6:138
Baburen, Dirck van *see Artists' Index*
'bachelor's year' 2:12
  Dürer's 2:12

backgrounds: in Bellini's works 1:82
  Caravaggio's use of 3:82
  Holbein and 2:84-5
  Van Dyck's use of 3:82
    architectural 3:83
Bacon, Francis *see Artists' Index*
Baden-Powell, Robert 5:41
  death of 6:106
Baglione, Giovanni *see Artists' Index*
Bahr, Hermann, on Vienna 9:100
Bailey, David 7:133, 134
Baille, Baptistan, Cézanne and 5:12
Bakst, Léon *see Artists' Index*
Bakunin, Mikhail 8:68-9
Baldung Grien, Hans *see Artists' Index*
Baldwin, Stanley, Prime Minister 7:107
Balen, Hendrick van *see Artists' Index*
Ball, Hugo, 6:47
  Klee and 6:47
Bandini, Smeralda, by Botticelli 1:*115*
Bangladesh 6:*136,* 138
Barber-Surgeon's Company, commission for Holbein 2:81
Barcelona School for Fine Arts *see* La Lonja
Barentsz, Jacob, voyages of 3:135
Bardi Chapel, Florence 1:16
Bargues technique 5:82
Barnard, Dr Christiaan 7:138
Barnum, Phineas T. 5:133
Barrie, J. M.: *Peter Pan* 9:74
Basilica of St Francis of Assisi 1:39
  Cimabue and 1:13
  problems of authenticating frescoes 1:14-15
Basilica del Santo, high altar (detail) 1:*77*
Basire, James, Blake and 4:45, *45*
Bath, Dowager Duchess of 9:15
Bastista, Fulgencio 6:74
Battenberg, Prince Henry of 5:138
'Battle of the Nations' (Leipzig, 1813) 4:105
Baud, 'Père' Courbet and 8:44
Baudelaire, Charles 5:99
  Courbet and 8:45
    portrait by 8:*46*
  on Delacroix 4:111
  theory formed by 9:69
  Le Salut Public 8:46-7
Bauhaus, The 6:46, 47; 7:36-9
  attacks on 7:38-9
  closure of 7:39
  crafts at 7:*38-9*
    importance of 7:39

declaration of intentions 7:36
  at Dessau 7:*37,*38
  financial success of 7:39
  funds cut off 7:38
  growing hostility to 6:48
  hounding of 7:17
  Kandinsky and 7:16-17
  Klee and 6:46
  Malevich and 7:49
  1923 exhibition 7:37
  research behind design 7:39
  staff of 6:*48;* 7:36-7
  student unrest 7:39
  unifying the arts 7:*38-9*
Bayeu, Francisco *see Artists' Index*
Bayeu, Josefa 4:13
  death of 4:16
  by Goya 4:*12*
Beardsley, Aubrey *see Artists' Index*
Beatles, The 7:*133,* 133-4, 138
Beaumont, Francis 3:102
Beckford, William 4:100
  Fonthill Abbey 4:*100, 101*
  Vathek: an Arabian Tale 4:100-101
Beckmann, Max *see Artists' Index*
Beethoven, Ludwig van 4:40
Belgium: and the Congo 5:*135*
  see also Low Countries, The
Belin, Zuan *see* Bellini, Giovanni
Bell, Alexander Graham 7:42
Bellini family *see Artists' Index*
Bellini, Gentile *see Artists' Index*
Bellini, Giovanni *see Artists' Index*
Bellini, Jacopo *see Artists' Index*
Bellini, Niccolosia 1:77
Bellio, Dr de, Pissarro and 5:99
Bellori: on Caravaggio and the Knights of Malta 3:16
  on Van Dyck 3:78, 79
    description of 3:81
    life-style in London 3:80-81
Beloff, Angeline 8:109
Bellmer, Hans *see Artists' Index*
Bembo, Cardinal Pietro, on Bellini's delaying tactics 1:80
Benedetto da Maiano *see Artists' Index*
Benedict XI, Pope: and Arena Chapel 1:14-15
  and Giotto 1:15-16
Bennett, Alan 7:135
Berchem, Nicholas, Ruisdael and 3:110
Berlin Academy, Friedrich and 4:80
Berlin Secession 9:*134*
  founders of 9:135
Bernard, Emile *see Artists' Index*
Bernardone, Giovanni *see* St Francis of Assisi
Bernadone, Pietro 1:36

Bernhardt, Sarah 8:*106*
Bernini, Gianlorenzo *see Artists' Index*
Bertoldo, and Michelangelo 1:*113*
Bessemers, Mayken Verhulst 2:111
   and Bruegel's sons 2:112
bestiaries, medieval 6:38
Bevans, Reginald 7:135
Bewick, Thomas *see Artists' Index*
Binet, Virginie 8:45, 48
Binsenstock, Elsbeth 2:77
   by Holbein 2:*79*
Black Death *see* plague
Blaen, Willem Jansz 3:135
Blake, Admiral 3:72
Blake, Peter *see Artists' Index*
Blake, Robert 4:45
Blake, William *see Artists' Index*
Blaue Reiter group 6:45, 47; 7:*14-15*
   and colour 6:45, 51
   exhibitions: intention of 7:15
      styles at 7:15
   founding of 7:15, *15*
   inspiration of 6:45
   Kandinsky and 7:15
   Klee and 6:45
      exhibits with 6:45
Bligh, Captain 5:*66*
block-making, Morris and 9:34
'blockbooks' 2:*37*
Blondin 5:132
blood: 17th-century discoveries about 3:134
   transfusion 5:70
blue pigment, amount specified in contracts 1:50
Boccaccio, on Giotto's art 1:18
Boccioni, Umberto *see Artists' Index*
Böcklin, Arnold *see Artists' Index*
bodegones 3:50-51
Boerhaave, Hermannus 3:134, *133-4*
Bohemia, Swedish invasion of (1648) 3:*137*
Böhm, Adolf *see Artists' Index*
Boitard, Clémence 6:13, *14*
   death of 6:14
Boleyn, Anne 2:78, 104
   execution of 2:79
Boleyn, Thomas, by Holbein 2:*85*
Bolivar, Simon 4:*138*
Bonaparte, Joseph 4:*39*, 42
Bonar Law, Andrew, Prime Minister 7:41
Bondone, Giotto di *see* **Giotto di Bondone**
Boniface VIII, Pope 1:*40*
   commission for Giotto 1:13-14
   failure of foreign policy 1:41

imprisonment of 1:42
   issues Papal Bull 1:41
   megalomania of 1:40-41
Bonington, Richard Parkes *see Artists' Index*
Bonnard, Pierre *see Artists' Index*
Bonnat, Leon *see Artists' Index*
book design (Böhm) 9:*102*
books: first great illustrated *see Nuremberg Chronicle*
   status of printed 1:116
Bora, Katherine von 2:71
Borgia, Cesare 1:105, 106
Borgia, Juan, Duke of Gandia 1:105
   created Duke of Benevento 1:106
   death of 1:*105*, 106
Borgia, Lucretia 1:105, *105*
   divorce proceedings 1:105-106
Borgias, the 1:104-106
   emblem of 1:*105*
Borgia pope *see* Alexander VI, Pope
Bosch, Hieronymus *see Artists' Index*
Boschini, Marco, on Velázquez 3:47
Boswell, James, in London 8:38-9
Bosworth, Battle of (1485) 2:100
Botha, Louis 6:42
Bothwell, Earl of 2:138
Botticelli, Sandro *see Artists' Index*
Boucher, Alfred, and La Ruche 6:100
Boucher, Catherine 4:45
Bougainville, Louis Antoine de 5:67
Bouger, André, and Redon 9:49
Boulanger, General 5:*102*, 104-106
Boullan, Abbé, Huysmans and 9:71
Bounty, mutiny on the (1789) 5:*66*
Bourdichon, Jean *see Artists' Index*
Bourges, Doctor Henri: Toulouse-Lautrec and 8:78
   portrait by 8:*79*
Braithwaite Martineau, Robert *see Artists' Index*
Brandenburg, Cardinal Albrecht of: and Cranach 2:48
   and Grünewald 2:48
Brandenburg, Elector of, and defeat of the Polish army (1656) 3:74, *74*
Brant, Sebastian: *Ship of Fools* 2:115
   Bruegel's use of 2:115
Braque, Georges *see Artists' Index*
Bratby, John *see Artists' Index*

Brazil, royal status 4:*106*
Brengbier, Barbara 2:45
Breschi (anarchist) 5:42
Brest-Litovsk, Treaty of (1918) 7:71
Breton, André 6:*110*
   Dali and 6:110
      attacks on politics 6:116
         charges against 6:112
   and Klee 6:47
   Miró and 7:77, 78
      denounces Miró and Ernst 7:78-9
      nickname for 6:113
      and Surrealism 6:111; 7:77
   Rivera and 8:113, *113*
   and Surrealism 6:114
      description of 6:114
      First Surrealist Manifesto 6:114
Breton, Jacqueline 8:113, *113*
Breuer, Josef, Freud and 6:68
Breuer, Marcel, and The Bauhaus 7:38
Briand, Aristide 6:40
Brik, Osip and Lili 7:73
Brisson, M, 5:136
Britain: and Afghanistan 5:137
   alliance with Russia (1941) 6:105
   and anarchist bomb attack (1894) 8:104
   Artists' Rifle Corps 9:42
   Atlantic Charter 6:105
   attacks on the Church 9:40
   birth of the BBC 7:42
   Blackpool Tower 8:*104-105*
   and Burma 4:*136-7*
   Chartist movement 8:*70*
   circus in 5:130-31, 133
   Combination Acts 4:135
   Common Market referendum 6:138
   Corn Laws 4:*103*
   Darwin debate 9:39-40
   Dogger Bank incident (1904) 9:73-4
   effects of war on 6:106
   and Fascism 6:73
   first Jewish peer 5:138
   Football League 5:104
   and France 5:106
      attitude to 8:104
      Entente Cordiale (1904) 9:*72*, 72-3
   foundation of National Gallery 4:*136-7*
   and Germany 5:106
   Gordon Riots 8:37
   Gothic Revival in 4:99, *99*
   and Greek War of Independence 4:135-6
   Home Rule Bill for Ireland (1914) 9:104

and India 8:41
      clashes with the French 8:*40*
      Government of India Act (1921) 8:*138*
   invasion scare 9:41
   Irish Question 9:104
   and Locarno Conference 7:104
   London: Dock Strike 5:74, *74*
      in Hogarth's time 8:36-9
      'Tube' the 5:*42*
   the Navy in 1808 4:40-41
   and North America 8:*40*, 41
   oil exploration 6:138
   Open Golf Championship 9:*40-41*
   'People's Budget' 6:*40*, 40-41
   'People's Convention' 6:106
   political activists in 4:66-9
   political crisis in (1909-10) 6:40-41
   protests against income tax 8:73-4
   race relations in 7:138
   refugees in 8:73
   restriction in the House of Lords 6:41
   Rolls-Royce formed 9:74
   and Spain: alliance with (1808) 4:42
      war with 4:*15*
   Spiritualism in 9:40-41
   and the Sudan 5:*134*, 136
   Suffragette movement 9:104-105, *106*
   the Swinging Sixties 7:132-5
   terrorism in 6:137
   Thames water 8:*72-3*
   Tower Bridge opens 8:*102*
   trams 9:39
   visit by King and Queen of Hawaii 4:138
   war with Turkey 7:72
   weather in 1860 9:39, 42
   workers' unrest in (1819) 4:71, 72-4
   and World War I 7:72-4
      Expeditionary Force 9:106
      recruitment propaganda 9:*104*
   in World War II 6:104-106
   see also England, Northern Ireland, Scotland
Brod, Max 7:106
Brodsky, Valentine 6:81
Brook, Peter: *Marat/Sade* 7:135
Brougham, Lord 5:36
Brouwer, Adriaen *see Artists' Index*
Brown, Ford Maddox *see Artists' Index*
Browning pistol 5:42
Bruant, Aristide 8:79, *100*
   by Toulouse-Lautrec 8:84, *91*
Brücke, Die: founders of 9:*138*

Munch and 9:117
Bruegel, Pieter, *see Artists' Index*
Brueghel, Jan, *see Artists' Index*
Brueghel, Pieter, the Younger, *see Artists' Index*
Brunelleschi, Filippo *see Artists' Index*
Bruno, Giordano 3:40, *40*
brush wash, Goya's use of 4:21
brushwork: Bellini's: effect of oil painting on 1:84
    Malevich's, in early works 7:50
Bruyas, Alfred: art collection 8:48
    commissions for portraits 8:48
    and Courbet 8:48
        portrait by 8:48
Bryant, Jacob: *New System of Mythology* 4:45
Buchan, John: *The Thirty-Nine Steps 7:74*
Buchon, Max: Courbet and 8:45
    exiled 8:48
Buckingham, George, Duke of 3:100
    assassination of 3:101
Bugenhagen, Johannes 2:69
Bulgaria, and World War I 7:73
Buller, Sir Redvers 5:40
Buñuel, Luis 6:*111*
    Dalí and 6:108, 135
    Un Chien Andalou 6:108, *111*, 135
    L'Age d'or 6:*111*
buon fresco 1:23
    see also fresco secco
burin, metal 2:20
Burliuk, David, and Futurism 7:46
Burne-Jones, Edward *see Artists' Index*
Burton, Sir Richard: *The Arabian Nights* 5:*135*
Butler, Samuel: *Hudibras* 8:20
Butts, Thomas 4:*48*
    and Blake 4:47-8
Byron, Lord 4:*131*, 135
    death of 4:133, *133*
    Delacroix and 4:111
Byzantine art/tradition: Giotto and 1:18

C

Cabot, John 1:*104*
Caillaux, Joseph 9:105
Cain and Abel 4:54, *54*
Cairo Conference (1921) 8:*136-7*
Calderon, Pedro 1:106
Calmette, Gaston 9:105
Calvert, Edward *see Artists' Index*

Calvinism, rise of 2:137
Cambio, Arnolfo, di, designs by 1:*40*
Campanile, Florence, Giotto and 1:*16*, 17
Campen, Jacob van: *Stadhuis, Amsterdam* 3:*137*
Campo Santo, Pisa, frescoes in 1:49
Canada: Canadian-Pacific Railway 5:*137*
    new Parliament buildings 9:*42*
    sells Niagara Falls (1885) 5:*136-7*
Caracciolo, Giovanni Battista *see Artists' Index*
Caravaggio *see Artists' Index*
Caravaggisti, The 3:36-9
    bias against 3:39
    brushwork 3:38
    greatest 3:39
Carducho, Vincenzo, on Caravaggio 3:39
Carew, Thomas 3:102
Carmelites, in Florence 1:68
Carnarvon, Lord 7:42
cassoni 1:115
    Botticelli and 1:110, 115
Carnot, Sadi, assassination of 8:*104*, 105
Carpaccio, Vittore *see Artists' Index*
Carranza, Venustiano 8:134
Carson, Sir Edward 9:104
Carter, Howard 7:42
Carus, Karl Gustav *see Artists' Index*
carving, Gauguin and 5:53
Casals, Pau 6:132, *133*
Casas, Ramon *see Artists' Index*
'Catch-me-who-can' 4:42
Caterina Cornaro, Queen of Cyprus 1:*103*
Catherine of Aragon 2:103, *103*, 104
    marriages 1:*104*
Catholic Church: corruption in 2:69-70
    and Luther 2:70-71
Cavallini, Pietro *see Artists' Index*
Cendrars, Blaise 6:101
    Chagall and 6:*78*, 79
    by Modigliani 6:*78*
ceramics: Chagall and 6:80, 81, *81*
    Miró and 7:80, 81
    Suetin and 7:48, *48*
Cervantes, Miguel de: *Don Quixote* 2:72
Cesari, Giuseppe, and Caravaggio 3:13
Cézanne, Louis-Auguste 5:12, *13, 16*
Cézanne, Paul *see Artists' Index*

Cha-U-Kao 5:*132*; 8:101
    by Toulouse-Lautrec 8:*97*
Chagall, Marc *see Artists' Index*
chalks, Holbein's use of 2:83
chambers of rhetoric *see rederijkkamer*
Chambre Ardente 2:74
Champfleury, Jules: breaks with friends 8:48
    Courbet and 8:45
Charcot, Jean-Martin, Freud and 6:68
Charles I, King of England 3:*100*,100-103
    abuse of Parliament 3:100-101, 100-103, 104-5
    court of 3:*101*
    execution of (1649) 3:138
    family 3:102
        by Van Dyck 3:*83*, 96-7
    position as prisoner 3:138
    in Spain 3:*69*, 100
    The Eikon Basilike 3:*103*
Charles II, King of Naples 1:41
Charles III, King of Spain: commission for Goya 4:13
Charles IV, King of Spain: abdication of 4:14, 41
    and Goya 4:13, 14, *14*
    popularity of 4:41
Charles V, Emperor: and Brussels 2:112
    coronation of in Aachen (1520) 2:17, *17*
        Dürer at 2:17
    and Council of Trent 2:73, *73*
    and Diet of Worms 2:41
    dominions of 2:72
    and Henry VIII's divorce 2:103
    and Luther 2:70
    and the Schmalkaldic League 2:73-4
Charles VII, King of France 1:73
Charles VIII, King of France: and Kingdom of Naples 1:111-112
Charles X, King of France 4:137
    coronation of 4:*137*
Charles X, King of Sweden 3:74
    and defeat of Polish army (1656) 3:74, *74*
Charles, Prince of Denmark 9:136
Charles Robert of Anjou 1:41
Charles de Valois, and revolt in Florence 1:42
Charter House, Wells Cathedral 1:42
Chassériau, Theodore *see Artists' Index*
Chatterton, Thomas 4:*100-101*, 101
Chekov, Anton: *The Cherry Orchard* 9:74

Cheron, Louis, Hogarth and 8:13
Chevreul, Eugène, on colour 4:117
chiaroscuro, Caravaggio and 3:20, *20*
Chiesa del Monte della Misericordia, paintings for 3:37
child labour 4:*70*
Chimiakin, Anja 7:13
China: Boxer Rebellion 5:*41*, 41-2
    end of Manchu dynasty 5:42
    invasion of Annam 5:135-6
Chirico, Giorgio de *see Artists' Index*
Chocquet, Victor: Cézanne and 5:34, 99
    and Renoir 5:99
Chopin, Frédéric 4:113, 116
    Delacroix and 4:112
        portrait by 4:*112*
Christian I, King of Denmark 1:*137*
Christian II, King of Denmark-Norway 2:*42*
    and Cranach 2:49
'Christian Elysium' 1:*83*
Christian, Fletcher 5:*66*
Christina of Denmark 2:81
    by Holbein 2:*98*
Christianity, and animals in art 6:37-8
Christopher, Duke of Bavaria pilgrimage of 2:44
'Christ's Bible' 4:77
Churchill, Charles, Hogarth and 8:17
Churchill, Winston 6:105
Cima da Conegliano, Giovanni Battista *see Artists' Index*
Cimabue *see Artists' Index*
circus 5:130-3
Clarence, George, Duke of, death of (1478) 1:*138*, *138*
Clark, Daniel 8:39
classical art: influence on Cimabue 1:12 revival of 1:18
Classicism, Rivera and 8:114
Clavaud, Armand: death of 9:48
    Redon and 9:45, 46
        portrait by 9:*46-7*
Clément, Rousseau and 6:13-14
Clement VII, Pope 2:*104*
    and Henry VIII's divorce 2:103
Cleopatra's Needle 4:73
Clericis Laicos 1:41
Clot, Auguste, Munch and 9:112, 116
Clouet, François *see Artists' Index*
Clovio, Guilio, and Bruegel 2:109
clown, the first 5:*131*
'Club of Seven' 9:100
Cochrane, Mr 8:73-4

Cock, Jerome *see Artists' Index*
Cocteau, Jean 5:132; 6:101
Coecke, Mayken 2:108, 111
Coecke van Aelst, Pieter *see Artists' Index*
Cohn-Bendit, Daniel 7:136
'College for the New Art, The', Vitebsk 7:48
Collins, Michael 7:42; 8:138
Collins, Wilkie 9:40-41
The Woman in White 9:40-41
colour: Bellini's technique with 1:84, 85
    Chagall and 6:78, 83
        'violet' pictures 6:83
    comparisons with light 7:20, 20
    Fra Angelico's skill with 1:50-51
    Gauguin and: changes in use of 5:50
        revolutionary use of 5:51
    Van Gogh and: changes his palette 5:82
        exaggerating 5:83, 83-4
    Kandinsky and 7:15, 18-19
        characteristics of 7:20
        early influences on 7:19
            of the Impressionists 7:13
        potential of 7:19
        relationships to shape 7:20
        theories about 7:16, 20
        'white' 7:37
    Klee and 6:51-2; 7:37
        as independent element 6:51
        influence of Delaunay 6:45
        in last works 6:52
        'orchestrating' 6:51
        preparation for 6:45
        writing on 6:46
    Malevich and: in early works 7:50
        in Suprematist works 7:52
    Munch and: critisism of use of 9:114
        symbolic use of 9:110
    Redon and 9:48
        bolder use of 9:49
        influence of Gauguin on 9:48
        writing on 9:49
    Riley and: ancient Egyptian 7:110-11, 112
        broadens her palette 7:111
        influence of Van Gogh 7:109
        influence of Seurat 7:110
        introduction of 7:115
        mixing 7:112, 115
        monochrome palette 7:110-111
        new inspiration 7:112-13
        standards for selecting 7:116-17

Rousseau and 6:21
    mood set by 6:21
    use of tones 6:21
Seurat and: effects of faulty materials 5:114
    mastering black and white 5:113
    'optical mixture' 5:112-14
Toulouse-Lautrec and: in later works 8:84
    number used in lithographs 8:82
Venetian fascination for 1:82
Commerson, Philibert, on the Tahitians 5:67
Commissar of Art for Vitebsk 6:79
Compagnia di San Luca, Botticelli and 1:109, 113
Compagnie des Isles d'Amérique 3:104
Condé, Prince de: and the Fronde 3:138
    and war with Spain 3:136-7, 137
Confessions of the Lutheran Faith 2:71
'Congress System' 4:135
Congress of Vienna (1815) 4:103-104
Conrad, Joseph 9:72
    Nostromo 9:72, 74
Constable, John *see Artists' Index*
Constructivists, principles of 7:49
Contarelli Chapel: Caravaggio paintings for 3:14
    reason for rejection of 3:19
contrapposto 1:83
conversos 4:34-5
Cook, Captain James 5:66
    and Tahiti 5:67, 68
Coornhert, Dirck 2:111
copperplate, Dürer and 2:20, 21
copying, Blake and 4:45, 45
Coram, Captain Thomas 8:16
    by Hogarth 8:19, 21
Cormon, Fernand *see Artists' Index*
Cornforth, Fanny 9:15, 16, 21
    by Rossetti 9:15
Corneille, Pierre 3:104
    Médée 3:104
Cornelisdr, Maycken 3:108
Cortona, Pietro da *see Artists' Index*
Cortés, Hernando 2:72
    and the Aztec Empire 2:42
Cross, Henri Edmond *see Artists' Index*
Coubertin, Baron Pierre de 8:105
Council of Trent 2:73, 73
Council of Troubles (in the Netherlands) 2:138

Counter-Reformation: effect on church building 3:13-14
    tradition in painting during 3:18-19
Courbet, Gustave *see Artists' Index*
Courbet, Juliette 8:44
Courbet, Régis 8:44
    by Courbet 8:44
Coypel, Charles-Antoine *see Artists' Index*
Cranach, Hans *see Artists' Index*
Cranach, Lucas *see Artists' Index*
Cranach, Lucas the Younger *see Artists' Index*
Crane, Walter *see Artists' Index*
Cranmer, Thomas 2:105, 106
Cranmer's Bible, title page 2:102, 103
Crippin, Hawley Harvey 6:42, 42
Croker, John and Frances, by Hilliard 2:140
Cromwell, Oliver 3:72, 103
    curbs the House of Commons 3:73-4
Cromwell, Thomas: and Holbein 2:79, 80
    and Thomas More 2:79
    and the Tudor administration 2:101
Cronje, General 5:40
Crossman, Richard 6:138
Cruikshank, George *see Artists' Index*
Cuba: revolt in 6:74
Cubism: Chagall and 6:82, 83
    Klee and 6:51
    Miró and 7:82
        views on 6:83
    range of subjects 6:83
    Rivera and 8:114
Cumberland, George, Blake and 4:53
Cuspinian, Anna 2:45
Cuspinian, Dr Johannes 2:45
    by Cranach 2:45, 50
Cuypers, Maria 3:76
Czechoslovakia: Soviet takeover of (1968) 7:138, 138
    Sudeten German Party 6:73
    see also Bohemia

D

Dada: in Barcelona 6:135
    founders of 6:47
Dadd, Richard: *The Fairy Feller's Master Stroke* 6:84
Dahl, Johann Christian: and Dresden Academy 4:81
    Friedrich and 4:81, 85

Dalí, Salvador *see Artists' Index*
Dalmau, Joseph: and Dalí 6:109, 132
    gallery 7:77
    Miró and 7:77
Dante, Alighieri 1:71
    Divine Comedy 1:42, 42, 71
        Blake and 4:49, 53
        Botticelli and 1:112, 113, 116
        Reginaldo degli Scrovegni in 1:24
    exile from Florence 1:42
    on Giotto 1:14, 15
Darnley, Lord Henry, murder of 2:138, 138
Darwin, Charles 9:42
    discussions on ideas 9:39-40
'daughters of inspiration' 4:48-9
Daumier, Honoré *see Artists' Index*
Davy, Sir Humphry 4:105
de Gaulle, President 7:136-7
Debussy, Claude: *La Mer* 9:136
'decadence', fashion for 5:110
Decadent movement, Redon and 9:47
'Defender of the Faith' 2:42
Degas, Edgar *see Artists' Index*
Dehmel, Richard 9:134
Del Monte, Cardinal: and Caravaggio 3:13, 14-15
    palace of 3:13, 15
Delacroix, Charles 4:108, 109
    posts 4:108
Delacroix, Eugène *see Artists' Index*
Delacroix, Victoire 4:108
Delaunay, Robert *see Artists' Index*
Delaunay, Sonia *see Artists' Index*
Delvaux, Paul *see Artists' Index*
Denbigh, Lord 3:100
Denis, Maurice *see Artists' Index*
Denmark: Copenhagen University 1:137
Descartes, René, on Amsterdam 3:135
Desnos, Robert, Miró and 7:77
Désossé, Valentin 8:79, 82, 83, 101
'Developing Process Exhibition, The', Riley and 7:109
Deverell, Walter 9:15
devotional painting, comparisons 4:85, 85
Deza, Diego 4:36
Diaghilev, Serge: *Romeo and Juliet* 7:78
Díaz, Felix 8:134
    and Madero 8:132-3
Díaz, President Porfirio 8:108, 132
Diderot, Denis, on the Académie Française 3:106

Diet of Worms (1521) 2:40-41, 41
and Luther 2:70, 70-71
Dinteville, Jean de see
Ambassadors, The (Holbein)
Director of the Catheral Works,
Florence 1:16, 17
Dix, Otto see Artists' Index
Dobson, William see Artists'
Index
Doesburg, Theo van see Artists'
Index
Doge of Venice 1:100, 101
Doge's Palace: decorations in
Great Hall 1:78, 81
restoration of 1:77
Dominican Order: commitments
1:69
in Florence 1:68-71
influence of 1:46
on fresco-painting 1:19
mental discipline in painting
1:50
Observationist 1:70
principles of 1:70-71
reforming zeal of 1:46
and San Marco Monastery,
Florence 1:47, 47-8
Dominico, Giovanni: Lucula
Noctis 1:46
Donatello see Artists' Index
Donovan, Terence 7:134
Doré, Gustave see Artists' Index
Doring, Christian, and Cranach
2:49
Dorpat, University of,
Kandinsky and 7:13
Dos Passos, John: Manhattan
Transfer 7:106
Dostoevsky, Fyodor: The Devils
9:114
Dot, Admiral 5:133
Drake, Edwin L. 9:40
drama, comparison of moments
of 4:116
Dresden Academy: and Dahl
4:81
and Friedrich 4:81
Professor of landscape 4:81
Dresden, Battle of (1813) 4:80
Dresden Romantics 4:78
Dreyfus, Alfred 8:102, 103, 106
Dubcek, Alexander 7:138
Duccio di Buoninsegna see
Artists' Index
duelling 5:103, 104-105
Dumas, Alexandre, on Delacroix
4:108
Dumas, Jean-Baptiste 4:136
Dunlop, John Boyd 5:102
Dupleix, Joseph 8:40
Dupuis, Eugéne 5:105
Durand-Ruel: and the
Impressionists 5:100
Redon and 9:49

Dürer, Albrecht see Artists' Index
Dürer, Albrecht, the Elder:
trade 2:12
by Dürer 2:13
Dusseldorf Academy, Klee and
6:48
Dutch painting, comparison of
7:84, 84
Dutschke, Rudi 7:137
Dyck, Anthony van see Van
Dyck, Anthony
dyeing, Morris and 9:34, 36

E

Early Christian art, Cavallini
and 1:19
East India Company, Officer of
3:40
Eaton, Daniel 4:69
Ecole des Beaux-Arts: Cézanne
and 5:13
Delacroix and 4:109
Redon and 9:46
Seurat and 5:108
Edward, Prince of Wales (later
Edward VII) 8:81
assassination attempt on 5:42
journey from America 9:42
Edward I, King of England 1:41
Edward IV, King of England,
and Duke of Clarence 1:137-8
Edward VI, King of England 2:74
coronation of 2:74
Edward VII, King of England,
death of 6:41
Edwards, Mary, by Hogarth 8:28
Egmont, Count, execution of
2:137-8
Egypt 6:48-9
anti-British riots 8:138
assassination of premier 6:42
hieroglyphs 6:52
Klee in 6:47-8
symbols of the gods 6:36, 37,
52
veneration of animals 6:36,
36-7
Eiffel, Alexandre Gustave 5:73,
102
Eiffel Tower 5:73-4
building the 5:102
Eighty Years War (1568-1648),
The 2:136-8
Einstein, Albert 9:138
Eisenstein, Sergei: The Battleship
Potemkin 7:104-105
El Greco see Artists' Index
electric chair 5:105
electricity, experiments with
5:104

'Eleven Years Tyranny, The'
3:104
Eliot, George 4:84
Elliot, T. S.: The Waste Land 7:42
Elizabeth I, Queen of England
2:103, 104
birth of 2:106
by Hilliard 2:87
and the East India Company
3:40
and Ireland 3:41
Eluard, Gala 6:110-111
with Dalí 6:112
Eluard, Paul: Dalí and 6:110-111
Miró and 7:77
Emin Pasha, rescue of 5:73
'end of the world' 2:14, 18; 5:103,
106
Engelhard, Josef, and
Hagenbund 9:100
Engels, Friedrich 8:71
England: capture of Jamaica
3:72
Civil War in 3:102-103, 138
battle of Marston Moor
(1644) 3:102-103
Dissolution of the
Monasteries 2:102
and Hundred Years War
(1337-1453) 1:73-4
London: 17th-century
3:100-101
steelyards 2:79
Tower of 2:81
Westminster pavement 2:89
Whitehall Palace: Holbein
wall painting for 2:80,
80-81, 86-7
Peterloo Massacre (1819) 4:68,
69, 70-71, 73-4
the plague in 1:73
portraiture in 17th-century
3:83-4
religion and politics 2:74
the Renaissance in 2:100
'Rump' Parliament 3:138
tastes of collectors in
17th-century 3:79
wars with Scotland (1637)
3:103
wars with Spain and France
3:72-3, 100
see also Britain
Engravers' Copyright Act,
Hogarth and 8:16
engraving: the art of 2:18-21; 4:52
Blake and 4:45
Dürer's 2:20-21
selling 2:14
Goya and 4:19
Hogarth and 8:12, 12, 13
13-14, 15
Miró and 7:81
see also printing/publishing

Ensor, James see Artists' Index
Eramus, Desiderius 2:69
on his fellow countrymen
2:132
Henry VIII and 2:100
by Holbein 2:77, 78
on Holbein's drawing of the
More family 2:82
Adages 2:115
Praise of Folly 2:78
Holbein and 2:76
Erfurt University, Luther at 2:68
Ernst, Max see Artists' Index
escalator, first 5:39
Esche, Herbert, by Munch
9:114-15
Esclavo, El see Pareja, Juan de
Essex, Earl of 3:41
and Elizabeth I 3:41-2
Este, Isabella d': commissions
for the Bellinis 1:79
by Leonardo 1:81
studiolo of 1:79
etching: Blake and 4:45
Chagall and 6:80
Dürer and 2:21
Goya and 4:19, 21
Hogarth and 8:20
Klee and 6:50
Miró and 7:81
Munch and 9:115
Redon and 9:46
Ruisdael and 3:111
Eugenius IV, Pope: and Florence
Cathedral 1:72, 72
and Fra Angelico 1:48
Euler, Leonhard 8:41
Europe: feeling of doom in 2:14
turmoil in 16th-century 2:138
see also individual countries
Evans, Mary Ann see Eliot,
George
Eve, discovering 2:52, 52
Evelyn, John 3:135
Everdingen, Allart van see
Artists' Index
Exhibition of Surrealist Art
(Paris, 1925) Klee and 6:47
Exposition Universelle de Paris
(1900) 5:39, 39, 72, 73-4
Rousseau and 6:14-15
Expressionists: Klee and 6:47
see also Blaue Reiter group

F

Falte, Camille 9:47
by Redon 9:47
'Family of Love' 2:111
famine, threat of (in the
Netherlands) 2:134

fantasy, comparisons of 4:20, 20; 6:84, 84
Fantin-Latour, Henry see Artists' Index
farming, in the Low Countries 2:133-4, 134
　harvest time 2:134, 134
Fascism, rise of 6:73-4
'Father of Impressionism' see Manet, Edouard
Faulkner, Charles 9:34
Fauré (singer), Manet and 5:99
Fauves: Chagall and 6:82
　Kandinsky and 7:19
　Miró and 7:82
Fayet, Gustave, Redon and 9:49
Feisal, King of Saudi Arabia 6:137
Felix, Eugen, and the Künstlerhaus 9:101
femme fatale, comparisons 9:20, 20
Fénéon, Félix: articles in Vogue 5:110
　and Neo-Impressionists 5:110
　and Seurat 5:109, 110
　and Signac 5:109
　painted by 5:109
Ferdinand II, Emperor, defeat of 3:137
Ferdinand V, King of Spain 1:137
　and heretics 1:138
　and the Inquisition 4:34, 34
Ferdinand VII, King of Spain 4:14, 41
　Goya and 4:41-2
　and the Inquisition 4:37
　and Napoleon 4:14
　restoration of 4:16
Ferrá, Dolores 7:76
Ferry, Jules 5:135-6
Fielding, Henry 8:14
　Hogarth and 8:14
　Joseph Andrews, preface 8:18
　Tom Jones 8:15
　Tom Thumb, frontispiece 8:14
Filiger, Charles see Artists' Index
Filipepi, Alessandro di Mariano de Vanni see Botticelli, Sandro
Filipepi, Giovanni 1:108
　death of 1:112
　trade 1:109
Filipepi, Mariano 1:108
　death of 1:108
Filipepi, Simone, and 'piagnoni' 1:113
Finney, Albert 7:133
Fiquet, Hortense: Cézanne and 5:14, 15, 16
　painted by 5:15, 24
'fiscal feudalism' 2:102-3
Fitzgerald, Francis Scott: The Great Gatsby 7:105, 106
　This Side of Paradise 7:105

Flajoulot, M., Courbet and 8:45
Flammerion, Camille 5:103
'Flanders Mare, The' see Anne of Cleves
Flaubert, Gustave, Redon and 9:45
Fletcher, John 3:102
Flöge, Emilie 9:79, 79-80
　by Klimt 9:94
Floquet, Charles 5:103, 104
'Florence of the North' see Germany: Nuremberg
Floris, Frans see Artists' Index
Fontaine, Arthur, Redon and 9:49
Footit and Chocolat 5:132, 132-3
Ford, President 6:138
foreshortening, Gozzoli's use of 1:49
Forget, Joséphine de 4:111
form, solid 1:23
fortification, Dürer and 2:17
Foundation Maeght, and Miró 7:81
Fra Angelico see Artists' Index
Fra Benedetto 1:46
Fra Domenico da Corella, on Fra Angelico 1:45
France: alliances 7:105
　　with Russia (1894) 8:104
　　with Scotland (1547) 2:74
　assassination of President Carnot 8:104, 105
　'Aux Quatre Vents' 2:110
　Avignon 1:42
　challenge to the Republic 5:105-106
　circus in 5:130, 131-2
　civil wars in see the Fronde
　colonialism 5:135-6
　comparisons of the Normandy coast 5:114, 114
　cult of the English 8:81, 81
　the Dreyfus affair 8:102, 103, 105-106
　duelling in 5:103, 104-105
　1848 revolution 8:71-2, 72
　Entente Cordiale (1904) 9:41, 72, 72-3, 138
　fall of the Third Republic 6:73
　and Far East crisis 9:72
　Le Figaro editor murdered 9:105
　the Fronde 3:137-8, 138
　and Germany: occupies the Ruhr (1921) 8:136
　　war debts 7:40
　Grande Jatte, La 5:108-109
　and India 8:41
　International Working-Men's Association 8:68
　Lascaux paintings 6:36, 36-7
　and Locarno Conference (1925) 7:104

and the Low Countries 2:134
Marseillaise 5:36
Monarchy v. Republic 8:74
1910 strikes 6:40
and North America 8:40, 41
occupation of Portugal 4:40
Paris: Café Guerbois 5:14, 99
　Commune 8:68, 69
　in the 1880s 5:78-9
　massacre in 4:68-9
　Montmartre 5:100, 101
　the Moulin Rouge 8:98-101
　night life in 8:84, 100, 100-101
　picture trade in 5:100-101
　revolt in (1830) 4:110
　riots in (1848) 8:46
　storming of the Bastille (1789) 4:66, 68
　strikes/violence in 5:105
　Ultras in 4:137
Paris-Rouen race 8:106
press scandal 8:105
Provence: in Cézanne's day 5:34-7, 34-5
　Pont du Gard 5:34-5
raids on anarchists 8:103
the Regency in 2:137-8, 138
Reign of Terror 4:68
and the Risorgimento 9:41
St Bartholomew's Eve Massacre 2:138
St Denis, Battle of 2:136-7
scandals 5:103, 104-5
Second Republic 8:46
separation of Church and State 9:74
17th-century territorial gains 2:137
and Spain 'oppression' of 4:14, 22-3, 38-42
　war with 2:71, 72-3
stand against Boniface VIII 1:41
Strasbourg, Dürer in 2:12
student riots 7:136-7, 137
and Tahiti 5:69
terrorism in 6:137
'22nd of March' movement 7:136
Vaux-le-Vicomte 3:72
Vendôme Column toppled 8:48-9, 49
war with China 5:135-6
workers' conditions in 8:66-9, 66-7
and World War I 9:104-5, 105-6
see also French Revolution
Francis I, King of France 2:72
　by Clouet 2:87
Franciscan Order 1:68, 71
　founding of 1:38
　influence on fresco painting 1:19

Franco, General 6:136, 138; 7:100, 100-103
Frankert, Hans, and Bruegel 2:117
Franz Ferdinand, Archduke, assassination of 9:105
freaks 5:132, 133
Frederick the Great of Prussia, and Silesia 8:40-41
Frederick the Wise, Elector of Saxony: and Cranach 2:45
　commission for 2:46
　portrait by 2:46
　types of work wanted 2:51
　and Dürer 2:14
　commissions for 2:14, 15
　and Luther 2:41-2, 46
　and Melanchthon 2:46
　pilgrimages 2:44
　and the Reformation 2:46
French Revolution 4:66
　Blake and 4:46
　centenary of 5:72-3
　effect on Provence 5:36
fresco, true see buon fresco
fresco-painting: Botticelli and 1:114, 114
　Caravaggio and 1:13, 21
　guide for 1:51
　ideal conditions for 1:52
　resurgence in Italy 1:19
　sequence for 1:52
　see also mural-painting
fresco secco 1:16
　see also buon fresco
frescoes: by Botticelli 1:114
　Fra Angelico's in San Marco 1:48
　Giotto's in the Arena Chapel 1:14, 15
　in Assisi 1:13
　in Rome 1:13-14
　in Santa Croce 1:16, 16
　Piero della Francesca's 1:22-3
Freud, Sigmund 5:41; 6:68, 112
　and Breuer 6:68
　and Charcot 6:68
　Dalí and 6:112, 112-3
　on classical painting 6:116
　influence on art 6:115
　disciples of 6:71
　and hysteria 6:68, 69-70
　theories 6:71
　development of 6:68
　at Vienna General Hospital 6:68
　Interpretation of Dreams 6:70
　Dalí and 6:108, 113
　Three Essays on the Theory of Sexuality 9:138
Frey, Agnes: and Dürer 2:12, 13
　painted by 2:15
Friars Minor see Franciscan Order

Friedrich, Adolf Gottlieb, by
   Friedrich 4:*76*
Friedrich, Caspar David *see*
   Artists' Index
Frink, Elizabeth *see Artists' Index*
Frizeau, Gabriel, Redon and 9:49
fruit/flowers: comparisons 2:*21*
   symbolic 2:*23*
Fry, Roger, and the
   Post-Impressionists 6:42
USS Fulton 4:*104-105*
furniture decoration, paintings
   as 1:*114*, 115, 9:35
Fuseli, Henry *see Artists' Index*
Futurists/Futurism: Dalí and
   6:109
   Malevich and 7:45-6, *45*
   Riley and 7:110
   second year of 6:42
   0.10 Exhibition 7:46

G

Gad, Mette Sophie 5:45, *45*
Gainsborough, Thomas *see*
   Artists' Index
Galerie Maeght, Miró and 7:81
Galerie Surréaliste 7:78
Galeries Lafayette, Rousseau
   and 6:21
Galí, Francisco, Miró and 7:76
Gallen-Kallela, Askeli *see Artists'*
   Index
Gallery One, Riley and 7:111
Gama, Vasco da 1:103, *106*
Gamble, Ellis, Hogarth and 8:12
Gandhi, Mrs Indira 6:138
Gandhi, Mahatma 7:*40*, 42
Garbo, Greta 9:138
gargoyles 4:*99*
Garibaldi, Giuseppi 9:41
Gauguin, Aline 5:44
Gauguin, Clovis 5:44
Gauguin, Paul *see Artists' Index*
Gautier, Théophile 5:99
Gay, John: *Beggar's Opera*,
   Hogarth and 8:14, 39
Gay-Lussac, J. L. 4:42
genre painting, increasing
   popularity of 9:44
Gentileschi, Artemisia *see Artists'*
   Index
Gentileschi, Orazio *see Artists'*
   Index
Geoffrin, Madame, salon of 8:*42*
George IV, King of England, and
   South America 4:*136*
George V, King of England 6:*41*
   accession of 6:41
George, Simon, of Quocoute, by
   Holbein 2:*83*, 85

Gérard, François *see Artists'*
   Index
'Gerard of the Night Scenes' *see*
   Honthorst, Gerrit van
Géricault, Théodore *see Artists'*
   Index
Germany: and army occupation
   8:*137*
   Augsberg 2:*48*, 77
      Cranach in 2:*48*, 49
   Berlin: The Black Piglet 9:111,
      132-5
   Blitzkrieg 6:105
   capture of Crete 6:105
   and the Dawes Plan 7:106
   Four Year Plan 6:*106*
   the Frankfurt Assembly 8:*74*
   freedom fighters 4:*80*
   hostility to the arts 6:48
      exhibition of Degenerate
      Art 6:48, *49*
   Imperial cities 2:36
      see also Nuremberg
   Munich as artistic centre 6:47,
      47
   National Socialism 6:72-3, *73*,
      80; 7:106, *106*
      and the Bauhaus 7:38, 39
      influence in 6:48
   Navy Bill 5:42
   and North Africa 6:*104*, 105
   Nuremberg 2:36
      the arts in 2:38-9
      as centre of commerce 2:37-8
      Chronicle 2:*36*, 39, *39*
      Cranach and 2:49, 51, 53
      Dürer's house in 2:15, *15*
      effect of Reformation in 2:17
      in the 15th century 2:*12*,
         36-9
      Great Council of 2:16, 17,
         37, 39
      honours Dürer 2:16
      living conditions in 2:36-7
      principal painter 2:38
      printing in 2:*37*, 38, 39, *39*
   payment of reparations 8:136
   political unrest in 7:36
   quarrel with France 5:106
   reconstruction of Cologne
      Cathedral 8:73
   Reichstag fire 6:72, *72*
   revolutions in 8:72
   Romanticism in 4:80-81
   and Russia 6:41-2
      'Operation Barbarossa'
         6:*105*, *105*
      treaties with 7:40-41; 9:138
   Schlieffen Plan 9:106
   structure of 15th-century 2:36
   struggle against Napoleon 4:80
   student riots in 7:137
   and South West Africa 9:74, *74*
   terrorism in 6:138

Treaty of Brest-Litovsk 7:71
   and Upper Silesia 7:40; 8:137
   and war debts 7:40
   Weimar Republic 7:105-106
   Wittenberg: Cathedral
      Church of 2:*46*
      Christian II in 2:49
      Cranach and 2:45-9
      modern 2:47
      as publishing centre 2:49
      University of 2.46, 47, 69
      and World War I 7:72-4;
         9:*104-105*, 105-106
Gérôme: Redon and 9:46
   Rousseau and 6:13-14, 21
   and *Two Majesties* 6:23
gesso 2:116
Ghiberti, Lorenzo *see Artists'*
   Index
Ghirlandaio, Domenico *see*
   Artists' Index
Gilray, James *see Artists' Index*
Giordano, Luca *see Artists' Index*
Giorgione *see Artists' Index*
Giotto *see Artists' Index*
Gisze, George, by Holbein 2:*86*
Giustiniani, Marchese, and
   Caravaggio 3:15
Gladstone, William, Prime
   Minister: fall of 5:137-8
   and the Sudan 5:136-7
Glidden, Carlos 9:*38*
'God of Wood, The' *see*
   Montañes, Juan Martinez
Godoy 4:41
Godwin, Mary 4:69
Godwin, William 4:66, 67, *69*
   Political Justice 4:69
Goebbels, Josef, and Chagall
   6:80
Goemans, Camille, Dalí and
   6:110
Goethe, Johann Wolfgang von,
   and Friedrich 4:*78-9*, 79
   and the Gothic Revival 4:101
   interests 4:101
   and Macpherson 4:101
   on Ruisdael 3:112
   Faust 4:41
   Von Deutscher Baukunst 4:101
Gogh, Cornelia van 5:76, 77
Gogh, Theo van 5:*80*, 81
   art gallery 5:81, 100
   and Gauguin 5:80
   and Van Gogh: helps with
      finances 5:78
      lives with in Paris 5:78-9
Gogh, Theodorus van 5:76, 77
   death of 5:78
Gogh, Vincent van *see Artists'*
   Index
Gogol: *Dead Souls*, illustrations
   for 6:80
gold, in contract 1:50

Golden Cross of Merit, Austrian,
   Klimt and 9:77
'Golden Head, The' 8:15
'gollilla' 3:71
goldsmiths: Dürer as 2.37
   patron saint of 1:*109*
Goldsmith's College, London,
   Riley and 7:109
Goncharova, Natalia *see Artists'*
   Index
Gongora, Luis de 3:46
   by Velázquez 3:45
Gonzaga, Cardinal Ferdinando,
   and Caravaggio 3:17
Gonzaga, Isabella, and Botticelli
   1:113
Gordon, General Charles 5:*134*,
   136-7
Gorin, Stanislas, Redon and
   9:*44*, 45
Gossaert, Jan *see Artists' Index*
Goshen, Colonel 5:133
Gothic novels 4:100-101, *101*
Gothic Revival 4:98-101, *101*
   first poem 4:99
   first great monument 4:*99*, 100
Goulue, La 8:*101*, 101
   Toulouse-Lautrec and 8:79
   by Toulouse-Lautrec 8:*82*, 94
Goupil's Gallery, Toulouse-
   Lautrec and 8:80
Gowrie, Lord 3:42
'Gowrie conspiracy' 3:42
Goya y Lucientes, Francisco de
   see Artists' Index
Goyen, Jan van *see Artists' Index*
Gozzoli, Benozzo *see Artists'*
   Index
Graef, Cornelis de, and Ruisdael
   3:111
Grande Medaille d'Honneur,
   given to Delacroix 4:113
Grant, Ulysses S., President
   5:*136-7*
Granvelle, Cardinal Antoine de
   2:*113*
   and Bruegel 2:112
Graveyard painter *see* **Friedrich,
   Casper David**
Gray, Thomas: *Elegy Written in a
   Country Churchyard* 4:99
Great Turk, The *see* Mehmet II,
   Sultan of Turkey
Greece: animals in mythology
   6:37
   cavalry 4:*132*
   Colonels gaoled 6:138
   Delacroix and 4:110
   War of Independence 4:130-33
      134, 135-6
   war with Turkey 7:42
   and World War I 7:73
Greene, Graham 9:74
Greenwich Naval College 8:*13*

Griffith, W. D.: *Birth of a Nation* 7:74, *74*
    Intolerance 7:*105*
Grimaldi, Marchesa Elena 3:*82*
    and Van Dyck 3:78, *82*, 83
Gris, Juan *see Artists' Index*
Gropius, Walter 7:*36*
    and the Bauhaus 7:36-8, 106
        resigns from 7:38-9
    and Kandinsky 7:36
    and Klee 7:36
    and Schlemmer 7:36-7
Gros, Baron Antoine Jean *see Artists' Index*
Grosvenor, Sir Richard, Hogarth and 8:17
Grünewald, Mathis *See Artists' Index*
'Guggems' *see* Siddal, Elizabeth
Guggenheim Foundation Grand International Prize, Miró and 7:81
Guelph Party 1:42
Guercino, Il *see Artists' Index*
Guérin, Marie 9:45
Guérin, Pierre-Narcisse *see Artists' Index*
Guiccioli, Teresa and Byron 4:131
Guido di Pietro *see* **Fra Angelico**
Guilbert, Yvette 8:*99*, 101
    by Toulouse-Lautrec 8:*83*
Guild of St Luke, Antwerp, Van Dyck and 3:76, 77
Guild of St Luke, Haarlem 3:108
    Ruisdael and 3:109, 136
Guildford, Sir Henry, commission for Holbein 2:*82*
Guillou, Jenny le 4:*110*, 113
Gutenberg's Bible 2:38
Guzman, Don Gaspar de (Olivares) 3:69
    by Velázquez 3:*68*

H

Haakon VII, King of Norway 9:136
Hadassah-Hebrew University, Jerusalem, Chagall and 6:*80*, 81
Hagenbund, members of 9:100
Haggard, Virginia 6:81
Halley's Comet 1:40, *41*
Halsman, Philippe: Dalí and 6:*111*
    'Atomicus' 6:*111*
Hamilton, Duke of 3:138
Hamilton, Richard *see Artists' Index*

Hampden, John 3:105
Hanseatic League: commission for Holbein 2:*80-81*
    London office of 2:79
Harington, James: *Oceana* 3:73
Haro, Don Luis de 3:70
Harvard University, and Miró 7:81
Hastings, Beatrice 6:101, 103
Hayem, Georges 5:*70*
Hayes, Colin *see Artists' Index*
Hayley, William, and Blake 4:48
Hazlitt, William on Hogarth 8:18
Hearst, Pattie 6:138
Hébuterne, Jeanne, by Marevna 8:*108-109*
Hedin, Sven, in Tibet 8:*106*
Heem, Jan Davidsz de *see Artists' Index*
Heemskerke, Martin van *see Artists' Index*
'Hell Brueghel' *see* Brueghel, Peter, the Younger
Hellfire Club, The 8:39
Hemingway, Ernest 7:102
Hennequin, Emile : death of 9:48
    Redon and 9:47
Henri IV, King of France, marriage 3:41, *42*
Henrietta Maria, Queen of England: by Van Dyck 3:*87*, *93*, *101* .
    description of 3:85
    portraits of 3:85
    temperament 3:102
Henry II, King of France 1:*73*
Henry II, King of Spain, and the Jews 4:34
Henry VIII, King of England 2:72, 100, *100*
    allegorical painting of 2:*102-103*
    and Anne of Cleves 2:81
    break with Rome (1533) 2:*102-103*
    and Christina of Denmark 2:81
    death of 2:74
    divorce 2:103, 104-106
    favourite painter 2:76
    and Hampton Court 2:101
    and Holbein 2:77
        Holbein's paintings of 2:86-7, *96*, *100*
    legend of 2:100-103
    and Luther 2:42
    marriage to Anne Boleyn 2:106
    passion for building 2:102
    palaces 2:102
    and the Pilgrimage of Grace 2:80-81
    propaganda against the Pope 2:102
    and Renaissance artists 2:100

Herbin, Auguste *see Artists' Index*
Herbster, Hans *see Artists' Index*
Herrera the Elder, Francesco de, and Velázquez 3:44
Heyman, Violette, by Redon 9:52, *53*
Hicks, Edward *see Artists' Index*
'high art', comparison of Caravaggio's work with 3:21
Hilliard, Nicholas *see Artists' Index*
Hindenburg, Paul von 7:105-106, *106*
Hiroshige, Utagawe *see Artists' Index*
Hirschfield, Morris *see Artists' Index*
Hitchcock, Alfred: *Spellbound* 6:113
Hitler, Adolf 7:106
    and 'degenerate' art 6:*49*
    propaganda 6:72
    rise of 6:72, 72-3
    Mein Kampf 7:106, *106*
Hoadley, Benjamin (Bishop of Winchester), by Hogarth 8:29
Hobbema, Meindart *see Artists' Index*
Hockney, David *see Artists' Index*
Hodler, Ferdinand *see Artists' Index*
Hoffmann, Josef
    and first Secessionist exhibition 9:101
    Stoclet Palace 9:*80-81*, 81
Hofmann, Ludwig von, and Berlin Secession 9:135
Hogarth, Edmund 8:12
Hogarth, Richard 8:12
Hogarth, William *see Artists' Index*
Hogenberg, Frans *see Artists' Index*
Holbein, Ambrosius 2:76
Holbein, Hans, the Elder *see Artists' Index*
Holbein, Hans, the Younger *see Artists' Index*
Holbein, Katharine 2:79
Holbein, Philip 2:79
Holland/United Provinces:
    Amsterdam: 'Silvere Trompet' 3:111
        Stadhuis 3:*137*
    European demand for engineers 3:132, 135
    genre subjects in 3:133
    importance of trade 3:134-5
    Protestant revolution in 3:132-3
    terrorism in 6:138
    and Truce of 1609 3:132
    see also Low Countries

Hollar, Wenceslaus *see Artists' Index*
Holper, Barbara 2:12
    by Dürer 2:*13*
Holy Roman Emperors: conflicts with the popes 1:41
homosexuality, Caravaggio and 3:13
Hondecoeter, Melchior *see Artists' Index*
Hondius, Jodocus 3:135
Honthorst, Gerrit van *see Artists' Index*
Horn, Count, execution of by Alva 2:137-8
Hornsey College of Art, London, Riley and 7:110
Houbraken, Arnold, on Ruisdael 3:109
    treatment of water 4:116
'House of the Deaf Man' *see* 'Quinta del Sordo'
'houses of the future' 7:48-9
Huerta, General 8:133
    caricature by Posada 8:*134*
Hugo, Victor, Delacroix and 4:111
Humanism/Humanist thought 2:76-7
    Cranach and 2:45
    Dürer and Italian 2:13-14
    foremost artist of 2:77
    Holbein and 2:78, *78*
    importance at Saxon court 2:47
    and intellectual pursuits 2:76
    in Nuremberg 2:38
    in Renaissance ideas 1:46
    Pope Nicholas V and 1:48
Humayun, the Great Mogul (Emperor of India) 2:72
Humbert I, King of Italy, assassination of 5:42
Hume, David 8:*41*
    Enquiry Concerning Human Understanding 8:41
    Philosophical Essays Concerning Human Understanding 8:41
Hume, Hamilton 4:138
Humphrey, Hubert 7:137
Hundred Years War (1337-1453) 1:73-4
Hungary, concessions from Austria 8:72
Hunt, Henry 'Orator' 4:68
Hunt, Leigh, Rossetti and 9:13-14
Hunt, William Holman *see Artists' Index*
Hunyadi, Matthias 1:*138*
Hus, John 1:73
Hussites, armed defiance of 1:73
Huygens, Christiaan 3:73, 133
    and astronomy 3:134
    pendulum clock 3:135, *135*

Huyghe, René, on Cézanne 5:18
Huysmans, Joris Karl: and
  Boullan 9:71
  Moreau and 9:69
  Redon and 9:47, 69
  and Symbolism 9:68
  A Rebours 9:47, 69
    model for central character
      9:68
hypnotism 6:69
hysteria, study of 6:68-71

I

Ibn Saud 6:42
Ibsen, Henrik: *Ghosts*, Munch
  and 9:112
  Hedda Gabler 9:135
    Munch and 9:112
icons, Venetian liking for 1:82
'Illuminated painting' 4:46-7
illumination: Blake and 4:46,
  50-53
  as devotional observance ﹀
    1:50-51
  Fra Angelico and 1:46, *50*
  Morris and 9:34
  Rossetti and 9:*19*, 20
  Rousseau and 6:20
impasto, Van Gogh and 5:83
Impressionism/Impressionists:
  first exhibition 5:98, 99-100
    Cézanne and 5:16
    reaction to 5:100
  formation of 9:44
  Van Gogh and 5:100
  Klimt and 9:78, 85
  Manet refuses to exhibit with
    5:99
  in Paris 5:98-101
    and Café Guerbois 5:99
  patrons 5:99
  Redon and: criticism of 9:44
    and last exhibition 9:48
  selling works 5:99
  Seurat exhibits with 5:110
  use of colour 5:82
    influence on Van Gogh 5:82
  working together 5:99
India: anti-British riots (1921)
  8:138
  constitution for 6:74
  Viceroy injured 6:42
Individual Psychology 6:71
'inferiority complex' 6:71
Ingres, Jean-Auguste-
  Dominique *see Artists' Index*
ink: Goya's use of 4:21
  Holbein's use of 2:83-4
Innocent III, Pope, and St
  Francis 1:38

Innocent X, Pope, and
  Velázquez 3:48
  by Velázquez 3:53
Inquisition, the 4:34-7, *37*
  and Goya's paintings 4:16, 34,
    34
  last victim of 4:37
  re-establishment of in Spain
    4:16
  and witchcraft 4:37
Institute of Artistic Culture:
  closure of 7:16
  Kandinsky and 7:16
instruction books, 17th-century
  3:134
insulin 7:42
International Exhibition,
  Barcelona 6:133
International Women's Year
  6:138
Ireland: Abbey Theatre founded
  9:74
  'Black and Tans' 8:138
  Blue Shirts 6:73
  civil war in (1922) 7:*40-41*
  the 'Curragh Incident' 9:104
  Home Rule 5:*106*, 138
    Bill for 9:104
  independence 7:41-2
  parliaments inaugurated
    8:*136-7*
  Sinn Fein 9:138
  war with Britain 8:137-8
Ireland, Northern *see* Northern
  Ireland
Irving, Sir Henry 9:138
Isabella, Archduchess, and Van
  Dyck 3:79
Isabella, Queen of Spain 1:*137*;
  4:34
  and heretics 1:138
Isherwood, Christopher 9:74
Isle, General Brière d' 5:135
Isle of Pheasants 3:49, *49*
Israel: Knesset, Chagall and 6:81
  terrorism in 6:137
Italy: Assisi 1:*37*
  Austrian forces driven out
    8:72
  and Ethiopia 5:*72*
  fascist coup in 7:41, *41*
  Fiesole monastery 1:*45*, 46
  Florence 1:*13*
    art in after Giotto 1:17
    Cathedral 1:*72*, 134
    change in attitude towards
      artists 1:113
    changing fortunes of
      1:111-12
    civil strife in 1:110
    family rivalries in 1:110
    in 1436 1:72-4
    importance to Pope
      Alexander VI 1:104

  influence of Savonarola on
    1:132
  monastic life in
    15th-century 1:68-71
  new bridges in 2:*136*
  the Ognissanti quarter
    1:108, *108-9*
  organization for the
    'embarrassed poor' 1:70
  Palazzo Vecchio 1:*40*, 137
  Pazzi Chapel 1:*136*
  Peruzzi Chapel 1:*16*
  plague in 1:17
  Platonic Academy 1:133,
    134
  republicanism in 1:134-5
  San Marco monastery 1:*47*,
    52
  teaching establishments in
    1:69
  White/Black struggle in 1:42
general strike 9:74
Gothic Revival in 4:99-100
Herculaneum: excavated 8:*40*
  Walpole on 8:42
invasion of Greece 6:104-105
'March on Rome' 7:41, *41*
Milan: and alliance against
  France 1:104
  war with Venice 1:102
Naples: and alliance against
  France 1:104
  Borgia alliance with
    1:105-106
  Castel Nuovo 1:16
  Charles VIII claims
    kingdom of 1:111-12
Ognissanti, Church of
  1:*112-13*
Orvieto Cathedral 1:*48-9*
  Fra Angelico and 1:48, *49*
Padua, artistic circle in 1:77
Pisa 1:*109*
  Botticelli in 1:109, *109*
Pompeii: excavation of 8:*40*, 42
  Villa of the Mysteries
    4:*40-41*
the *Risorgimento* 9:41
Rome: Botticelli in 1:115
  during the Counter
    Reformation 3:13-14
  painters' academy *see*
    Accademia di San Luca
  Palazzo Madama 3:13, *15*
  Piazza Navona 3:*136*
  terror in 1:*104-105*
Serenissima see Venice/
  Venetian Empire
and Spanish Civil War 7:102
unification of 8:72-3; 9:41
Venice *see* Venice/Venetian
  Empire
Villa Castello 1:*118*
and World War I 7:73-4

Itten, Johannes, and the
  Bauhaus 7:36
  leaves 7:37
  life-style 7:36
Ivan the Terrible, Tsar of Russia
  2:*106*
Ivan III, Grand Duke of
  Muscovy 1:*137*

J

Jack of Diamonds group 7:*45*
'Jack the Ripper' 5:74, *103*, 105
Jacob, Max 6:101, *103*
  by Marevna 8:*108-109*
Jacobson, Daniel: Munch and
  9:113
  painting of 9:*115*
Jaeger, Hans, by Munch 9:*110*
James, Edward, Dalí and 6:112
James, Henry: *The Golden Bowl*
  9:74
James I, King of Scotland,
  murder of 1:74
James V, King of Scotland 2:74
James VI, King of Scotland 3:42
Japan: attack on Pearl Harbor
  6:*104-105*, 106
  war with Russia 9:*72-3*, 73-4,
    36-8
  propaganda for 9:*137*
Japanese prints: Klimt and 9:84-5
  Munch and 9:12
Jarry, Alfred 6:15
  and Rousseau 6:15, *15*
  destroys paintings by 6:15
Jaurès, Jean 9:105
Jawlinsky, Alexei von *see Artists'
  Index*
Joan of Arc, burning of 1:73
Joffre, 'Papa' 7:72
John VI, King of Brazil 4:*106*
John Casimir, King of Poland
  3:72
John Frederick, Elector of
  Saxony 2:49
  capture of 2:74
  and Cranach 2:49
    painted by 2:*46*
'John Moore's Liverpool
  Exhibition', Riley and 7:111
John the Steadfast, Elector of
  Saxony, by Cranach 2:*46*
Johnson, Amy 6:106
Johnson, Joseph 4:66, 67
Johnson, Samuel: *Dictionary* 8:15
  on London 8:36
Jonas, Justus 2:*69*
Jones, Ernest 6:71
Jonghelinck, and Bruegel 2:112
Jonson, Ben 3:102

Jordaens, Jacob *see Artists' Index*
Joyant, Maurice, Toulouse-
   Lautrec and 8:80
Joyce, James 6:106
   Ulysses 7:42
Juan Carlos I, King of Spain 6:*138*
   accession of 6:136
Jubilee Year, first papal 1:*40*
Juel, Jens, Friedrich and 4:77
Juell, Dagny 9:*134*, 134-5
Jugend, Die 6:44
Jugendstil 6:44
   and Phalanx group 7:15
Jujol: Parc Guell 6:*133*
July Uprising 4:*110*
Jumbo the Elephant 5:*136*
Juncosa, Pilar 7:79
Jung, C. G. 6:71, *71*
   theories 6:71
Junkers, Hugo 7:74
Juniet, Père, by Rousseau 6:33

K

Kafka, Franz: *The Trial* 7:106
Kahlo, Frida *see Artists' Index*
Kalm, Peter, on London 8:37
Kamehameha II, King of Hawaii
   4:*138*
   in England 4:138
Kandinsky, Nina 7:15
Kandinsky, Wassily *see Artists'*
   Index
'Kandinsky Society' 7:17
Keeler, Christine 7:132
Kelmscott Press 8:37
   Chaucer 8:37
Kemal, Mustafa (Atatürk) 7:*40*,
   42, 106; 8:138
Kennedy, Jacqueline 7:138
Kennedy, Robert 7:137, *137*
Kennington, Eric *see Artists'*
   Index
Kent, William: Holkham Hall
   8:42
Kerensky, Alexander 7:70
Kersting, Georg Friedrich *see*
   Artists' Index
Keyser, Thomas de *see Artists'*
   Index
Khnopff, Fernand *see Artists'*
   Index
Ki Koine, Michel 6:101
Kiev School of Art, Malevich
   and 7:*44*, 45
'king' *see* **Klimt, Gustav**
King, Martin Luther 7:137
King Kong 6:72-3
Kipling, Rudyard 5:*105*
Kirchner, Ernst Ludwig *see*
   Artists' Index

Kisling, Möise *see Artists' Index*
Kitaj, R. B. 7:134
Kitchener, General 5:41
Klee, Mathilde 6:44
Klee, Paul *see Artists' Index*
Klimt, Ernst (brother) *see Artists'*
   Index
Klimt, Ernst (father) 8:76
Klimt, Georg 8:76
Klimt, Gustav *see Artists' Index*
Kliun, Ivan and Jack of
   Diamonds group 7:45
'Knight George' *see* Luther,
   Martin 2:42
Knights of Malta, and
   Caravaggio 3:16, *16-17*
Knirr, Edwin, Klee and 6:44
Knobloch, Madeleine 5:111
   by Seurat 5:*111*
Knossos, excavation of 5:42
Knox, John 2:*73*, 74
Koberger, Anton 2:*38*
   and Dürer 2:14, 39
   and Nuremberg Chronicle
      2:39
   and Nuremberg Council 2:39
   press of 2:14, 39
   production of 2:39
Kodak No. 1 camera 5:74
Kokoschka, Oscar *see Artists'*
   Index
Korea, and *Pueblo* 7:138
Kosegarten, L. T., Friedrich and
   4:77
Krämer, Johann, and
   Hagenbund 8:100
Kremègne, Pinchus 6:101
Krohg, Christian, Munch and
   9:109
Kronach 2:44, *44-5*
Kruchenykh, Alexei *see Artists'*
   Index
Kruger, Paul 5:40, 41
Kubin, Alfred, and *Blaue Reiter*
   group 6:45
Kubrick, Stanley: *2001: A Space*
   Odyssey 7:138
Kunstgewerbeschule, Vienna,
   Klimt and 9:76
Künstlerhaus: Felix and 9:101
   founding of 9:100
   Klimt and 9:78

L

La Fontaine, illustrations for
   Fables 6:80
La Lonja, Barcelona, Miró at 7:76
La Tour, Georges de *see Artists'*
   Index

Lacombe, Georges, *see Artists'*
   Index
LaLa, Miss 5:132
Lama, Zanobi del, commission
   for Botticelli 1:109
Lamarck, Jean Baptiste: *Histoire*
   Naturelle des Animaux 4:105
landscape: Bellini and 1:84, *86-7*
   Bruegel and 2:109, 112
   Cézanne and 5:15
   comparisons of 3:116, *116*
      of winter 2:116, *116*
   composition of religious 1:84,
      84
   Cranach and 2:45, 50
   Dürer and 2:*14-15*, 23
   Dutch: early categories of
      3:114
      first style of 3:112
      tradition of 3:108
   Fra Angelico and 1:54
   Friedrich and 4:77-8, 82-5
   by Giorgione? 1:*136*
   Van Goyen and 3:112
   increasing popularity of 9:44
   Klimt and 9:80
   Millais and 9:19
   Monet and 5:99
   of the spirit 4:82-5
   Romantic era 4:82
   Rossetti and 9:19
   Rousseau and 6:18, 19
   Isaack van Ruisdael and 3:108
   Ruisdael and 3:112-14, 116-17
      constructs more complex
      3:114
   Ruysdael and 3:108
   Van Dyck and 3:79
      in portraits 3:82
   Van der Velde and 3:112
Landseer, Sir Edwin *see Artists'*
   Index
Langlois, François, by Van Dyck
   3:*82-3*
Lanier, Nicholas, 3:*80*
   by Van Dyck 3:*80*
Larionov, Mikhail Fedorovich
   see Artists' Index
Larsen, Tulla 9:112
   by Munch 9:*112*
Lasky, Martin 7:133
'last of the medieval popes' *see*
   Boniface VIII, Pope
Laud, Archbishop 3:103
Laufberger, Ferdinand: Klimt
   and 9:76
   class of 9:76
Laurencin, Marie *see Artists'*
   Index
Laurent, Ernest *see Artists' Index*
lawn tennis 5:*104-105*
Lawrence, D. H. 8:*138*
   The Rainbow 7:74
   Women in Love 8:138

Lawrence, Sir Thomas *see Artists'*
   Index
Le Nôtre, André 3:*72*
Le Valentin *see Artists' Index*
League of Nations 7:107
   Geneva Protocol 7:106-107
Lebanon, massacre of the
   Maronites 9:*42*
Leake, Anna 5:133
Leavens, Harriet, by Phillips
   6:*20*
Leewenhoek, Anton van 3:*133*
   and the microscope 3:134
Léger, Fernand *see Artists' Index*
Légion d'Honneur: Courbet and
   8:48
   Delacroix and 4:113
   Redon and 9:49
   Rousseau and 6:16
Lehar, Franz: *The Merry Widow*
   9:*138*
Lemon, Margaret 3:81
   by Van Dyck 3:*78*
Lenin, V. I. 7:69, *69*, 70
Lens, Battle of (1648) 3:137
Leo X, Pope 2:*70*
   and Henry VIII 2:42
Leonardo da Vinci *see Artists'*
   Index
Leoni, Ottavio *see Artists' Index*
Leopold II, King of Belgium
   5:*135*; 8:48
Léotard, Jules *see Artists' Index*
Lesseps, Vicomte Ferdinand de
   5:71, *72*
Levassor, Emile 5:*70*
Leyden, Lucas van *see Artists'*
   Index
Lhote, André, Rivera and 8:109
'Liberty Boy' 4:66
Liebermann, Max *see Artists'*
   Index
light/shade: Giovanni Bellini's
   perception of 1:78, 82-5
   Caravaggio's use of 3:20-21, 36
   experiments on speed of 5:103
   Fra Angelico and 1:46
   Ruisdael's use of 3:116-17
   Van Dyck's use of 3:84-5
   Venetian fascination with 1:82
Limbourg brothers *see Artists'*
   Index
Lincoln, Abraham, President
   9:*38*, 41
Linde, Dr, Munch and 9:112
line: Botticelli and 1:116, 117
   masters of 1:*117*
   Dürer's mastery of 2:20-21, *21*
   Holbein and 2:86
   Seurat and 5:*113*, 114
Linnel, John, and Blake 4:49
Lipchitz, Jacques *see Artists'*
   Index
Lipi, Filippino *see Artists' Index*

Lipi, Filippo *see Artists' Index*
Lissitzy, El *see Artists' Index*
literature: Bruegel's use of
    subjects from 2:115
    Gothic forgeries 4:101
    role in Gothic Revival 4:99
lithography: first great master of
    4:21
    Goya and 4:17, 21
    Miró and 7:80, 81
        from 'Art for Research' 7:98
        'The Lizard with Golden
            Feathers' 7:83
        from 'Seers' 7:99
    Munch and 9:116
    Redon and 9:46-7
    Toulouse-Lautrec and 8:82
'Little Jewel' *see* **Toulouse-
    Lautrec, Henri de**
Lloyd George, David, Prime
    Minister 7:41; 8:138
    fall of 7:41-2
    and the 'Irish Question' 7:41-2
    'People's Budget' 6:40, 40-41
Loeb, Pierre, gallery 7:78
Lomellini Family, The 3:83
    by Van Dyck 3:82, 83
Lorca, Federico Garcia, Picasso
    and 6:108
Lorenzetti, Pietro *see Artists'
    Index*
Lotto, Lorenzo *see Artists' Index*
Loubet, M. 5:39
Louis XIV, King of France 3:137,
    138
    marriage 3:49
Louis XVII, King of France
    4:137-8
Louis-Napoleon Bonaparte 5:44;
    8:66, 67
    in Britain 8:74
    elected president 8:74
    and Proudhon 8:67
    see also Napoleon III, Emperor
        of France
Louis Philippe, King of France:
    exile in England 8:73
    overthrow of 8:46, 67, 71, 72
    rising against 8:66
Lovelace, Richard 3:102
Low Countries: Antwerp 2:109
    artist's workshop in 2:109
    Dürer in 2:17, 17
    importance of harbour 2:109
    as a painting centre 2:109
    see also Guild of St Luke,
        Antwerp
    Brussels 2:112
        Bruegel in 2:111-12
        importance in 16th century
            2:112
    Castle of Egmond, Ruisdael
        and 3:108-109, 112-13
    division of land in 2:133

Dürer in 2:16-17
    invasion of by Spain 2:133,
        133, 136, 136-9
    Fall of Breda 3:71
    Leyden: Guild of Physicians
        and Surgeons 3:134
        University 3:132-3, 135
            anatomy theatre 3:132-3
    life expectancy in 2:134
    map of 2:108
    political unrest in 2:112-13
    16th-century peasant life
        2:132-5
    see also Belgium; Holland
Loyola, St Ignatius 2:41
Ludendorff, General 7:106
Ludwig I, King of Bavaria,
    abdication of 8:73
Ludwig II, King of Bavaria, and
    Courbet 8:48
Lüeger, Karl, and the
    Secessionists 9:102
Lusitania, sinking of the 7:74
Luther, Martin 2:40-42
    arrest of 2:17
    becomes a monk 2:68
    and Cranach 2:68
        sits for 2:47
    and the Diet of Worms
        2:40-41, 41, 70, 70-71
    Dürer and 2:16, 21
    Elector of Saxony and 2:46
    first attack on Church 2:16
    followers 2:69
    marriage 2:71
    '95 Theses' 2:40, 47, 68, 69
    and the papal bull 2:70, 70
    and the Reformation 2:68-71
        'Reformation Treatises'
            2:40-41
    translation of the Bible 2:47
        Cranach and 2:49
        title page 2:40, 71
    university education 2:68
        at Wittenberg 2:47, 69
Luther altarpiece (Cranach) 2:71
Lutheran propaganda 2:69
Lüthi, Hanny *see Artists' Index*
Luzán, José, and Goya 4:12
Lycée Imperial, Paris 4:108
Lydgate, John 1:74, 74

M

Macadam, John Loudon
    4:102
MacDonald, Ramsay, Prime
    Minister, and the Geneva
    Protocol 7:106-107
Macmillan, Harold 7:135
Mach, Ernst 5:103

Macpherson, James 4:101, 101
Madero, Francisco I, 8:132, 132-3
Madonna and Child, formal
    images of 1:82
Madrid Academy, 4:13-14
    Goya and 4:13
maestro pintor de ymagineria,
    Velázquez as 3:45
Magellan, Ferdinand, 2:14
Magritte, René *see Artists' Index*
Mahdi, the 5:136
Mahler, Alma 9:79
Maitland, Edward 5:103
majesty, comparisons of images
    of 2:87, 87
Makart, Hans *see Artists' Index*
Maler, Hans 2:44
Malevich, Kasimir *see Artists'
    Index*
Mallarmé, Stéphane: death of
    9:48
    and Symbolism 9:68
    by Munch 9:68, 111
Malphigi, Marcello 2:134
mandala 6:71
Mander, Karl/Karel van *see
    Artists' Index*
Manet, Edouard *see Artists' Index*
Manetti, on Fra Angelico 1:45
Manfredi, Bartolommeo *see
    Artists' Index*
Manifesto of Futurist Artists 6:42
Mannerism, spread of 2:52-3
Mantegna, Andrea *see Artists'
    Index*
Manuel II, King of Portugal 6:41
mapmaking/mapmakers,
    17th-century Dutch 3:134-5,
    135
    new standards in 3:132
Marc, Franz *see Artists' Index*
Margarita, Infanta of Spain, by
    Velázquez 3:54, 67
Maria Luisa, Queen of Spain
    4:14
    by Goya 4:14
Maria Theresa, Empress of
    Austria, 8:41
Maria Theresa, Infanta,
    marriage of 3:49
Marino, Giovanni Battista, and
    Caravaggio 3:15
Marq, Charles, Chagall and 6:80
marranos 4:34-5, 37
Marshall, P. P. 9:34
Martin, John *see Artists' Index*
Martini, Simone *see Artists' Index*
Marx, Karl 8:69, 71
    and the 'First International'
        8:68, 69
    The Communist Manifesto 8:71,
        71
    The Poverty of Philosophy
        8:68

Mary, Princess 2:103
Mary, Queen 6:41
Mary, Queen of Scots 2:74, 138,
    138
Masaccio *see Artists' Index*
Masson, Andre *see Artists' Index*
Massys, Quentin *see Artists'
    Index*
Masuccio: on 15th-century
    monastic life 1:68
Matisse, Henri *see Artists' Index*
Matout, Louis *see Artists' Index*
Matsch, Franz *see Artists' Index*
Matthew (ship) 1:104
Matta, Echaurren Roberto *see
    Artists' Index*
Matyushin, Mikhail, Malevich
    and 7:47
    Victory over the Sun 7:47
Maugham, W. Somerset: *Of
    Human Bondage* 7:74
Maurier, George du: *Trilby* 8:105
Mauve, Antona, and Van Gogh
    5:78, 82
Mavrocordato, Prince 4:132
Maximilian I, Emperor: death of
    2:16
    and Dürer 2:15-16
    posthumous portrait by 2:16
    painting project for 2:38-9
Mayakovsky, Vladimir *see
    Artists' Index*
Mazarin, Cardinal 3:74; 137
    and the Fronde 3:138
Mazdazna, Itten and 7:36
Mazeppa's Ride 5:130, 132
Mazo, Juan Bautista Martinez
    del 3:48, 53
mechanical aids for portraiture
    2:84
Medici, Catherine de': marriage
    of 2:16
Medici, Cosimo de': commission
    for Fra Angelico 1:51
    and Florence 1:133
        and San Marco monastery
            1:47-8, 69-70
Medici, Guiliano de': and Pazzi
    conspiracy 1:136
        murder by 1:110, 136
Medici, Lorenzo de': death of
    1:134
    and Florence 1:109-110, 133
        government of 1:111
    and Pazzi conspiracy 1:110,
        136
    and Savonarola 1:134
    upbringing 1:133
Medici, Lorenzo di Pierfrancesco
    de' 1:119
    and Botticelli 1:109, 118, 119
        commissions for 1:116-17
    leaves Florence 1:112
    villa of 1:118

Medici, Marie de', marriage of 3:41, *42*
Medici, Piero de' 1:*135*
　and French invasion 1:134
　　cedes stronghold 1:112
　and Florence 1:111
Medici dynasty 1:*132-3*
　sculptor to 1:*137*
Medina del Campo, Treaty of (1487) 1:104
Mehmet II, Sultan of Turkey:
　and the Bellinis 1:78, 138
　by Gentile Bellini 1:*101*
Meier-Graefe, Julius 9:134
Meister, Joseph 5:138
Melanchthon, Philip 1:*104-105*; 12:69
　and Dürer 2:16
　　epitaph to 2:17
　Elector of Saxony and 2:46
　　and Luther's ideas 2:47
　　and the Reformation 2:16
Melly, George 7:133
Mendicant orders 1:*69*
　dislike of 1:68
　see also Carmelite Order; Dominican Order; Franciscan Order
Mendoza, Cardinal, and the treatment of heretics 1:138
Menelik II, Emperor of Ethiopia 5:72
Mengs, Anton *see Artists' Index*
Menken, Adah 5:130, 131-2
Merchants' Guild, Florence, commission for Botticelli 1:109
Mercure de France, and Rousseau 6:15
Merisi, Fermo di Bernardino 3:12
Merisi, Michelangelo *see* **Caravaggio**
Meryon, Charles *see Artists' Index*
Messina, Antonella da *see Artists' Index*
Metternich, Prince 4:135
Metzinger, Jean 6:101
Mexican Revolution 8:132-5
　Convention of Aguas Calientes 8:134-5
Mexico: authoritarian regime in 8:132
　Decena Trágica 8:134
　Díaz regime 8:108
　new constitution 8:135
　a *Pulqueria* 8:116
　tradition of wall painting 8:116, *116*
　　murals for public buildings 8:110-11
Meyer, Hannes: and the Bauhaus 7:38-9
　direction of studies 7:39
　Torten estate 7:38

Meyer, Heinrich, and Friedrich 4:79
Michelangelo *see Artists' Index*
Michelson and Morley 5:103
microscopes/microscopy, 17th-century 3:*133, 134*
Mies van der Rohe, Ludwig: and the Bauhaus 7:39
　Seagram Building 7:*39*
Milan, Duke of, and Botticelli 1:111
Millais, John Everett *see Artists' Index*
Miller, Jonathan 7:135
Miller, Roger 7:132
Millet, Jean-François *see Artists' Index*
Milner, Sir Alfred 5:40
mining, new machinery 4:*70*
Miró, Dolores 7:79
Miró, Joan *see Artists' Index*
Miró, Miguel 7:76
Mistral, Frédéric 5:36, *36*
Mocenigo, Giovanni 3:40
Mocenigo, Pietro, and the Turks 1:138
'modelling' lines 2:19
Modigliani, Amedeo *see Artists' Index*
Mohammed II of Turkey *see* Mehmet II
Moholy-Nagy, Laszlo *see Artists' Index*
Moilliet, Louis 6:45
Monaco, Lorenzo *see Artists' Index*
monasteries/monastic life, 15th-century 1:68-71, *70*
　as dens of iniquity 1:*68*
　flouting the rules 1:68
　recreations 1:71
Mondrian, Piet *see Artists' Index*
Monet, Claude *see Artists' Index*
Monroe Doctrine 4:136-7
Montañes: *Crucifix* 3:46
Monte Carlo 5:36, *36-7*
Montesquieu: *L'Esprit des Lois* 8:41
Montesquiou, Count Robert de 9:68
Montez, Lola 8:73
　organization of 6:51
Moors, the Inquisition and 4:37
moral narratives, comparisons in 8:20, *20*
More, Thomas: circle of friends 2:83-4
　execution of 2:79
　family, by Holbein 2:*78, 85*
　and Henry VIII 2:100
　　and marriage of 2:78-9
　Holbein and 2:77-8
　　portrait by 2:83, *92*
　and Oath of Supremacy 2:79

Moréas, Jean: and Symbolism 9:68
　manifesto of 9:68
Moreau, Gustave *see Artists' Index*
Morgunov, Alexei *see Artists' Index*
Mornay, Count Charles de 4:110, 112
Morocco, revolt in 8:138
Morosov, Ivan: art collection 7:45
　Malevich and 7:45
Morris, Jane 9:16, 21, *36*
　Rossetti and 9:36
　　by Rossetti 9:*16*
Morris, William *see Artists' Index*
Morris & Co 9:34-7
　commissions from Webb 9:35
　1861 prospectus 9:35
　founder-members 9:34
　range of products 9:35, *36*
mosaic 1:19
　comparison of Byzantine 9:*84, 84*
　by Giotto 1:*19*
　Klimt and 9:76
Moscow University, Kandinsky at 7:13
Moser, Kolomon 9:*100*
　and 'Club of Seven' 9:100
　illustration for *Ver Sacrum* 9:*103*
Mother Shipton 5:106
Motherwell, Robert *see Artists' Index*
Mountjoy, Lord Deputy 3:41
Mozart, Wolfgang Amadeus:
　Klee and 6:44, *45*
　The Magic Flute 4:*104*; 6:45
Muffel, Jacob, by Dürer 2:*19*
Mühlberg, Battle of (1547) 2:49, 72-3
Müller, Johann 1:*74*
　in Nuremberg 2:37,38
Munby, Arthur 9:40
Munch, Christian 9:108
Munch, Edvard *see Artists' Index*
Munch, Peter Andreas 9:108
Munich Royal Academy, Kandinsky at 7:14
Münster, Treaty of, ratification of (1648) 3:136
Münter, Gabriele 7:14, 15
mural painting: Early Christian, influence on Cimabue 1:12
　Hogarth and 8:16, *16*
　in Mexico: tradition of 8:116, *116*
　　revival in 8:110-11
　Miró and 7:*94-5*
　Riley and 7:*113*
　Rivera and 8:110-11
Murat, Joachim 4:22

Murer, and Pissarro 5:99
Murillo, Bartolomé Esteban *see Artists' Index*
Mus, Decius, commission for Rubens 3:77
Musée Granet, and Cézanne 5:37
Museum of Modern Art, New York: Chagall and 6:81
　'Responsive Eye Exhibition' 7:111
　Rivera exhibition 8:112
Mussolini, Benito 7:41, *41*
　and World War I 7:73-4
　criticism of 6:15
Mytens, Daniel *see Artists' Index*
mythology, master of 1:114-17

N

nabi aux belles icônes, le see Denis, Maurice
Nabis, the: Gauguin and 9:48, *48-9*
　inspiration of 9:71
　members of 9:49
　Redon and 9:48, *48-9*, 49
Nadar *see* Tournachon, Gaspard Félix
naive painters 6:20, *20*
Nalanson, Misia 8:79
Nansen, Fridtjof 5:103
Napoleon I, Emperor of France:
　in Spain 4:14, 16
　escape from Elba 4:*102*, 104-105
　exile to St Helena 4:106, *106*
　and Macpherson 4:101
　and Tsar Alexander I 4:*42*
Napoleon III, Emperor of France:
　and Italian unification 9:41
　and Salon des Refusés 5:98-9
narrative sequences 1:22-3
Nash, John: Brighton Pavilion 4:*104*
National Gallery, London, Riley and 7:113
Naturalism/Naturalists:
　comparisons of style 2:*21*
　Redon's criticism of 9:44
navigational equipment 3:135
Naylor, James 3:73-4
Nazarenes, the 4:141
Neo-Classicism: development of 8:42
　Friedrich and 4:77
Neo-Impressionists 5:110
Netherlands, the: the Inquisition in 4:36-7
　see also Low Countries

Neue Künstlervereinigung München, Kandinsky and 7:15
Neve, Ethel le 6:42
'New Learning' 2:100
New Zealand 3:135, *137*
Newfoundland, made a Crown Colony 6:74
Nicholas I, Tsar of Russia 4:*81*
and Friedrich 4:*81*
Nicholas II, Tsar of Russia: abdication 7:68, 70
accession of 8:*102-103*
army refuses to support 7:69
and dispute with Germany 6:42
Rasputin and 7:68
Nicholas V, Pope: chapel of 1:*48*
and Fra Angelico 1:48
commission for 1:48, *48*
and Humanist ideals 1:48
Nietzsche, Friedrich 5:103-104
Nieuwerkerke, Comte de, and Courbet 8:47
Nightingale, Florence 6:42
Nixon, Richard, President, election of 7:137
non-representation art *see* abstract art
Nordheim, Sondre 9:*39*
North, Robert, *Colour Moves* 7:*112-13*, 113
Northern Ireland: civil rights movement in 7:138
North-West Passage, quest for 1:*104*
Norway: political autonomy 9:136
Nostradamus 2:74
'notary' *see* **Seurat, Georges-Pierre**
Notti, Gherardo delle *see* Honthorst, Gerrit van
nudes: Dürer's study of 2:14, 19-20, *20*
first German life-size 2:*20*
Velázquez' only 3:48, *62-3*
Nuremberg Chronicle 2:36-9, *36, 39*

O

oak panels, Bruegel and 2:116
Oberreid, Hans, commission for Holbein 2:*82*
Oberreid Altarpiece, The (Holbein) 2:*82*
Obregón, Alvaro 8:134
Obstfelder, Sigbjorn 9:134-5
Odysseus (Greek freedom fighter) 4:*133*
Offenburg, Magdalena 2:77

oil paint/oil painting: Bruegel and 2:116
Friedrich and 4:79-80
qualities of 1:84
Olbrich, Joseph *see Artists' Index*
Old Masters: Courbet and 8:51
Hogarth and 8:17
Olivares, Count of *see* Guzman, Don Gaspar de
Olympic Games 8:*105*
Onassis, Aristotle 7:138
Op Art, Riley and 7:*110*
imagery in 9:52
Orazco, José Clemente *see Artists' Index*
Orazco, Pascual 8:133
Orcagna, Andrea *see Artists' Index*
Order of St Olav, Munch and 9:113
'Orphism' 6:78
Ortelius, Abraham 2:*110*
and Bruegel 2:110, 111
Theatrum Orbis Terrarum 2:110, *110*
Orton, Joe: *Entertaining Mr Sloane* 7:135
Orwell, George 7:102
on Dalí 6:111
Oscar II, King of Sweden-Norway 9:136
Osman I, Sultan of Turkey 1:*41*
Ospidale della Consolazione 3:13
Ossian *see* Macpherson, James
Ottoman Empire: attacks on Italy 1:138
threat to Venetian Empire 1:102-103
see also Turkey

P

Pacheco, Francisco *see Artists' Index*
Pacheco, Juana, and Velázquez 3:45
Pacher, Michael *see Artists' Index*
Paderewski, Jan, death of 6:106
Paine, Tom 4:66, 66-8
The Age of Reason 4:69
Common Sense 4:66-7
The Rights of Man 4:67
painter-monks 1:46
painter-poets 4:52, *52*
painters' guild *see* Guild of St Luke
Paisley, Ian 7:138
Palestinian Giant *see* Goshen, Colonel
Palmer, Samuel *see Artists' Index*

Palomino, Antonio: on Pareja 3:48
on Velázquez 3:44, 50-51
as Ambassador to Rome 3:49
'freeness' of technique 3:52
and Rubens 3:47
pamphlets/pamphleteers 4:66-9
cover by Malevich 7:*50-51*
Panama Canal, building of 5:47
Gauguin and 5:47, *47*, 71
paying for 5:*70-71*, 71-2
scandal over 5:105
Pani, Alberto J., and Rivera 8:110
papal authority, threats to 1:41-2
Papal States, and alliance against France 1:104
paper, improvement in manufacture 2:39
Parc Guell (Gaudí/Jujol) 6:*133*
Pareja, Juan de 3:48, *49*, 53
by Velázquez 3:*48*, *64*
The Baptism of Christ 3:48
The Calling of St Mathew 3:*49*
'Parigots' 5:36
Parnell, Charles 5:74, *106*
Paris Salon: Cézanne and 5:13, 16
Courbet and 8:45, *46*
Delacroix and 4:109-110, 111, 112, 113
Seurat and 5:109
Paris Universal Exhibition *see* Exposition Universelle de Paris
Pars, Henry: and Blake 4:45
drawing school 4:45
Pasteur, Louis 5:138, *138*
Pater, Walter, and 'rediscovery' of Botticelli 1:117
Patriarch of Venice, and Dürer 2:14
patrons: Botticelli's 1:109
Giotto's 1:16-17
first secular 1:14
patterns, Venetian fascination for 1:82
Paul III, Pope: alliance with Emperor Charles V 2:73
by Titian 3:52
and Council of Trent 2:73, *73*
Paul VI, Pope 7:138
Pavlova, Anna 5:*138*
Pazzi, Francesco 1:137
Pazzi, Jacopo 1:137
Pazzi conspiracy 1:110, *136*, 136-7
punishment for 1:*111*
peasant life: comparisons in painting 8:53, *53*
16th-century 2:132-5, *135*
Peasants' War 2:17, 48, 71
Péladan, Joséphin, and Symbolism 9:70

Pen, Jehuda *see Artists' Index*
pencil, Goya's use of 4:21
pendulum clock, invention of 3:135, *135*
Pershing, General 8:135
perspective: Bellini and linear 1:85
Botticelli and 1:113
Caravaggio and 3:20
Dürer and 2:14
writing on 2:17
Fra Angelico's use of 1:46, 51
Gozzoli's use of 1:49
Mantegna and 1:83
Peru: Cuzco 2:105
Peruzzi, Giovanni, commission for Giotto 1:16, *16*
Peterzano, Simone, and Caravaggio 3:12
Petrograd State Free Art Workshops, Malevich and 7:47
Petronio, Captain 3:16
Pforr, Franz *see Artists' Index*
Phalanx group 7:14
Kandinsky and 7:*14*, 15
Philip II, King of Spain: and Bosch 4:20
and Brussels 2:112
and the Low Countries 2:134, 136-7
Philip IV, King of France 1:*42*
defiance of the Pope 1:41
Philip IV, King of Spain 3:68-71
character of 3:69-70
and duties of kingship 3:70
family, by Velázquez 3:53, *70*
heirs 3:69, *70*, 71
and hunting 3:*68-9*, 69
as literary patron 3:68
mistresses 3:69-70, *70*
and Velázquez 3:46
painted by 3:*51*, 68
Phillips, Ammi *see Artists' Index*
'piagnoni' 1:113, 135
Picasso, Pablo *see Artists' Index*
Pico della Mirandola 1:135
Piero della Francesca *see Artists' Index*
Pierozzi, Antoninus, life of 1:70
Pierre Matisse Gallery, Miró and 7:80
pigments: amount specified in commissions 1:50
technique of applying for *buon fresco* 1:23
pigtails 4:39
Piles, De, on Van Dyck's portraits 3:85
Pilgrimage of Grace, Henry VIII and 2:80-81
Pinkie, Battle of (1547) 2:74
Piper, Sir David, on Filippo Lippi 1:117

Piranesi, Giambattista *see Artists' Index*
Pirckheimer, Willibald, and Dürer 2:12, *14*
   on his last years 2:17
   on his wife 2:13
   in Nuremberg 2:38
Pisanello, Antonio *see Artists' Index*
Pisano, Andrea *see Artists' Index*
Pisano, Giovanni *see Artists' Index*
Pissarro, Camille *see Artists' Index*
Pitt, William, the Younger, Prime Minister 4:66, 68
Pius II, Pope, and holy crusade 1:*103*
Pizarro, Francisco 2:*105*
plague: the Black Death 3:72-3
   in England 1:*73*
     Holbein dies of 2:81
     in London 2:81
   in Nuremberg 2:13
Plehve, Vyacheslav 9:73
Poe, Edgar Allan, Redon and 9:45
Pointillism 5:112-15
   Seurat and 5:109
     first experiment in 5:113
Poland: plebiscite in 8:136-7
   treaty with Russia 8:137
   and the Ukraine 8:137
   and Upper Silesia 7:40
Polidori, Frances Mary 9:12
Pollaiuolo, Antonio *see Artists' Index*
Pollaiuolo, Piero de *see Artists' Index*
Pollaiuolo Brothers *see Artists' Index*
Pollock, Jackson *see Artists' Index*
Pomare V, King of Tahiti 5:*48*
   Gauguin and 5:48, *48*
Pompidou, Georges, dismissed by de Gaulle 7:137
Pontier, Auguste-Henri, and Cézanne 5:37
Poor Clares 1:38, *39*
Popova, Lyubov Sergeevna *see Artists' Index*
portraits, comparisons of:
   equestrian 3:85, *85*
   papal 3:52, *52*
   see also individual portraits
Portugal: declared a republic 6:41
   French occupation of 4:40
   independence from Spain 3:69
   revolution in 6:41
   threat to Venetian trade 1:103
Posada: caricature of Huerta 8:*134*

Post-Impressionists/Post-Impressionism 5:50, 101
   Chagall and 6:82
   exhibition in London 6:42
   Fry and 6:42
   Miró and 7:82
poster art: in Barcelona 6:134
   Miró and 7:*79*, 83
     Aidez Espagne 7:79, *91*
   Toulouse-Lautrec and 8:*78-9*, 79
Poussin, Nicolas *see Artists' Index*
poveri vergognosi, organization for 1:70
'predella', Linaiuoli altarpiece 1:51
Pre-Raphaelite Brotherhood 9:14-15
   'rediscovery' of Botticelli 1:113
press gang 4:40
Pride, Colonel 3:138
   'Pride's Purge' 3:138
'primitive' painters: Bruegel and 2:114
primitive worlds, comparison 5:53, *53*
Princeteau, René, Toulouse-Lautrec and 8:77
Princip, Gavrilo 9:105
printing/publishing: in Antwerp 2:109
   Cranach and 2:49
   Morris and 9:34
   Munch and 9:112
   Nuremberg and 2:*37*, 38, 39, *39*
   popularity of 2:37
Priuli, Girolamo, on new trade routes 1:103
Profumo, John 7:132
Prokofiev, Serge: *The Love of Three Oranges* 8:138
propaganda, artists and 2:80
proportion: Dürer and perfect 2:19-20
     writing on 2:17, 21
'props', Van Dyck's use of 3:84
Proudhon, Pierre: Courbet and 8:45, *66*
     interpretation of works by 8:47
   philosophy 8:66
   and the workers' revolution 8:66-9
   Du Principe de l'Art 8:68
   Le Représentat du Peuple 8:67
   What is Property? 8:66
Proust, Marcel 7:42
proverbs, Bruegel's use of 2:115
Prussia: and Peace of Aix-la-Chapelle 8:40-41, *40-41*
   royal family and Goya 4:14
Przybyszewski, Dagny 9:112

Przybyszewski, Stanislaw, Munch and 9:111, 133
   painted by 9:*133*
psychoanalysis, birth of 6:70-71
Puccini, Giacomo 5:*40*
   Madame Butterfly 9.74, *74*
   Tosca 5:40
pulpit, San Andrea, Pistoia (Pisano) 1:*40*
Puvis de Chavannes, Pierre *see Artists' Index*

Q

Quant, Mary, 7:*132*, 133-4, *134*
'Quinta del Sordo' 4:16, *17*
Quistrop, Johann Gottfried, and Friedrich 4:77

R

Rabelais, François: *Gargantua* 2:*104*
   Pantagruel 2:*104*
rabies, vaccine for 5: 138, *138*
Rabin, Sam, Riley and 7:109
Radcliffe, Ann 4:*101*
Raerburg, Malevich and 7:45
Raet, Marie de, by Van Dyck 3:*91*
Raffles, Sir Thomas Stamford 4:*71*
Rahman, Sheik Mujibur 6:138
Raphael Sanzio *see Artists' Index*
Rasputin 7:68, 69
'Rayonnism' 7:46
Raysac, Madame de 9:46, *46*
real tennis 2:101
Realism/Reality 8:45
   Courbet and 8:45
   protests against 8:46
   the shock of 8:50-53
Realist movement, leader of 8:50
Rebull, Santiago, Rivera and 8:114
Redbeard the Pirate 2:*105*
Redon, Arï: by Redon 9:*48*
   on his father 9:49
Redon, Bertrand 9:44
Redon, Odilon *see Artists' Index*
Reformation: destruction of Holbein's works during 2:83
   Dürer and 2:16
   effect on art in Basel 2:77
   Elector of Saxony and 2:46
   the Inquisition and 4:37
   Luther and 2:68-71
   religious extremists in 2:*78-9*
   Scottish 2:73

Reformation Treatises (Luther) 2:40-41
Reinhardt: Munch and 9:112, *134-5*, 135
religion, spread by pictures 2:68
religious wars, 16th-century 2:138
Rembrandt van Rijn *see Artists' Index*
Renaissance: animals 6:38
   symbols of learning 2:89
Reni, Guido *see Artists' Index*
Renoir, Auguste *see Artists' Index*
Responsive Eye Exhibition, Riley and 7:111
Reverdy, Pierre, criticism of Rivera 8:109-110
'Reviser of Indecent Paintings' 4:12
Reymerswaele, Marinus van *see Artists' Index*
Ribera, Jusepe de *see Artists' Index*
Ricevuta di Lapo del Pela (Ciuta) 1:14
Richard Feigen Gallery, Riley and 6:111
Richard III, King of England 2:10
Richardson, Samuel: *Clarissa* 8:41,42
   Pamela; or Virtue Rewarded 8:41
Richelieu, Cardinal 3:*104*
   and the Thirty Years War (1618-48) 3:105-106
Riesener, Henri, and Delacroix 4:109
Riley, Bridget *see Artists' Index*
Rinversi, Anna 1:76
Rio de Janeiro, founding of 2:*138*
Rivera, Diego *see Artists' Index*
Robbia, Luca della *see Artists' Index*
Robert of Anjou, King of Naples, and Giotto 1:16-17
Roberts, Lord 5:40
Rockefeller Center, Rivera and 8:113, *113*
Rodchenko, Alexander Mikhailovich *see Artists' Index*
Roller, Alfred, and Hagenbund 9:100
Romanesque period: animals in art of 6:38
   Miró and 7:77, 82
'Romanists' 2:109
Romantic era/Romantic movement: animals 6:38-9
   Friedrich and 4:80-81
   leading painter 9:50
     most important German painter see Friedrich, Caspar David
   spirit of 4:111-12
   waning in France 9:44

Rommel, General 6:*104*,105, 106
Roosevelt, Franklin D,
    President: inauguration of
    6:*74*
    and the New Deal 6:74, *74*
    and repeal of the Eighteenth
    Amendment 6:73
Roosevelt, Theodore, President
    9:*73*, 74
Rops, Félicien *see Artists' Index*
Rosenfeld, Bella 6:79, 81
    and Chagall 6:*78-9*
Ross, Mrs Nellie 7:106
Rossetti, Christina 9:12, *17*
Rossetti, Dante Gabriel *see
    Artists' Index*
Rossetti, Gabriele Pasquale 9:12,
    13, 13
Rossetti, Maria 9:12
Rossetti, William Michael 9:12,
    17
Rothschild, Sir Nathaniel 5:138
'Rough Wooing' 2:74
Rousseau, Henri *see Artists'
    Index*
Rousseau, Julien 6:12
Rowlandson, Thomas *see Artists'
    Index*
Rowley, Thomas *see Chatterton,
    Thomas*
Roy, Pierre *see Artists' Index*
Royal Academy, London: Blake
    and 4:45
    Rossetti at 9:13, *13*
Royal College of Art, London,
    Riley at 7:109
Royal Tapestry Manufactury,
    Madrid 4:13, *13*
Rubens, Peter Paul *see Artists'
    Index*
Rudolph, Crown Prince of
    Austria, suicide of 5:*70*, 72-3
Ruisdael, Isaack van 3:108
Ruisdael, Jacob van *see Artists'
    Index*
Rusiñol, Santiago 6:134
Ruskin, John *see Artists' Index*
Russell, John, Van Gogh and
    5:101
Russia: and Afghanistan 5:137
    Allied forces in 7:71
    army demoralized 7:68, 69
    and Austrian expansion 6:41
    Brest-Litovsk, Treaty of 7:71
    civil wars (1918-20) 7:71
    and Czechoslovakia 7:138,
    138
    detente in space 6:*136*, 138
    Duma: abolition of 7:71
    power of 7:69
    February Revolution (1917)
    7:68-81, *68-9*
    Federation of Leftist Artists
    7:47

and France 8:103-104
and Germany 6:41-42
    German invasion of (1941)
    6:105, *105*
    treaty with 7:40-41, 9:138
and Greek War of
    Independence 4:135-6
illiteracy campaign 7:70
the Kronstadt Rising (1921)
    8:137, *138*
May Day 7:71
Moscow as an art centre 7:45-6
'1905 Revolution' 9:*136-7*, 137
New Economic Policy 8:137
People's Commissariat for
    Enlightenment, Kandinsky
    and 7:16
plight of the peasants 7:*68*,
    68-9
Potemkin mutiny 9:137
rise of the Bolsheviks 7:*69*,
    69-71; 8:137
and Spanish Civil War
    7:101-102
spreading propaganda 7:*71*
suppression of the avant-
    garde 7:16
and Tibet 9: 72-3
treaty with Poland 8:137
war with Japan (1904) 9:*72-3*,
    73-4, 136-7, *137*
widespread unrest in 7:69-71
and World War I 7:72-3;
    9:105,106
Russian Academy of Artistic
    Sciences, Kandinsky and 7:16
'Russian primitivist' movement:
    leaders of 7:45
Russian Revolution: Chagall
    and 6:79
    demand for art during 7:47, *47*
    and easel painting 7:48
    plotting for the 6:103
Ruthven, Alexander 3:42
Ruthven, Mary: and Van Dyck
    3:81, *81*
Ruysdael, Jacob Salomonsz *see
    Artists' Index*
Ruysdael, Salomon van *see
    Artists' Index*
Rysselberghe, Theo van *see
    Artists' Index*

S

sacra conversazione: Bellini and
    1:84
    Fra Angelico and l:*51*
    masterpiece of *see* San Giobbe
    Altarpiece
St Antonino 1:47

St Benedict 1:*70*
St Bernardino, in Venice 1:76
St Eloi 1:*109*
St Francis of Assisi 1:36, 36-9
    burial place of 1:18
    by Giovanni Bellini 1:79, 84, *90*
    by Giotti 1:*19*, 38
    by Sassetta 1:*36*, 37
    founding an order 1:38
    pilgrimage of Egypt 1:38
    Canticle to the Sun 1:39
St Lorenz, Nuremberg 2:36
St Martin's Lane Academy:
    Hogarth and 8:13
    method of copying 8:20
St Nicholas Eve, feast of 2:*135*
St Peter's Square, Rome
    (Bernini) 3:72
St Sebald, Nuremberg 2:36
Saint-Saëns, Camille: *The
    Carnival of Animals* 8:138
Salon des Artistes
    Indépendants: Chagall and
    6:78
    exhibits at 6:79
    Rousseau and 6:14
    Toulouse-Lautrec and 8:78
Salon d'Automne, Redon and
    9:49, 72
Salon painting, convention in
    8:50
Salon des Refusés, opening of
    5:98-9
Salon de la Rose+Croix 9:70, *71*
Salter, Elisabeth 4:*109*, 111
San Andrea, Pistoia, pulpit 1:*40*
S. Antonio de la Florida,
    commission for Goya 4:14
S. Cassiano Altarpiece, Messina
    1:*80*
San Domenico, Cortona,
    commission for Fra Angelico
    1:47
San Domenico, Fiesole 1:*44*
    sinopia found at 1:*51*
San Luigi dei Francesi, Rome
    3:14, *14*
San Pietro Martire: triptych 1:46
    bill for painting 1:46
San'Onofrio, Cardinal,
    commissions Reni 3:*105*
Sand, George 4:113
    Delacroix and 4:112
    by Delacroix 4:*113*
Sanderson & Co, and Morris
    9:37
Sant Lluch circle, Miró and
    7:76-7
Santa Croce, Florence:
    Altarpiece 1:36
    Giotto frescoes in 1:16, *16*
    detail 1:*18-19*
Santa Maria della Croce al
    Tiempo 1:*54-5*

Santa Maria della Salute, Venice
    3:*106*
Santa Maria della Scala, rejection
    of Caravaggio paintings 3:17
Santa Maria Novella, Florence
    1:*68*
    Botticelli painting for 1:109
    crucifix for 1:*18*
Santi Giovanni e Paolo, Venice
    1:*81*
Sanudo, Marin, on Giovanni
    Bellini 1:81
Saraceni, Carlo, and Caravaggio
    3:36-7
Sass's Art School, Rossetti and
    9:13
Sassetta, Stephano di Giovanni
    see Artists' Index
Sassoon, Vidal 7:*133-4*, 134
Satie, Eric: *Parade* 6:135
Saturn, discovery of rings/
    moons 3:*73*, 134
Sausmarez, Maurice de, Riley
    and 7:110
Savonarola 1:71, 104, *132*, 132-5
    criticism of the Medici 1:133-4
    denounces the pope 1:104, 135
    and destruction of Florence
    1:111
    excommunication of 1:112-13
    execution of 1:*132*, 135
    followers *see* 'piagnoni'
    and French invasion (1494)
    1:112
    study cell of 1:*71*
Schedel, Hartmann, and
    Nuremberg Chronicle 2:39
Schiavone, Giorgio 1:106
Schiele, Egon 9:*80*
    Klimt and 9:80, *80*
Schinkel, Friedrich: design for
    The Magic Flute 4:*104*
Schlegel, Friedrich 4:78
Schlemmer, Oscar: and the
    Bauhaus 7:36-7
    Gropius and 7:36-7
    Triadic Ballet 7:36, *37*
Schmalkaldic League 2:73
Schmidt-Rottluff, and *Die Brücke*
    9:138
Schönberg, Arnold: and *Blaue
    Reiter* group 7:15
    Kandinsky and 7:14, *14-15*,
    15-16, *16*
Schongauer, Martin *see Artists'
    Index*
School of Applied Arts, Vienna
    see Kunstgewerbeschule
School of Fine Arts, Madrid,
    Dalí at 6:108-109
School of the Imperial Society
    for the Protection of Fine
    Art, Chagall at 6:77-8
'School of Paris' 6:103, *103*

scientists, 17th-century Dutch 3:113-14
Scopes, John A. 7:106
Scorel, Jan van *see Artists' Index*
Scotland: alliance with France (1547) 2:74
　Reformation in 2:73
Scott, Sir Walter 4:*134-5*
　Delacroix and 4:111
Scott, William Bell *see Artists' Index*
Scrovegni, Enrico degli: by Giotto 1:*24*
　commission for Giotto 1:14-15, 22
　private chapel for *see* Arena Chapel
Scrovegni, Reginaldo degli 1:24
sculpture: influence of classical on Cimabue 1:12
　Miró and 7:*82-3*
Seagram Building (Mies van der Rohe) 7:*39*
Secession/Secessionists 6:47; 9:100-103
　acceptance of 9:102-103
　aims of 9:101-102
　commissions for 9:103
　exhibitions: first 9:101, 102-103
　　14th 9:*100*
　　hall for 9:*100, 101*,102
　founder-members 9:101
　Die Jugend 6:44
　　Klee and 6:44
　Klimt and 9:78
　　poster for 9:*79*, 101
　　rift with 9:80-81
　Liebermann and 9:110
　members of 9:*100*
　President of 9:78, 101
　railway art 9: *102*
　setting up of 9:78
　Simplicissimus 6:44
　Ver Sacrum 9:101
　　illustration for 9:*103*
　　proclamation in 9:102
Sedgley, Peter *see Artists' Index*
Segatori, Agostina 5:101
Segondet, Madame 6:100
self-expression, Goya and 4:21
self-portraits, first independent 2:12-13
　see also individual artists
Selve, Georges de *see Ambassadors, The* (Holbein)
Sergantini, and the Secessionists 9:101-2
Serte, José Luis, Miró and 7:81
Sérusier, Paul, and the Nabis 9:49
Servite Order, Brescia, and Fra Angelico 1:47
Seurat, Antoine-Chrisostôme 5:108

Seurat, Georges-Pierre *see Artists' Index*
Seymour, Edward 2:74
Seymour, Jane, by Holbein 2:*97*
Sforza, Francesco, Marchese di Caravaggio, *major domo* to 3:12
Sforza, Giovanni 1:105
sfumato, Holbein's use of 2:82
Shackleton, Ernest 7:42; 9:*106*
Shakespeare, William: *Hamlet* 3:40-41
'Shakespeare of Painting, The' *see* **Hogarth, William**
Shchukin, Sergei: art collection 7:45
　Malevich and 7:45
Shelley, Mary: Frankenstein 4:101, *101*
Shelley, Percy Bysshe 4:69, *69*
　Declaration of Rights 4:69
　The Mask of Anarchy 4:69, *69*
Shiloh, King, devotees of 4:71
'Ship Money' 3:*101*, 104, *105*
Sholes, Christopher 9:*38*
shop card (Hogarth) 8:12, *12*
Shrimpton, Jean 7:134, 135
Sicily, revolution in (1848) 8:71
Siddal, Elizabeth 9:14, 15
　death of 9:16
　model for Rossetti 9:14
Sigismund, King of Bohemia 1:73, *73*
Signac, Paul *see Artists' Index*
Signorelli, Luca *see Artists' Index*
Silva, Jerónima de 3:44
Silva, Juan Rodríguez de 3:44
silversmiths/silversmithing: artists and 2:37
　in Nuremberg 2:37
sinopia, by Fra Angelico 1:*51*, 52
Siqueiros, David Alfaro *see Artists' Index*
Sistine Chapel: before painting of ceiling 1:*110*
　painting of the 1:110-11
Sixtus IV, Pope 1:*111*
　and the Sistine Chapel 1:110-11
　and the Pazzi conspiracy 1:110
skiing, birth of competitive 9:39
Smith, Adam, on London 8:36
Smollett, Tobias: *Roderick Random* 8:41
'snivellers' *see* '*piagnoni*'
Snyders, Frans *see Artists' Index*
soap opera, 18th-century 8:41-42
Société des Artistes Indépendants 5:109
　first exhibition 5:109
　Redon and 9:47-8
Society of Antiquaries, master-engraver to 4:45
Solomon R. Guggenheim Museum, Miró and 7:81

Solzhenitsyn, Alexander 7:*136*
Sophia, Princess, description of Henrietta Maria 3:85
sorcery, in 15th-century 1:138
Sorgh, Hendrick: *The Lutanist* 7:*84*
Soulé, Samuel 9:*38*
Soutine, Chaim *see Artists' Index*
South Africa: diamond mines in 5:*106*
　discovery of gold in 5:40
　political parties in 6:42
　and World War I 7:74
South African War (1899-1902) 5:*38*, 39-41
　Ladysmith, Relief of 5:40
　Mafeking, Relief of 5:*38*, 40-1
　Spion Kop, Battle of 5:40
Spain: alliance with Britain 4:42
　art patronage in 4:12
　Barcelona: as art centre 6:134-5
　　café life 6:*134*, 134-5
　　as cultural centre 7:82
　　revival of 6:132-5
　Carlist rebellion (1860) 9:*40*
　censorship in 4:37, *37*
　civil war in (1936-39) *see* Spanish Civil War
　declaration of republic 7:100
　decline of 3:69, 72-3
　defence of Catalonia 7:*101*
　Edict of Faith 4:35
　extravagance of the court 3:69
　French 'oppression' of 4:14, 38-42
　highest class of painter in 3:45
　ineffectiveness of government 7:100-101
　influence of French Revolution on 4:14
　Inquisition: effect on cultural life 4:37
　　reestablishment of 4:16
　and the Low Countries 2:134
　　invasion of 2:*133*, 136-8
　　makes peace with 3:136
　Madrid: as centre of the arts 4:12-14
　　Buen Retiro 3:68-9, 70, *70-71*
　　French troops in 4:14, *16*, 38-9
　　important painters in 4:12
　　uprising in 4:16, *18-19, 22-3, 30-31*, 42
　　royal court at 3:45
　Moors in 1:138
　repressive atmosphere of 4:16
　Seville 3:*44*
　　in the 17th-century 3:44
　　and South America 4:136
　treatment of heretics 1:138
　Jews 4:34-5
　war with France 3:71, 72-3

Spanish Civil War (1936-39) 6:*135, 135*; 7:100-103
　bombing of Guernica (1937) 7:103
　International Brigades 7:102, 103
　Madrid Massacre (1936) 7:*103*
　Miró and 7:79
　refugees from 7:102, *102*
　storming the Alcázar 7:*100-101*
Stadler-Stölzl, Gunta: and the Bauhaus 7:38
　weaving by 7:*38-9*
Stäel, Nicolas de *see Artists' Index*
stained glass: Chagall and 6:80, *80*
　Miró and 7:81
　Morris and 9:34, 35, *35*
Stalin, Josef 6:105
Stanley, Henry Morton 5:*73*, 74
Stavisky, Serge Alexandre 6:73
Stayner, Captain Richard 3:73
Steen, Jan *see Artists' Index*
Stefaneschi, Cardinal Jacopo, commission for Giotto 1:*15*
Stephens, John 7:134
Steuben, M., Courbet and 8:45
Stevenson, Robert Louis 5:103
still-life painting 9:44
stippling: Blake and 4:45
　Friedrich and 4:85
Stoclet, Adolphe 9:81
Stöhr, Ernst, and Hagenbund 9:100
Stoneborough-Wittgenstein, Margaret, by Klimt 9:*97*
Strachey, Lytton: *Queen Victoria* 8:138
Strauss, Richard: *Salome* 9:138
Stravinsky, Igor 6:40
　The Firebird 6:40
　　Chagall and 6:81
　　costume design for 6:*40-41*
　Petrushka 6:40
　The Rite of Spring 6:40
Stresemann, Gustav 7:*104*
Strindberg, August 9: *132, 133*
　Getting Married 9:133
　　Munch and 9:111,133
Strozzi Chapel, Florence, painting for 1:*54*, 54-5
Stuart, John McDouall 9:41
Stubbs, George *see Artists' Index*
Stuck, Franz von *see Artists' Index*
studia generale, standards of 1:69
studiolo of Isabella d'Este 1:79
Stumpf, Lily 6:45, *45*
Sturm, Der, Chagall and 6:79
Sturm Gallery, Der, Kandinsky and 7:16
Stuyvesant Foundation, Riley and 7:111
Suarez, Pino 8:134

Sudan, war in 5:136
Suetin, Nikolai *see Artists' Index*
Suleiman the Magnificent
  2:*40-41*
Suprematism: and the applied
  arts 7:48-9
  derivation of name 7:46-7
  early titles 7:52
  legacy of 7:48, *48*
  logic of 7:52
  origin of style 7:46
Surrealists/Surrealism 6:110, *110*
  in Barcelona 6:135
  Chagall and 6:82, 83
  Dalí and 6:*109*, 110
    doubts about 6:116
    effect on 6:114
    importance to 6:111
  exhibitions: Dalí and 6:112
    first 7:104
  First Surrealist Manifesto
    6:114; 7:77
  International Exhibition 6:112
  'only authentic' 6:113
  precursors of 6:116, *116*
  theoretical foundations 6:83,
    114
  and World War II 6:113
Sussex, Countess of, on Van
  Dyck's painting of 3:85
Sweden: and alliance with
  England 3:74
  invasion of Bohemia 3:*137*
  17th-century territorial gains
    3:137
  and the Thirty Years War
    3:105-106
Sweerts, Hieronymous, and
  Ruisdael 3:111
'Swiftest of Painters' *see*
  Cranach, Lucas
Switzerland: Basel 2:*13, 79*
    attitude to art in 2:78
    Dürer in 2:12, *13*
Symbolists/Symbolism 9:68-71
  Chagall and 6:*77*
  champion of 9:48
  characteristics 9:69
  and the frieze 9:115
  great decade of 9:71
  Klimt and 9:68
  leaders 9:68
  Munch and 9:110
  Northern 2:*21*
  and the 'real world' 9:69-70
  Redon and 9:47, 48, 50
  Salon 9:70, *71*
  subjects: popular 9:*50*
    femme fatale 9:71
  Les Vingt and 9:48
  and Wagner 9:71
  La Revue Blanche 9:69
Synge, J. M.: *Riders to the Sea* 9:74
Syria, Druze rebellion in 7:*104*

T

Tagore, Sir Rabindranath 6:*104*
Tahiti 5:*48*, 66-9
  Cook charts 5:*67*
  Gauguin in 5:48-9
  Matavai Bay 5:*67*
  Royal Family 5:*68*
    Princess Poedua 5:*68*
Taillasson, Jean-Joseph, on
  Ruisdael 3:112
Talleyrand, Charles, and
  Delacroix 4:108, *109*
Tanguy, Père: and the
  Impressionists 5:99
  Van Gogh and 5:101
    painted by 5:*88*
Tanguy, Yves 6:141
Tanning, Dorothea 6:141
tapestry cartoons, Raphael:
  influence on Flemish painters
    2:112
  sent to Brussels 2:112
tapestry manufacture: Goya and
  4:13, *13*, 18
  I. van Ruisdael and 3:108
  Rubens and 3:77
  in Spain 4:13, *13*
  Van Dyck and 3:78
  Lady and the Unicorn 6:*36-7*
Tapié de Céleyran, Dr Gabriel,
  by Toulouse-Lautrec 8:*86*
Tasman, Abel 3:*135, 135*
Tasmania, discovery of 3:135,
  135
Tassi, Agostino 3:38
Tatlin, Vladimir *see Artists' Index*
tax-collectors, Netherlandish
  2:*133*
Taylor, Warrington 9:36
Teha'amana 5: *50-51*
telescopes, 17th-century 3:134
Telford, Thomas 4:*135*
tempera 2:116
  Bellini and 1:82
  qualities of 1:83-4
'Temple of Realism' 8:45, 46-7, *47*
Teniers, David *see Artists' Index*
tennis: 16th-century 3:*16*
  see also lawn tennis; real tennis
'tenth muse, the' 1:*81*
Terborch, Gerard *see Artists'
  Index*
Terbrugghen, Hendrick *see
  Artists' Index*
terrorism, international 6:137-8
Tesla, Nikola 5:*104*
Tetzel, John 2:69
'That Daring Young Man on the
  Flying Trapeze' *see*
  Léotard, Jules
Thatcher, Margaret, Prime
  Minister 6:138
Thaulow, Frits, Munch and 9:109

Thirty Years War (1618-48): end
  of (1648) 3:136
  protagonists 3:105
  Spanish defeats in 3:69
Thornhill, Jane, and Hogarth
  8:14, *14-15*
Thornhill, Sir James *see Artists'
  Index*
Thoth (sculpture, Egyptian) 6:*52*
three-field system 2:133
Tibet: Russia and 9:*72-3*
Ticheef, Elisabeth 7:12
Ticheef, Lydia 7:12, *13*
Tiepolo, Giambattista *see Artists'
  Index*
Tissot, James *see Artists' Index*
Titian *see Artists' Index*
Toerten estate (Meyer/Gropius)
  7:38
Tolstoy, Lev Nikolaevich 6:*40*
  death of 6:42
Tommasoni, Ranuccio, and
  Caravaggio 3:16
tone/texture: Dürer's use of 2:20
  Holbein and 2:84
Toorop, Jan *see Artists' Index*
'Topsy' *see* Morris, William
Torquemada, Tomás de 1:138;
  4:34
  successor to 4:36
Torrigiano, Pietro *see Artists'
  Index*
Toulouse-Lautrec, Henri de *see
  Artists' Index*
Tournachon, Gaspard Félix 5:*99*
  and the Impressionists 5:98
travel, in 15th-century 2:13
'Tres Grandes, Los' 8:111
Trevithick, Richard 4:42
trial by torture 4:35
triptychs, of San Pietro Martire
  1:46
Tristan, Flora 5:44, *44*
Trotsky, Leon 7:70, *70*; 9:137
  Rivera and 8:112, 113, *113*
Truce of 1609 3:132
Trudeau, Pierre 7:138
Tudor dynasty by Holbein 2:80,
  80, 86-7
Tucher, Elsbeth, by Dürer 2:*25*
Tunisia 6:*46*
  Klee in 6:45-6
tupapaus 5:*50-51*
Turenne, Marshal 3:73
Turkey: and Albania 6:42
  and Arabia 6:42
  Constantinople (Istanbul)
    1:*102*; 3:74
  new state of 7:*40*, 42
  war with Greece 8:138
Turner, J. M. W. *see Artists' Index*
Tutankhamun, tomb found
  7:*42, 42*
Twain, Mark, death of 6:42

Twenty, The *see* Vingt, Les
Twiggy 7:*134, 134*
typewriter, first 9:*38*
Tyrone, Earl of 3:*41*
Tzara, Tristan 7:*78*
  L'arbre des voyageurs 7:*78*

U

Uccello, Paolo *see Artists' Index*
unconscious, discovering the
  6:68-71
unemployment, early 19th-
  century 4:70-74
Union of Berlin Artists *see* Verein
  Berliner Künstler
United States *see* America
Urizen 4:*52*
Utrillo, Maurice *see Artists'
  Index*
Utrillo, Miquel 6:134

V

Valadon, Suzanne 8:*78, 78*
  The Blue Room 8:*78*
Valdes Leal, Juan de *see Artists'
  Index*
Valera, Éamon de 8:*138*
Valla, Lorenzo, on Fra Angelico
  1:*49*
Vallotton, Felix *see Artists' Index*
Van Dyck, Anthony *see Artists'
  Index*
Van Gogh, Vincent *see* **Gogh,
  Vincent van**
Vanderbank, John, Hogarth
  and 8:13
Varley, John, and Blake 4:49
Vasarély, Victor *see Artists' Index*
Vasari, Giorgio: on Botticelli
  1:108,110-111, 113, 117
  on Fra Angelico 1:*44*, 44-5, 74
  on Giotto 1:15-17
  on Filippo Lippi 1:46
  title page of *Lives of the Artists*
    1:*44*
Vasconcelos, José 8:110, 135
'Vava' *see* Brodsky, Valentine
Velázquez, Antonio 3:49
**Velázquez, Diego Rodriguez
  de Silva y** *see Artists' Index*
Velázquez, Francisca 3:45, 48
Velázquez, Ignacia 3:45
Velde, Esaias van de *see Artists'
  Index*
'Velvet Brueghel' *see* Brueghel,
  Jan

Venice/Venetian Empire 1:*76, 100*, 101-102
  and alliance against France 1:*104*
  the Renaissance in 1:*79*
  Ca d'Oro 1:*72*
  changes in 1:*79*
  Collegio 1:*101*
  commission for Verrocchio 1:*111*
  Dürer in 2:*14-15*
    commission from German merchants in 2:*14*
  in the 15th-century 1:*76*
  galley fleet 1:*101*
  Grand Council 1:*101*
  greatest 15th-century painter *see* **Bellini, Giovanni**
  honours Giovanni Bellini 1:*79*
  liking for formal religious images 1:*82*
  naval supremacy of 1:*102-103*
  official artist 1:*81*
  period of turmoil 1:*100-103*
  political system 1:*100-101, 101*
  portraits of Doges 1:*85*
  16th-century 2:*44*
  secular painting in 1:*79*
  Signoria 1:*101*
  trading links 1:*101, 103*
  Turkish threat to 1:*102-103*
  use of Constantinople 1:*102*
  war with Milan 1:*102*
  wedding the sea 1:*100*
Venice Biennale Grand Prize: Miró and 7:*81*
  Riley and 7:*111*
'Venus pudica' (sculpture) 1:*119*
Vercellini, Francesco 3:*77*
Verein Berliner Künstler, Munch and 9:*110, 135*
Verlaine, Paul, and Symbolism 9:*68*
Vermeer, Johannes *see Artists' Index*
Veronese, Paolo *see Artists' Index*
Verrocchio, Andrea del *see Artists' Index*
Versailles, Treaty of (1919) 8:*136-7*
Vetsera, Baroness Marie, suicide of 5:*70, 72-3*
Viaud, Paul, and Toulouse-Lautrec 8:*87*
Victoria, Queen of England 4:*72*
  by Landseer 3:*85*
  death of 5:*42*
  marriage of youngest daughter 5:*138*
  and the Sudan 5:*136, 137*
Vidal, Gore: *Myra Breckinridge* 7:*138*
Vienna University 2:*45*
  Cranach and 2:*45, 45*

Viennese Artists' Association *see* Künstlerhaus
Vietnam, US withdrawal from 6:*136-7, 137*
Vigeland, Gustav 9:*133*
Villa, Pancho 8:*133, 133, 134*
Vinci, Leonardo da *see Leonardo da Vinci*
Vinaver, Max, Chagall and 6:*78*
Vingt, Les (Les XX) 5:*110*
  Redon and 9:*48*
  themes 9:*48*
  Toulouse-Lautrec and 8:*78*
Viot, Jacques, Miró and 7:*78*
Vitebsk Art School: Malevich and 7:*48*
  renamed 7:*48*
Vitry, Jacques de, on the Franciscans 1:*38*
Vollard, Ambroise: and Cézanne 5:*17*
  organizes show for 5:*16*
  painted by 5:*17*
  Chagall and 6:*80*
  Redon and 9:*49*
Vorobëv-Stebelska, Marevna *see Artists' Index*
Vos, Kee 5:*78, 78*
Vroom, Cornelis *see Artists' Index*
Vuillard, Edouard *see Artists' Index*

W

Wael, Cornelis de, by Hollar 3:*79*
Wael, Lucas de, by Hollar 3:*79*
'waggoners' 3:*135*
Waghenaer 3:*135*
Wagner, Otto 9:*100*
  Majolika Haus 9:*103*
  ornamental facade 9:*103*
Wagner, Richard: the Symbolists and 9:*71*
  Parsifal, Kundry in 9:*71*
Walden, Herwath, and Chagall 6:*79*
Waller, Edmund 3:*73*
Wallis, Captain Samuel 5:*66-7*
Wallis, Henry *see Artists' Index*
Walpole, Horace 4:*98* 100
  on Herculaneum 8:*42*
  Strawberry Hill 4:*99, 100*
  The Castle of Otranto 4:*100*
Warham, William, Archbishop of Canterbury 2:*78*
  Holbein and 2:*77*
  drawn by 2:*84*
'warriors of God, the' *see Hussites*
War of Liberation (German, against Napoleon) 4:*80*

Wars of the Roses, end of (1485) 2:*100*
Wassilieff, Maria 6:*103*
watercolour: Dürer and 2:*13*
  in England 9:*20*
  Friedrich and 4:*84*
  Holbein's use of 2:*83*
  Kandinsky and 7:*17*
  Rossetti and 9:*15*
    technique with 9:*20*
  Van Dyck and 3:*79*
Waterloo, Battle of (1815) 4:*102-103, 104, 105*
Watts-Dunton, Theordore 9: *17*
weaving: Morris and 9:*34*
  experiments with 9:*36*
Webb, Philip 9:*34*
Webber, John *see Artists' Index*
Weimar, Duke of, and Friedrich 4:*79*
Weimar Friends of Art 4:*79*
Weiss, Leocadia: in France 4:*16-17*
  Goya and 4:*16*
    painted by 4:*17*
Welles, Orson: *Citizen Kane* 6:*106, 106*
Wellington, Duke of 4:*14, 16, 105*
  by Goya 4:*28*
Wells, John 7:*135*
Werner, Anton von 9:*135*
Westphalia, Peace of (1648) 3:*136*
Whistler, James McNeill *see Artists' Index*
Wiener Werkstätte, and Stoclet Palace 9:*81*
Wignacourt, Grandmaster Alof de 3:*16*
  by Caravaggio 3:*17*
Wilberforce, Samuel 9:*39-40*
  and *Essays and Reviews* 9:*40*
Wild, Jonathan 8:*39*
Wilde, Oscar, by Toulouse-Lautrec 8:*81*
Wilding, Alexa 9:*16*
Wilheim II, Kaiser of Germany 5:*41, 105-106, 106*; 9:*136*
  and Alsace-Lorraine 5:*106*
  and disputes with Russia 6:*42*
  and *Entente Cordiale* 9:*138*
  and world power status 9:*138*
Wilkes, John, Hogarth and 8:*17*
Wilkie, David, Delacroix and 4:*111*
Wilson, Daniel 5:*105*
Wilson, Harold 7:*132, 133*
Wilson, Woodrow, President and the Mexican Revolution 8:*134*
Windsor drawings (Holbein) 2:*84, 84-5*
wings, fantastic 1:*52*
winter scenes: model for in the Low Countries 2:*112*

witchcraft, the Inquisition and 4:*37*
Witte, Sergei 9:*137-8*
Wolgemut, Michael *see Artists' Index*
Wollstonecraft, Mary 4:*66, 67-8, 69*
  Vindication of the Rights of Woman 4:*67*
Wolsey, Cardinal Thomas 2:*101*
  downfall of 2:*103*
women with flowers, comparisons 9:*52, 52*
woodcuts: Cranach and 2:*45*
  Dürer and 2:*12, 14*
  Kandinsky and 7:*19*
  Munch and 9:*116*
Woolf, Virginia 6:*106*
  Mrs Dalloway 7:*106*
Woolner, Thomas, emigration of 9:*16*
working people, comparisons of 9:*116, 116*
Works of the Commune, Florence, governor of 1:*17*
workshops: in Antwerp 2:*109*
  Cranach's: output 2:*52, 53*
  14th-century practices in 1:*13*
Wotton, Mary, Lady Guildford, by Holbein 2:*91*
Wren, Sir Christopher 4:*99*
Wyatt, Margaret, Lady Lee, by Holbein 2:*83*

Z

Zadine, Ossip 6:*101*
Zapata, Emiliano 8:*134*
  by Rivera 8:*133*
Zapatista Landscape – The Guerilla (Rivera) 8:*114*
Zazal, Madame 5:*130-31*
Zborowski *see Artists' Index*
Zeeland, Dürer in 2:*16-17*
Zeppelin, Count Ferdinand von 5:*39, 42*
0.10 Exhibition of Futurist Painting 7:*46*
  progression of works in 7:*52*
Zeuxis: *Still-Life* 3:*21*
Zidler, Charles 8:*98*
  and Toulouse-Lautrec 8:*100*
Zola, Émile 5:*99*
  Cézanne and 5:*12, 14, 16*
  on L'Estague 5:*36*
  L'Oeuvre 5:*16*
  La Terre 5:*14, 14*
Zurburan, Francisco *see Artists' Index*
Zvantseva School, Chagall and 6:*78*

Index of Artists

A

Albers, Josef 7:140
Alberti, Leon Battista 1:72
  Della Pittura 1:72
Alenza, Leonardo 4:140
Altdorfer, Albrecht 1:140
Amigoni, Jacopo 8:16
  Hogarth and 8:16
Anquetin, Louis 5:140
  influence of Japanese prints
    8:78
  Van Gogh and 5:101
  Toulouse-Lautrec and 8:78
Archipenko, Alexander 6:101
Arp, Jean (Hans)
  Kandinsky and 7:19
  Klee and 6:47
  Miró and 7:78
Artigas, Joseph Llorens 7:76-7
Avercamp, Hendrick
  Winter Scene, Skaters 2:116
'Avida Dollars' *see* Dalí, Salvador

B

Baburen, Dirck van 3:39
Bacon, Francis
  Pope I 3:52
Baglione, Giovanni
  on Caravaggio 3:14-15, 17, 39
  Life of Caravaggio 3:14
Bakst, Leon
  and the Ballets Russes 6:78
  Chagall and 6:77
  The Firebird 6:41
  Schérézade 6:77

Baldung Grien, Hans 2:140
Balen, Henrick van 2:76
Bayeu, Francisco 4:12, 18
Beardsley, Aubrey 9:140
  Salome 8:103; 9:87
  The Yellow Book 8:103
Beckmann, Max 8:140
Belin, Zuan *see* Bellini, Giovanni
Bellini family 1:78
  early work together 1:76
  last project together 1:77
  link with Mantegna 1:77
  trips to Padua 1:77
  Christ on the Cross 1:76
Bellini, Gentile 1:76, 140
  bequest to his brother 1:81, *81*
  commission from Isabella
    d'Este 1:79
  death of 1:81
  and the Doge's Palace 1:77
  drawing of by his brother 1:78
  and the Great Turk 1:78
  influence of Donatello 1:77
  influence of Mantegna 1:77
  as state painter to Venice 1:78
  Mehmet II 1:101
  *St Mark Preaching to the
    Alexandrians* 1:80-81
  View of Cairo 1:79
  see also Bellini family
Bellini, Giovanni
  Ariosto on 1:79
  attempts new composition
    1:85
  attitude to young artists 1:80
  by Belliniano 1:75
  bequest from his brother 1:81,
    81
  challenge to supremacy of 1:81
  character 1:80-81

commissions: from Isabella
  d'Este 1:79-81
delaying tactics over work 1:79
  on *Virgin and Child* 1:79-80
drawing of Gentile 1:78
Dürer and 1:80; 2:14-15, 19, 22
early training 1:76, 82
as established artist 1:77
experiments with *sacra
  conversazione* 1:84
family life in Venice 1:79
and 'fancy of fable' 1:79
finishes brother's work in
  Doge's Palace 1:78
finishes *St Mark Preaching to
  the Alexandrians* 1:80-81
formula for Virgin and Child
  paintings 1:82
gallery guide 1:139
grouping figures 1:84-5
influence of Donatello 1:77, *77*
influence of Giorgione 1:80
influence of Mantegna 1:77,
  82-3
  in *Agony in the Garden* 1:83
influence of Messina 1:78, 83-4
influence of Piero della
  Francesca 1:78
influence of St Bernadino 1:76
influence of Titian 1:80
key dates 1:77
and landscape 1:84, *86-7*
last years 1:80-81
and linear perspective 1:85
major transformation in work
  1:78
as official painter in Venice
  1:79
and oil painting: to enrich
  paintings 1:78, 83-4

painting on a design by
  Donatello 1:82-3
perception of light 1:82-5
and portraiture 1:78, *83*, 85
pupils 1:80-81, 82, 85
sacred allegory 1:*83*
subjects preferred 1:80
tomb 1:*81*
trademarks 1:85
use of his father's sketchbooks
  1:*86*
use of pure colour 1:85
use of Renaissance advances
  1:82
and Venetian Artists' guild
  1:79
and Venetian liking for formal
  images 1:82
The Agony in the Garden 1:*88-9*
The Baptism of Christ 1:*83*, 85
Christ with Two Angels 1:77
The Coronation of the Virgin
  1:79
*Dead Christ Supported by Four
  Angels* 1:82-3
The Doge Leonardo Loredan
  1:85, *96*
The Feast of the Gods 1:85
Frari Altarpiece 1:93
*Madonna and Child between St
  Catherine and St Mary
  Magdalene* 1:94-5
The Madonna of the Meadow
  1:81, *86-7, 98*
  details 1:*86-7*
Murano Altarpiece 1:*8*
Pesaro Altarpiece 1:*78*
Pietà 1:*87*
The Pilgrimage of the Soul 1:*83*
St Francis 1:79, 84, *90*

San Giovanni Crisostomo
    Altarpiece 1:81
San Giobbe Altarpiece 1:79,
    85, *92*
San Zaccaria Altarpiece 1:81,
    97
Transfiguration 1:79, 84, *91*
Virgin and Child 1:82
*Virgin and Child with St John the
    Baptist and a Female Saint* 1:84
    detail 1:*85*
Young Woman with a Mirror
    1:81, 85, *99*
see also Bellini family
Bellini, Jacopo 1:76, 140
    sketchbooks: bequest of 1:77
        images used by Giovanni
            Bellini 1:*86*
        images used by Mantegna
            1:77
    workshop of 1:76
    Madonna and Child 1:*78*
    see also Bellini family
Bellmer, Hans 6:140
Benedetto da Maiano
    roundel of Giotto 1:*17*
Bernard, Emile 5:140
    Gauguin and 5:*47*
    influence of Japanese prints
        8:78
    and Redon 9:49
    Toulouse-Lautrec and 8:78
        painted by 5:*47*
    Van Gogh and 5:79, 101
        sketched by 5:*83*
Bernini, Gianlorenzo 3:140
    Bust of Charles I (copy) 3:*87*
    Fountain of the Four Rivers 3:*136*
    St Peter's Square, Rome 3:72
Bewick, Thomas
    and animals 6:38, 39
Blake, Peter, and Riley 7:109
Blake, William
    on animals 6:39
    apprenticeship 4:45, *45*, 50
    and Basire 4:45, *45*
    by his wife 4:*44*
    commissions: from
        Cumberland 4:*53*
        from Hayley 4:48
        from *Ladies' Magazine* 4:45
        from Linnell 4:49
        sets of prints 4:47
    and copying 4:45
    death of 4:49
    at drawing school 4:45
    early training 4:45
    and engraving 4:45
    and etching 4:45
    and the Fall of Man 4:51
    family 4:45
        effect of brother's death on
            4:45
        visions of brother 4:45

and fairies 4:48
in Felpham 4:*47*, 48
finances 4:46
    Linnell and 4:49
    payment for *Book of Job* 4:49
    payments from Butts 4:47-8
and freeing the spirit 4:52-3
and illumination 4:46, 50-3
    'illuminated painting' 4:46-7
and imagination 4:52
influence of Bryant 4:45
influence of Gothic art 4:45, 50
influence of Michelangelo 4:50
influence of the Old Masters
    4:50
influence of Raphael 4:50
key dates 4:44
Klee and 6:45
in Lambeth 4:47
last days 4:49
and Linnell 4:49
marriage 4:45, 47
    help from his wife 4:47
on nature 4:48
as object of veneration 4:49
and Paine 4:68
painting method 4:50
and Palmer 4:49
patrons 4:47
    Butts 4:47-8
    Hayley 4:48
personal symbolism 4:50
as poet 4:50
politics 4:46-9, *47*
and print-making, secret
    technique 4:51
pupil 4:45
and religion 4:46
returns to London 4:49
    and Soho 4:*45*, 45-6, *46-7*
as revolutionary 4:46, 66-9
and Royal Academy 4:45
and stippling 4:45
trademarks 4:53
tried for assaulting soldier
    4:48-9
and Varley 4:49
and Westminster Abbey
    4:44-5
works: last design 4:*53*
    sources 4:51-2
    on his work 4:53
The Ancient of Days 4:56
*The Body of Abel Found by Adam
    and Eve* 4:54, *54-5, 62-3*
    details 4:*55*
    study for 4:*54*
The Book of Job 4:49, 53
    *Satan Smiting Job with Sore
        Boils* 4:53, *53*
    detail 4:*53*
Canterbury Pilgrims 4:48, *48-9*
Canute 4:51
The Dance of Albion see Glad Day

Divine Comedy 4:49, 53
    Beatrice addressing Dante 4:*64*
    The Inscription over Hell Gate
        4:*65*
    The Simoniac Pope 4:*61*
The Ghost of a Flea 4:47
Glad Day 4:*60*
God Judging Adam 4:47, *57*
Good and Evil Angels, The 4:*8*
Jerusalem 4:49, 66-9, *67*
    title page 4:*51*
King Sebert 4:45
Milton 4:49
Nebuchadnezzar 4:52, *59*
Newton 4:51-2, *58*
Pity 4:*50-51*
Satan, Sin and Death 4:51
Songs of Experience 4:47, *50*
Songs of Innocence 4:47, *50*
    colour quality in 4:50-51
The Spirits of Fountain Court
    4:*49*
'visionary heads' 4:51
visiting card 4:*53*
Boccioni, Umberto
    and Futurism 6:42
    Elasticity 10:*63*
Böcklin, Arnold 9:140
    The Island of the Dead 9:*70*
Böhm, Adolf
    and Hagenbund 9:100
    book design 9:*102*
    embroidery design 9:*102*
Bombois, Camille 6:140
Bondone, Giotto di *see* **Giotto
    di Bondone**
Bonington, Richard Parkes 3:141
    and Delacroix 4:111
Bonnard, Pierre 5:140
    and the Nabis 9:49, 71
    on Redon 9:48
    Toulouse-Lautrec and 8:79
Bonnat, Léon
    Munch and 9:109, *109*
    Toulouse-Lautrec and 8:77, 82
Bosch, Hieronymus
    Bruegel and 2:110-11, *111,
        114, 115*
    Philip II and 4:20
    revival of interest in 2:110-11
    The Garden of Earthly Delights
        6:*116*
    The Temptation of St Anthony
        4:*20*
Botticelli, Sandro
    altarpieces, audience for
        1:115-16
    apprenticeship 1:109, *109*
    approach to antiquity 1:113
    assistants 1:110
    burial place 1:*112-13*
    and *cassone* panels 1:110, 115
    catalogues of works 1:114
    comment of brother on 1:110

commissions: for Church of
    Ognissanti 1:*113*
    first documented 1:109, *109*
    for Merchant's Guild 1:109
    for his patron 1:109
    to paint Pazzi conspirators
        1:110
    for Pierfrancesco de' Medici
        1:112, *113*, 116-17
    for Pisa Cathedral 1:109
    from Zanobi del Lama 1:109
and Compagnia de San Luca
    1:109, 113
criminal charges against 1:113
Dalí and 6:16
and Dante's *Divine Comedy*
    1:112, *113*, 116
and *David* (Michelangelo)
    1:113
death of his father 1:110
dispute with neighbours 1:108
and Duke of Milan 1:111
and Filippo Lippi 1:109
first documented work 1:*109*
and fresco painting 1:114, *114*
gallery guide 1:139
honorary position in Florence
    1:113
as illustrator 1:*113*, 116
influence of antiquity 1:113
influence of Filippo Lippi
    1:116
influence of Savonarola 1:112,
    135
key dates 1:108
in last years 1:113
and line 1:116
links with the Medici 1:109
most remarkable paintings
    1:115
and mythology 1:114-17
number of surviving paintings
    1:114
'off the peg' paintings 1:115
patrons 1:109
    and mythologies 1:116
personal worries 1:112
in Pisa 1:109, *109*
popularity of Madonna and
    Child paintings 1:110
pupils 1:110
    and sale of work by 1:110-11
    star 1:112, *112*
'rediscovery' of 1:113, 117
reputation 1:109
peak of reputation 1:111, 115
recommended to Isabella
    Gonzaga 1:113
rivals in Florence 1:111
in Rome 1:110, 115
    and the Sistine Chapel 1:115
sexual activities 1:113
and study of 'science' of
    painting 1:113, 117

style of painting 1:113
  consistency of 1:116
  distinctive feature of 1:117
  gracefulness of 1:116
  increasingly 'old-fashioned'
    1:117
  use of archaic devices 1:117
subjects painted 1:114-17
summons from the Pope
  1:110-11
trademarks 1:116
type of clientele 1:115
types of work 1:*108*, 110
workshop 1:108
  apprentice in 1:112
  copying works 1:110
  method of working 1:114-15
The Adoration of the Magi 1:109,
  110, 115
Abundance (drawing) 1:*114*
The Annunciation 1:129
The Bardi Altarpiece 1:126
The Birth of Venus 1:115, 117,
  118-19, 122-3
  details 1:*118, 119*
Fortitude 1:109, *109*
The Lamentation 1:130
The Madonna of the Book
  1:*116-17*
  detail 1:*116*
Madonna of the Magnificat 1:128
Mars and Venus 1:*114-15*, 115
The Mystic Nativity 1:117, *131*
Portrait of a Young Man 1:124
Primavera 1:109, 115, 116,
  120-21
Punishment of the Rebels 1:110,
  111
Saint Augustine 1:113
San Barnaba Altarpiece 1:*127*
self-portrait 1:*107*
Smeralda Bandinelli 1:115
Venus and the Graces 1:114
Young Man with a Medal 1:125
Bourdichon, Jean
  The Hours of Anne of Brittany
    (detail) 2:*21*
Braithwaite Martineau, Robert
  The Last Day in the Old Home
    8:*20*
Braque, Georges 6:51
  Klee and 6:49
  Malevich and 7:45, 51
Bratby, John
  and Riley 7:109
Brouwer, Adriaen
  and Hogarth 8:19
Brown, Ford Madox
  9:16, *16*
  and Morris & Co 9:34, 35
  and Rossetti: and 'Guggums'
    9:13, 20
  style 9:13
  The Last of England 9:16

Bruegel, Pieter
  and Antwerp
    painters' guild 2:108
  apprenticeship 2:108-109
  in Brussels 2:111-12
    and political unrest in
      2:112-13
  and Clovio 2:109
  and Cock 2:110
  and Coecke van Aelst
    2:108-109
  commissions: from
    Jonghelinck 2:112
  and contemporary taste 2:112
    detailed notes 2:*117*
  and development of oil
    painting 2:116
  and 'Family of Love' 2:111
  gallery guide 2:139
  improvement of
    draughtsmanship 2:116
  influence of Alps 2:110, *111*
  influence of Bosch 2:110-11,
    111, 114, 115
  influence of Italian art 2:112,
    114, 116
  influence of political unrest on
    2:113
  influence of the *rederijkkamer*
    2:115
  in Italy 2:109-110
  key dates 2:108
  and landscape 2:112
    collaboration on 2:109
  marriage 2:108, 111
  naer het leven drawings 2:117,
    117
  and Ortelius 2:110, 111
  patrons 2:112
    Cardinal Granvelle 2:112,
      113
    effect on style 2:116
  and popular literature 2:115
  and the 'Primitive' painters
    2:114
  and printmaking 2:110
    landscape series 2:110, *111*
  produces greatest works 2:112
  public image 2:108
  and religion 2:111
  reputation after death 2:113
  and *Ship of Fools* 2:115
  sons 2:112-13
  by Spranger 2:*107*
  style: change in 2:112, 116-17
    'old-fashioned' 2:114
  subjects 2:108, 114
    in final years 2:113
    narrative approach to 2:114
    sources 2:115-16
  and tempera 2:116
  trademarks 2:117
  trips in the country 2:117
  use of oak panels 2:116

  Big Fish Eat Little Fish
    (engraving) 2:111, *111*
  Carnival and Lent, influences
    on 2:115-16
  The Conversion of St Paul
    2:128-9
  The Corn Harvest 2:125
  The Fall of Icarus 2:120-21
    influences in 2:115
  The Harvest 2:134
  Haymaking 2:124
  Hunters in the Snow 2:112
  The Massacre of the Innocents
    2:113, *127*
  The Misanthrope 2:*115*, 2:116
  Months of the Year 2:112
  Netherlandish Proverbs 2: 118-19
    details 2:*118, 119*
    influences on 2:115
  Parable of the Blind 2:111, 115,
    116, 117
    medium for 2:116
  The Peasant Dance 2:117, *131*;
    8:*53*
  The Port of Naples (detail)
    2:*108-109*
  self-portrait 2:115
  The Temptation of St Anthony
    (engraving) 2:*114*
  Two Monkeys 2:115
  Wedding Dance in the Open Air
    2:*114*
  The Wedding Feast 2:130
Brueghel, Jan 2:113
  Isabella of Bourbon 3:69
Brueghel, Peter, the Younger
  2:112
  Peasant Wedding 2:132-3
  The Village Market 2:134-5
Brunelleschi, Filippo
  and Florence Cathedral 1:72,
    72
Burne-Jones, Edward 9:*36*, 141
  description of ideas 9:21
  family, with Morris 9:*36*
  and Morris & Co 9:34-5
  and the Pre-Raphaelites 9:34
  and Botticelli 1:117
  Rossetti and 9:16
  Kelmscott Chaucer 9:37
  The Golden Stairs 1:117

C

Calvert, Edward 4:140
Canaletto, Antonio
  The Horses of San Marco in the
    Piazzetta 10:*55*
Caracciolo, Giovanni Battista
  and Caravaggio 3:37
  The Liberation of St Peter 3:37

Caravaggio
  apprenticeship 3:12
  and d'Arpino 3:*12*, 13
  bias against 3:39
  and Cesari 3:13
  and chiaroscuro 3:20, *20*
  commissions:
    for Chiesa del Monte della
      Misericordia 3:37
    for Chiesa Nuova 3:19-20
    for Contarelli Chapel 3:14,
      14, 19
    after Contarelli Chapel
      success 3:14
    for Del Monte 3:14
    papal 3:12
    rejection of religion 3:21
  in court 3:14-15, *15*
  death of 3:17
  and Del Monte 3:13
  disregard for convention
    3:18-21
  drawings 3:21
  family 3:12
  and fresco-painting 3:21
  fight at the Campo Marco 3:16
  finances, in Rome 3:13
  followers *see* Caravaggisti, the
  friends and companions
    3:15
  gallery guide 3:139
  and Gentileschi 3:36
  in hospital 3:13
  influence on 17th-century art
    3:36, 39
  key dates 3:13
  and the Knights of Malta
    3:16-17, *16-17*
    as Knight of the Order
      of Obedience 3:16
  last days 3:17
  by Leoni 3:36
  life-style 3:14, 44
  in Malta 3:16, *16-17*
  and Marino 3:15
  models: corpses as 3:21
    for Del Monte paintings
      3:13
    mistress as 3:*15*
    prostitutes as 3:13
  in Naples 3:16, *16-17*, 17
    influence of style in 3:37-9
  and the Old Masters 3:16
  papal pardon for 3:16, 17
  patrons: Del Monte 3:13, 15
    Marchese Giustiniani 3:15
  and perspective 3:20
  and Peterzano 3:12
  in prison 3:17
  in Rome 3:12, 12-13
    employers in 3:*12*, 13
    flight from 3:16-17
    lifestyle in 3:13
  sexuality 3:13

in Sicily 3:17, *37*
style: and Counter
    Reformation's traditions
    3:18-19
    followers and 3:36-9
    naturalism of 3:18-21
    spread of in Europe 3:38-9
    use of light 3:20-21, *36*
subjects, of early paintings
    3:13
technique 3:21
trademarks 3:20
works: comparisons with
    'high art' 3:21
    effect of modern on 3:20
    for the open market 3:13
    sense of violence in 3:18
Bacchus 3:18
Beheading of St John the Baptist
    3:16, *16, 18-19*
    sense of violence in 3:18
The Calling of St Matthew
    3:20-21
    use of light in 3:21
The Conversion of St Paul 3:30
    use of light in 3:21
The Crucifixion of St Peter 3:31
David with the Head of Goliath
    3:35
The Death of the Virgin 3:34
    rejection of 3:17
    replacement for 3:36-7
    rumours about 3:21
The Entombment of Christ
    3:19-20, *32*
The Gipsy Fortune Teller 3:24
Grandmaster Alof de Wignacourt
    3:16, *17*
Judith Beheading Holofernes 3:27
    sense of violence in 3:18
The Madonna di Loreto 3:33
Madonna del Palafrenieri (detail)
    3:15
Martyrdom of St Matthew 3:14
Medusa 3:19
The Musicians 3:14
Raising of Lazarus, 3:21
The Rest on the Flight into Egypt
    3:25
The Sacrifice of Abraham 3:18, *26*
self-portrait 3:11
    as Bacchus 3:13
Seven Works of Mercy 3:37
Still-Life 3:18, *21*
Supper at Emmaus 3:19, 22,
    22-3, 28-9
Victorious Cupid 3:13, *19*
Carpaccio, Vittore 1:14, 140
    The Laying Out of Christ 1:*84*
Carus, Karl Gustav 4:140
Casas, Ramon 6:134
    Picasso 6:132
Cavallini, Pietro 1:140
    and 'natural' style 1:19

Cézanne, Paul
    and Baille 5:12
    character 5:13
    and colour 5:19
        in later paintings 5:20
    critical events for 5:16
    death of 5:17, *17*
    and Degas 5:14
    depressions 5:13
    dictum on nature 7:51
    and Ecole des Beaux-Arts 5:13
    education 5:12
        friends at school 5:12
    eccentricity 5:14
    and L'Estaque 5:15, *36*
    fame 5:17, *17*
    family 5:12, *13*
        death of his father 5:16
        fear of his father 5:12
        illegitimate son 5:15
        influence of his sister 5:16
        paintings of his sister 5:13
    favourite props 5:22, *23*
    finances: for art studies 5:12
        on death of his father 5:16
    gallery guide 5:139
    in Gardanne 5:*15*
    and geometry of nature 5:16,
        18-21
    Van Gogh and 5:101
    and Hortense Fiquet 5:14
    importance of particular
        places 5:21
    and Impressionists:
        dissatisfaction with 5:18
        and first exhibition 5:16
    key dates 5:12
    and landscape of Provence
        5:34-5
    as law student 5:12
    letters, to Chocquet 5:34
    Malevich and 7:51
    and Manet 5:13-14
    marriage 5:*15,* 16
    models 5:21
    and Musée Granet 5:37
    on the official system 5:18
    as outdoor painter 5:18, *18*
    in Paris 5:12-13, 34
        behaviour in 5:13, 14
        on the Guerbois group 5:14
        and other artists in 5:13-14
    and Paris Salon 5:13
        failure at 5:16
    patron 5:99
    pilgrimages to 5:16-17
    and Pissarro 5:14, *15,* 15-16
    and poetry 5:12
    in Pontoise 5:15, *15*
    and Provence 5:21, 34-5
        and dialect of 5:36
    as a recluse 5:16-17
    Rivera and 8:114
    sitters, tolerance to 5:21

    and still-life 5:20-21
        method of setting up 5:22,
        22
    on studio paintings 5:18
    studios 5:17, *23, 37*
        last 5:*16-17, 17*
    style: changes 5:16
        development of 5:18-19
    subjects: changes 5:15
        in the 1860s 5:14
        favourite 5:34
        himself as 5:18, *18*
        landscapes 5:15
    in Switzerland 5:16
    technique 5:19-20
        'flat-depth' 5:18-19
        Impressionist 5:18
        in later paintings 5:20
        with palette knife 5:18
        use of light and shade 5:19
        use of paint 5:18, *19*
        use of repeated paint marks
        5:18
        use of photographs 5:21
    trademarks 5:21
    and Vollard 5:16
        painting of 5:*17*
    working method 5:16
    works: emotional strain in 5:21
        freedom of later 5:20
        principal inspiration 5:34
        time taken on 5:19-20
    and Zola 5:12, 14, *14*
        ends friendship with 5:16
        letter to 5:18
Apples and Oranges 5:22, *22-3,*
    30-31
    details 5:*22, 23*
Boy in a Red Waistcoat 5:25
    auction of 5:*17*
The Card Players 5:26-7
Château at Médan 5:18, *21*
    detail 5:*21*
Le Château Noir 5:*9*
Girl at the Piano 5:13
The Great Bathers 5:21, *32*
The Great Pine 5:*28*
Harlequin 5:*19*
Lake at Annecy 5:*29*
*Madame Cézanne in a Red
    Armchair* 5:*24*
A Modern Olympia 5:18, *18*
Mont Sainte-Victoire 5:18-19, *33*
*Paul Alexis Reading to Emile
    Zola* 5:14
portrait of Ambroise Vollard
    5:*17*
Portrait of Mme Cézanne 5:15
self-portrait 5:*11*
Still-life with Basket of Apples
    5:22
Still-life with Onions 5:*19*
The Turn in the Road 5:19, *20*
Woman with a Coffee Pot 5:*20*

Chagall, Marc
    and abstraction 6:83
    aims in art 6:84
        in his autobiography 6:82,
        83
    in America 6:81, *81*
    and Apollinaire 6:79
    apprenticeship 6:76, *77*
    assistants/craftsmen 6:81
    and Bakst 6:*77*
    and Bella Rosenfeld 6:78-9
    in Berlin, exhibition in 6:79
    and Cendrars 6:*78,* 79
    and ceramics 6:80, 81, *81*
    and colour 6:88
        experiments with 6:78
        'violet' pictures 6:83
    Commissar for Art for Vitebsk
        6:79
    commissions: Bible
        illustrations 6:80
        Dead Souls 6:80
        Fables 6:80
        for Hadassah-Hebrew
            University 6:*80,* 81
        for the Knesset 6:81
        for Metz cathedral 6:80, 81
        monumental paintings 6:81
        mosaics 6:81
        in Moscow 6:79
        Nôtre Dame, Assy 6:80
        for the Paris Opéra 6:81
        for Rheims cathedral 6:81
        stained glass 6:80, *80,* 81
        tapestries 6:81
        theatre/ballet 6:81
        from Vollard 6:80
    and the Cubists 6:102
        first encounter 6:83
        influence of 6:78-9, 82
        writing on 6:81
    death of 6:81
    and the Delauneys 6:78
    dislike of excesses 6:103
    education 6:76
    exhibitions, in London 6:81
    family 6:76
        birth of his daughter 6:79
        death of his wife 6:81
        description of his father 6:76
        illegitimate son 6:81
    finances, in Paris 6:101
    first teacher 6:76, *76*
    and form, experiments with
        6:78
    in France: and the countryside
        6:79
        in the south 6:80-81, *81*
        in Vence 6:81, *81*
    gallery guide 6:139
    in Holland 6:80
    in the Holy Land 6:80
    influence of childhood images
        6:84

influence of the Fauves 6:82
influence of Gauguin 6:82
influence of icons 6:83
influence of the Post-
    Impressionists 6:82
influence of the Surrealists
    6:82, 83
influence of Symbolism 6:77
key dates 6:77
and Marq 6:80
marriage 6:79
    second 6:80
and Modigliani 6:103
muse/critic (Bella) 6:79, 79
and Nice 5:37
and 'painterly' paintings 6:78
in Paris 6:78-9
    exhibitions in 6:80
    at La Ruche 6:77, 78, 101-102
    paintings taken 6:80, 103
    studio in 6:77, 78
and Pen 6:76, 76
rate of working 6:79
and real/imaginary 6:82-4
rebellion against 6:79
in Russia 6:79
in St Petersburg 6:6-7
and Salon des Indépendants
    6:78, 79
at School of the Imperial
    Society for the Protection of
    Art 6:77-8
and 'School of Paris' 6:103
    training in 6:77
and still-lifes 6:83
style 6:82
subjects: on choice of 6:84
    circus 6:84
    home town 6:79
    inspiration for 6:82
    recurring 6:84
    sources of 6:83
    his wife 6:79
and his symbolism 6:84
teaching 6:79
trademarks 6:85
and Valentine Brodsky 6:80,
    81
views on painting 6:83
and Vinaver 6:78
and Virginia Haggard 6:81
and Vitebsk Art School 7:48
Walden and 6:79
working methods: in Paris
    6:78, 84, 101
works: biblical pictures 6:81,
    84
    burnt by Goebbels 6:80
    categorizing 6:84
    chronology of 6:84
    effect of political unrest on
        6:80
    later 6:81
    principles of 6:83

at Zvantseva School 6:78
The Acrobat 6:92
Biblical Message 6:81
The Birthday 6:90-91
Bouquet with Flying Lovers 6:96
Equestrienne 6:93
The Fiddler 6:83
I and the Village 6:85, 85
    detail 6:85
    influence of Cubism 6:83
My Fiancée with Black Gloves
    6:82
Over Vitebsk 6:88-9
Poet Reclining 6:82-3
To Russia, Asses and Others 6:87
Self-portrait with Seven Fingers
    6:86
Solitude 6:94-5
    mood of 6:80
The Three Candles 6:97
Twelve Tribes of Israel 6:80
    Benjamin 6:99
    Joseph 6:98
White Crucifixion 6:84
    mood of 6:80
Chassériau, Thédore 3:141
Chirico, Giorgio de 6:140
    Dalí and 6:108, 109
    subjects 6:108
Cima de Conegliano, Giovanni
    Battista
    The Rest on the Flight into Egypt
        1:84
Cimabue 1:140
    in Assisi 1:13
        and Basilica of San
            Francesco 1:13, 39
    in Florence 1:12, 13
    and Giotto 1:12-13, 12-13
    influences on 1:19
        of classical art 1:12
    powers of expression 1:20
    in Rome 1:12
Clouet, François
    Francis I 2:87
Cock, Jerome 2:140
    and Bruegel 2:110
    and pastiches of Bruegel's
        work 2:110-11
Coecke van Aelst, Pieter 2:140
    and Bruegel 2:108-109
    and publishing 2:109
Constable, John
    Delacroix and 4:111
    on Ruisdael's approach to
        landscape 3:113-14
    winter 3:117
    Water-mill at Gillingham 3:116
Cormon, Fernand
    artists in studio of 8:78
    Van Gogh and 5:79, 101
    Toulouse-Lautrec and 8:77, 82
Cortona, Pietro da 3:140
Cross, Henri Edmond 5:140

Courbet, Gustave
art training 8:44
    at Besançon Art Academy
        8:45
'Assyrian' profile 8:54
and the avant-garde 8:45
and Baudelaire 8:45
beliefs in art 8:51
in Besançon 8:46-7
breaks with the past 8:48
and Bruyas 8:49
    painting of 8:48
and Buchon 8:45
caricature of 8:47
and Champfleury 8:45
and class divisions 8:44
commissions: from Comte de
        Nieuwerkerke 8:47
    from Dutch dealer 8:45
and the Commune 8:49
death of 8:49
description of 8:45
on 1848 8:72
in Etretat 8:48
exhibitions: one-man 8:48, 53
    'Pavilion of Realism' 8:50
    throughout Europe 8:48
exile in Switzerland 8:49, 49
fame, basis of 8:50
family 8:44
    his son 8:45, 49
finances 8:45
and Flajoulot 8:45
in Frankfurt 8:48
and French government:
    picture bought by 8:46
    stand against 8:47-8
gallery guide 8:139
health, after imprisonment
        8:49
hostility towards 8:47
imprisonment 8:49, 49
influence of local countryside
        8:44, 44-5
and 'intellectual liberty' 8:47
key dates 8:44
'living art' 8:50
on his loneliness 8:45-6
manifesto 8:50
mistress 8:45, 48
and Monet 8:48
and Old Masters 8:51
paints: mixing 8:52
    use of 8:51-2
in Paris 8:45
    art studies in 8:45
    and the Brasserie Andler
        8:45
    friends in 8:45
    letter to his parents 8:45
    life-style 8:45
and Paris Salon 8:46
    first submission to 8:45
    less reliant on 8:48

patron 8:48, 48
philosophy 8:53
and popular insurrection 8:46
prizes 8:46, 48
and Proudhon 8:45, 47
reaction against academic
    painting 8:50-53
on Realism 8:53
reason for travelling 8:48
recognition: early attempts at
        8:45
    official acclaim 8:46-7
    outside Paris 8:48
and Republican Arts
    Commission 8:48-9, 49
as revolutionary artist 8:69
and State interference in
    art 8:47, 48-9
and Steuben 8:45
and students 8:51
studio: methods of teaching
    in 8:51
    in Paris 8:54
style: in forest scenes 8:53
    in landscapes 8:52-3
    shallow picture space 8:53
    single images 8:53
subjects 8:46, 49, 50
    abandons Romantic 8:46
    painted in Trouville 8:48
    photographic source 8:55
    'threat' to new regime 8:47
    ugly 8:50-51
trademarks 8:52
in Trouville 8:48
and Vendôme Column 8:48-9,
    49
and Virginie Binet 8:45
and Whistler 8:48
and workers' revolution 8:66
working methods: from
    photographs 8:50
    from popular prints 8:50
    use of palette knife 8:52
works: first to be exhibited
        8:45
    size of 8:50
and the World Exhibition 8:47
After Dinner at Ornans: prize
    for 8:46
    purchaser 8:46
The Bathers 8:52
    detail 8:53
    purchaser 8:48
    ugliness of 8:50
Bonjour Monsieur Courbet see
    The Meeting
Brasserie Andler 8:47
Burial at Ornans 8:46, 56-7
    criticism of 8:47
    methods of painting 8:50
    real subject of 8:74
    shallow picture space 8:53
    starts painting 8:47

Cliffs at Etretat after the Storm 5:*114*; 8:65
The Hammock 8:*50-51*
The Kill 8:51
The Meeting 8:58
The Painter's Studio 8:48, 54, *54-5, 60-1*
   details 8:*55*
   methods of painting 8:50
Peasants of Flagey Returning from the Fair, Ornans 8:50
Portrait of Alfred Bruyas 8:48
Portrait of Baudelaire 8:46
Portrait of Régis Courbet 8:44
Proudhon and his Children 8:66
self-portrait 8:*43*
Self-portrait with a Black Dog 8:*45*
self-portrait in prison 8:49
The Sleepers 8:64
The Sleeping Spinner 8:48; 10:57
Still-life with Apples and Pomegranate 8:*51*
The Stonebreakers 8:52
The Studio, method of painting 8:50
Sunset on Lake Geneva 8:51
The Trellis 8:63
The Winnowers 8:59
Young Ladies on the Banks of the Seine 8:62
Coypel, Charles-Antoine and *Don Quixote* 8:20
Cranach, Hans 2:48
   self-portrait 2:*48*
   Monkey (sketch) 2:*48-9*
Cranach, Lucas
   assistants 2:46, 52
   in Augsburg 2:*48*, 49, 74
   birthplace 2:44, *44-5*
   as businessman 2:48, 49
      printing firm 2:49
   and Christian II 2:49
   commissions, from Electors of Saxony 2:46, 49
   as court painter 2:50-51
   early life 2:44
   early work 2:50
   and the Electors of Saxony 2:45-7, 50-51
   family 2:45-6, 48-9, *48-9*
   in his father's workshop 2:44
   filing system for portraits 2:52
   finances 2:49
   first signed/dated work 2:45
   gallery guide 2:139
   granted coat of arms 2:46
   and the Humanists 2:45
   influence of Dürer 2:45, 50
   influence of Italian ideas 2:50, 51
   influence of Mannerism 2:53
   Italian contemporaries 2:50
   key dates 2:44

and landscape 2:45, 50
last great works 2:53
and Luther 2:47-8, 68
   closeness of friendship 2:47
   paints 2:47
   publishes Bible of 2:49
map of travels 2:47
marriage 2:45
in the Netherlands 2:46, 51
and the nude 2:51
   growing importance of 2:53
in Nuremberg 2:49
paints Charles, later Holy Roman Emperor 2:46
partnership with Döring 2:49
patrons 2:46-7
   Catholic 2:48
   on pilgrimage 2:44-5
   sensibilities of 2:51
portraits: change in style of 2:53
   demand for 2:52
signature 2:49
use of sketches 2:52
speed/efficiency of 2:50-53
style: of figures 2:50
   'quaintness' of 2:50
   range of gestures/actions 2:50
subjects 2:47, 48
   first classical 2:51
   most characteristic 2:51
   mythological 2:47, 48
   portraits 2:51
   Reformation 2:53
   for Saxon court 2:51
summons from the Emperor 2:49
temperament 2:51-2
trademarks 2:53
in Vienna 2:45
   works in 2:50
in Weimar 2:49
in Wittenberg: duties at the court 2:46
   first painting in 2:46
   lifestyle in 2:49
   as mayor of 2:49
and woodcuts 2:45
   influence of Dürer in 2:*50*
working methods, for portraits 2:52
workshop 2:45, 48-9
   sons and 2:48, 49
   supervision of 2:52
Cathedral Church, Wittenberg 2:*46*
Crucifixion 2:50, *50*
Dr Johannes Cuspinian and his Wife Anna 2:45, *45*
The Electors of Saxony 2:46
The Fee 2:65
Frederick the Wise 2:71

The Garden of Eden 2:62-3
The Golden Age 2:52-3
   detail 2:*53*
Johannes Cuspinian 2:50
The Judgement of Paris 2:51, *54*, 54-5, *64*
   details 2:*54, 55*
   original sketch 2:*54*
Judith with the Head of Holofernes 2:59
Lucretia 2:51
Luther Altarpiece 2:71
The Martyrdom of St Catherine 2:46, 51, *51*
Missale Pataviense 2:50
The Penance of St Jerome 2:56
Reclining Water Nymph 2:66-7
The Rest on the Flight into Egypt 2:57
self-portrait 2:*43*, 53
St Stephen (woodcut) 2:50, *50*
The Stag Hunt 2:60-61
The Torgau Altarpiece 2:50-51
   influence on 2:51
Venus and Cupid as the Honey Thief 2:9
Virgin and Child with a Cake 2:52
The Virgin of the Grapes 2:58
Cranach, Lucas, the Younger 2:48
   and his father's studio 2:49
Crucifixion 2:*49*
Crane, Walter
   and the Secessionists 9:101-102
Cruikshank, George 8:140

D

Dadd, Richard
   The Fairy Feller's Master Stroke 6:*84*
Dalí, Salvador
   on his ambitions 6:108
   and his art 6:114
   'American Campaign' 6:113
   and *The Angelus* 6:112, *114*, 115-16
   automatic painting 6:110-11
   in Barcelona 6:132
      inspiration from architecture 6:133
   and Botticelli 6:116
   and Breton 6:110
      attacks on politics 6:116
      charges against 6:112
      and importance to Surrealism 6:111
      nickname for 6:113
   and Buñuel 6:108, *111*
   and Chirico 6:108, 109

on his classical period 6:116
commissions: in America 6:113
   for films 6:113
and Dalmau 6:132
   and the Dalmau Gallery 6:109
education 6:108
and Eluard 6:110-11
family 6:108
   and his dead brother 6:*108-109*
   painting of his father 6:*109*
first exhibition 6:109, 132
and free association 6:115
and Freud 6:108, 112, *113*
   on classical paintings 6:116
   influence of 6:112, *112-12*, 115
and Gala Eluard 6:110-11, *112*
and Goemans 6:110
greatest ambition 6:112
and Halsman 6:*111*
and hidden meanings in art 6:112
imagery, development of 6:115
influence of the Futurists 6:109
influence of the Old Masters 6:116
inspiration from the atom bomb 6:*114-15*, 116
interpretation of paintings 6:112, *114*, 115-16
in Italy 6:116
and James 6:112
key dates 6:108
and Lorca 6:108
and madness 6:108, 110, 115
in Madrid 6:108-109
and Miró 6:110
and *Mona Lisa* 6:116
and new art movements 6:108
in New York 6:113
   description of 6:113
in Paris 6:110
patron 6:112
personality 6:108
and photography:
   'handmade' 6:115
   photographic portraits 6:*111*
and Picasso 6:108, 110
   inspiration from 6:110
and Raphael 6:116
and School of Fine Arts, Madrid 6:108-109
   suspension/expulsion from 6:109
showmanship 6:112, 113
style: experiments with 6:109-110
   return to classicism 6:113, 116

and Surrealism 6:*109*, 110, 112, 113, 114
techniques: multiple image 6:115
   'paranoiac-critical method' 6:115-16
   perfecting 6:108
   photo-realist 6:115
trademarks 6:117
and Uccello 6:116
and Velázquez 6:116
and Vermeer 6:109
works: Cubist 6:110
   first 6:108
   portrayal of Lenin 6:112
   reacts against early 6:112-13
   structure of 'classical' 6:116
as writer 6:111-12
   The Secret Life of Salvador Dalí 6:111
L'Age d'or 6:108
Animated Still Life 6:130-31
The Apotheosis of Homer 6:128-9
The Architectonic Angelus of Millet 6:114
The Artist's Father 6:109
'Atomicus' 6:*111*
Un Chien Andalou 6:108
Christ of St John of the Cross 6:126-7
Dismal Sport 6:113
The Face of Mae West 6:113, 115
The Ghost of Vermeer of Delft, Which Can Be Used As a Table 6:115
Girl Seated Seen from the Rear 6:118
Impression of Africa 6:116
The Madonna of Port Lligat 6:114-15, 116
The Metamorphosis of Narcissus 6:115, *122-3*
Palladio's Corridor of Thalia 6:116
The Persistence of Memory 6:120-21
The Phantom Chariot 6:114
Premonition of Civil War 4:20
Spain 6:117
The Temptation of St Anthony 6:124-5
Woman at the Window at Figueras 6:119
Daumier, Honoré 8:140
   and Bismarck 8:*141*
Degas, Edgar 5:98
   Cézanne and 5:14
   and circus 5:132
   influence on Van Gogh 5:79
   and Parisian life 8:82-3
   and Seurat 5:108, 110
   Toulouse-Lautrec and 8:84
   At the Ambassadeurs 8:*84*
   The Rehearsal 10:60

Delacroix, Eugéne
   and the Académie des Beaux-Arts 4:113
   and animals 6:39
   awards 4:113
   beliefs in painting 4:116
   and Bonington 4:111
   caricature of 4:*112*
   and Chopin 4:113, 116
      portrait of 4:*112*
   and colour 4:115-16, 117, *117*
   commissions: Chapelle des Saintes-Anges 4:*112*, 113
      Galerie d'Apollon 4:*112*
      working sketch 4:*115*
      government 4:112-13
      Library of Bourbon Palace 4:112
      Salon de la Paix 4:112
      Salon du Roi 4:112
   distractions 4:113
   early life 4:108
   and Ecole des Beaux-Arts, Paris 4:109
   in England 4:111
   failing health 4:111-12, 113
   family 4:108, *109*
   friends/friendships 4:113
      lasting 4:112-13
      and George Sand 4:113
      portrait of 4:*113*
   gallery guide 4:139
   by Géricault 4:*108*
   and Greek War of Independence 4:110
   and Hugo 4:111
   influence of Britain on 4:111
   influence of Constable 4:111
   influence of Géricault 4:109
   influence of Gothic art 4:109
   influence of Persian art 4:*118*
   influence of Rubens 4:116, 117
   journal 4:110, 113
      on finding subjects 4:117
      on theories of art 4:117
   key dates 4:108
   and Lawrence 4:111
   love affairs 4:111
      and Elisabeth Salter 4:*109*
   models, Greek 4:*118*
   and music 4:108
   nature 4:111
   and Neo-Classical style 4:116
   in North Africa 4:110, 112
      watercolour studies in 4:*111*
   and the Paris Salon 4:109-110, 111, 113
   publishing activities 4:113
   Redon and 9:50
   and Romanticism 4:110-11; 9:50
      and 'Romantic' writers 4:110

Rousseau and 6:21
schooldays 4:108
and Scott 4:111
and sketching 4:109, 115
studio 4:*112*, 113
subjects 4:116-17
   sources of 4:110, 111
trademarks 4:117
training 4:109-110, 114-15
and Wilkie 4:111
withdrawal from society 4:113
working method: for salon paintings 4:115-17
   use of sketches 4:114
works: best known 4:112
   first major 4:109-110
   magnitude of 4:112-13
   number at death 4:114
and the zoo 4:*109*
The Barque of Dante 4:110, *120-21*
   buyer 4:110
   representation of water in 4:116
The Death of Sardanapalus 4:111, *124-5*
   preliminary sketches 4:114
Elisabeth Salter 4:*109*
The Execution of Doge Marino Faliero 4:123
   use of colour in 4:117
The Expulsion of Heliodorus from the Temple 4:113
Frédéric Chopin 4:*112*
George Sand 4:*113*
The Giaour and the Pasha 4:114
Horse Attacked by a Tiger 4:*115*
Horses Emerging from the Sea 4:*129*
Jenny le Guillou 4:*110*
The Jewish Wedding 4:127
Liberty Leading the People 4:112, *126*
The Lion Hunt 4:*14-15*; 9:*44-5*
   Redon copies 9:45
The Massacre of Chios 4:110, 118, *118*, 122, 135
   details 4:*118-19*
self-portrait 4:*107*
The Taking of Constantinople 4:*128*
Women of Algiers 4:*116-17*
   detail 4:*117*
Delaunay, Robert
   Chagall and 6:78
      ideas 8:109
      Rivera and 8:109
   Klee and 6:45, 51
   and light 6:51
   Rivera and 8:114
   The City of Paris 6:*78-9*
Delaunay, Sonia
   Chagall and 6:78
Delvaux, Paul 6:140

Denis, Maurice 5:140
   and the Nabis 9:49, 71
   Homage to Cézanne 9:*48-9*
Dix, Otto 8:140
Dobson, William 3:140
Doesburg, Theo van 7:140
Donatello
   Bellini painting on design by 1:*82-3*
   and Florence Cathedral 1:72
   Passion scenes from the Maestà 1:23
   Santo reliefs 1:77
Doré, Gustave 8:140
Duccio di Buoninsegna 1:140
Dürer, Albrecht
   in Aachen 2:16-17
   abandons painting 2:15
   and animals 6:38, 39
   in Antwerp 2:17
   apprenticeship 2:12
      as goldsmith 2:12, 37
      travels after 2:12
      work during 2:39
   and art theory 2:21
   artistic/spiritual crisis 2:16
   on artist's curiosity 2:18
   and Bellini: praise from 2:14-15
      Dürer on 1:80
   Bresdin and 9:46
   and collecting 2:17
   commissions, from Elector of Saxony 2:14, *15*
      from German merchants in Venice 2:14
      from Maximilian I 2:15-16
   and copperplate 2:20, 21
   Cranach and 2:45, 50
   difficult years 2:16-17
   early life 2:12
   effect of mother's death on 2:16
   epitaph by Melanchthon 2:17
   family chronicle 2:17
   in his father's workshop 2:12
   finances: annuity from Charles V 2:16, 17
      annuity from Maximilian I 2:16
      during journey to the Netherlands 2:16
      high expenses 2:16
   first great work *see The Apocalypse*
   gallery guide 2:139
   on German artists 2:13
   and Giorgione 2:14
   godfather 2:*38*
   and graphic work 2:15
   greatest works 2:20
   and important works of art 2:16
   influence of Bellini 2:19
      tribute to 2:22

influence of Leonardo 2:19
influence of Mantegna 2:19
influence of Pollaiuolo 2:19
interest in nature 2:21
in Italy 2:13-14
   see also in Venice
   on Italian artists 2:13, 15
key dates 2:13
and Koberger 2:14
and landscape 2:*14-15, 23*
and Luther 2:16, 21
last years 2:17
and Mantegna 2:14
marriage 2:12, 13, 15
mastery of line 2:20-21, *21*
and mechanical aids 2:84
and minute detail 2:20
and the natural world 2:20
in the Netherlands 2:16-17
Northern traditions 2:18, 19
and the nude 2:14
in Nuremberg: buys house in
   2:15, *15*
   gift to council of 2:17
   honoured by 2:16
   and importance of 2:36
obsession 2:16
on his own abilities 2:21
and perspective 2:14
and Pirckheimer 2:12
   visits in Pavia 2:13-14
and proportion 2:19-20
as publisher 2:14
   of his own treatises 2:21
   selling engravings 2:14
   selling woodcuts 2:14
   uses Koberger's press 2:39
   work for other 2:12
and rudiments of Italian
   Renaissance 2:14
and Schongauer 2:12
   learns technical secrets of
   2:12
scope of work enlarged 2:20
sketchbooks of travels 2:16
spread of fame 2:14, 15
and status of the artist 2:14-15
studies of the nude 2:19-20, *20*
style, mixture of 2:19
support of new movements
   2:17
and symbolism 2:21
trademarks 2:21
on use of detail 2:20
variety of work 2:14
in Venice 2:14-15
   and artists in 2:14
   asked to stay in 2:15
   copies nudes in 2:19
   visitors to studio 2:14-15
and watercolour 2:13
woodcut illustration 2:12
   perspective in 2:19
   technique for 2:18-19

writings: advice for young
   artists 2:17
   on fortification 2:17
   memoirs 2:17
   on perspective 2:17
   on proportion 2:17, 21
   published works 2:17
in Zeeland 2:16-17
Adam 2:21
The Adoration of the Magi 2:28-9
   Italian influence in 2:19
The Adoration of the Trinity
   2:*31; 4:85*
Agnes Frey 2:15
The Apocalypse 2:18
   The Four Horsemen 2:18
   Northern traditions in 2:19
   printing of 2:39
The Apocalypse of St John 2:14
Birth of Mary, Rossetti and 9:22
Crab 2:14
Eve 2:52
The Fall of Man 2:19, *20*
   detail 2:*21*
The Feast of the Rose Garlands
   2:22, *22-3, 30*
   details 2:*22, 23*
   people in 2:23
   preparatory study 2:23
   symbolism in 2:23
The Four Apostles 2:17, *34-5*
   inscription on 2:17
Frederick the Wise, Elector of
   Saxony 2:15
Girolamo Tedesco 2:23
Hands of an Apostle 2:18
The Hare 2:20, *26*
The Heron 2:18
Jacob Muffel 2:19
The Knight, Death and the Devil
   2:20, *32*
The Large Piece of Turf 2:27
Melencolia I 2:16, 20, *33*
Nuremberg Woman 2:37
Portrait of Elsbeth Tucher 2:25
portrait of his father 2:13
Portrait of Maximilian I 2:16
Portrait of Michael Wolgemut
   2:37
portrait of his mother 2:13
Portrait of Willibald Pirckheimer
   2:14
St Jerome in his Study 2:20
self-portrait 2:11, 14, *22, 24*
   silverpoint 2:12
Triumphal Arch 2:16
Triumphal Procession 2:38-9
View of Arco 2:23
Virgin with the Pear 2:19
vision of the end of the world
   2:17
Wehlsch Pirg 2:*14-15*
Dyck, Anthony van *see* **Van
Dyck, Anthony**

E

El Greco
   Rivera and 8:109
Ensor, James 9:140
   Klee and 6:45
Ernst, Max 6:141
   Miró and 7:78
   Célèbes 8:*136*
   The Temptation of St Anthony
   6:*140*
Esclavo, El *see* Pareja, Juan de
Everdingen, Allart van 3:*110*
   Ruisdael and 3:114

F

Fantin-Latour, Henri
   Redon and 9:46
Filiger, Charles 5:140-41
Filipepi, Alessandro di Mariano
   di Vanni *see* **Botticelli, Sandro**
Floris, Frans 2:140
Fra Angelico
   and Archbishop of Florence
   1:48
   on the art of painting 1:74
   beatification of 1:45
   and Capella della Madonna di
   San Brizio 1:48
   collaborators 1:48
   commissions: from Guild of
      Linen Weavers of Florence
      1:45
      important secular 1:47
      from Nicholas V 1:48, *48*
      for San Domenico, Cortona
      1:47
      for Santa Maria della Croce
      al Tempio 1:*54-5*
      for Santa Trinita, Florence
      1:47
      for the Servite Order,
      Brescia 1:47
      for Strozzi Chapel 1:*54-5,
      58-9*
   comparison with Filippo
      Lippi 1:69
   death of 1:49
   early phase of works 1:50-51
   features of style 1:50
   first Renaissance masterpiece
   1:47
   gallery guide 1:139
   and Humanist ideas 1:46
   influence of Masaccio 1:47
   influence of Monaco 1:46-7
   influence of the Renaissance
   1:51-3
   key dates 1:44
   key work in development 1:51

and landscape painting 1:54
and light/shade 1:46
and manuscript illumination
   1:46, *50*
and narrative unity 1:46
in Orvieto 1:48
and perspective 1:46, 51
as prior of Fiesole 1:49
as professional artist 1:50-3
pupil 1:48, 49,*49,* 53
reality of figures 1:46
relationship with Nicholas V
   1:48
in Rome 1:48
   assistants in 1:53
and *sacra conversazione* 1:51
and San Marco monastery:
   decoration of 1:*47,* 48
   life in 1:69
by Signorella? 1:*43*
teacher? 1:46-7
trademarks 1:52
treatment of angels 1:52
use of assistants 1:47, 52, 53
Vasari on 1:44-5
views on personality 1:45-6
woodcut of 1:44
The Adoration of the Magi 1:51
Annunciation 1:47, 51, *56-7,
   62-3*
Annunciation (illumination)
   1:*50*
Coronation of the Virgin 1:47, *61*
The Deposition from the Cross
   1:47, *54, 54-5, 58-9*
   details 1:*54-5*
   rhetorical gestures in 1:55
The Flight into Egypt 1:*66*
*The Lamentation over the Dead
   Christ* 1:*54-5*
Last Judgement (unfinished)
   1:49
Linaiuoli Altarpiece 1:45, 47,
   51
*The Martyrdom of St John the
   Evangelist* 1:51
Massacre of the Innocents 1:*67*
Noli Me Tangere 1:*60*
St Lawrence Distributing Alms
   1:*65*
*St Lawrence Receiving the
   Treasures of the Church* 1:*64*
St Peter Preaching 1:51
St Stephen and St Lawrence
   frescoes 1:48, *48*
San Marco Altarpiece 1:51
Scenes from the life of St Nicholas
   1:*50-51*
*Virgin and Child with Saints
   Dominic, John the Baptist,
   Peter Martyr and Thomas
   Aquinas* (details) 1:*52-3*
Fragonard, Jean-Honoré
   The Bathers 10:*56*

Friedrich, Caspar David
Academy training 4:77-8
on art 4:78, 81
attempted suicide 4:78-9
and Berlin Academy 4:80
by Kersting 4:82
character 4:76-7
and colour 4:81, 85
in Copenhagen 4:77-8
and Dahl 4:81
death of 4:81
in Dresden 4:78, 81
effect of Romanticism on 4:81
and Eldena abbey 4:77, 77
family 4:76-7, 81
gallery guide 4:139
and Gothic architecture 4:98
and Gothic revival 1:101
and Gottfried 4:77
growing reputation 4:79-80
influence of Dahl 4:85
influence of 'Dresden
    Romantics' 4:78
influence of Juel 4:77
influence of home life on
    painting 4:81
influence of Kosegarten 4:77
and Kersting 4:84
    painted by 4:79, 82
key dates 4:77
and landscape 4:77-8
marriage 4:81
media used 4:79-80
    oil sketches 4:85
    use of sepia 4:76, 79, 82,84-5
    and watercolour 4:85
and nature 4:82
patriotism 4:80
patrons: Nicholas I 4:81
preoccupations 4:77
problems with figures 4:84-5
and Prussian claims to Saxony
    4:103-104
religious symbols 4:83-4
and Rügen 4:77, 77
in his studio 4:82, 82
subjects 4:78, 83
trademarks 4:85
travels in the mountains 4:79,
    79
wins prize in Weimar 4:78, 79
working methods 4:81, 82-3,
    84-5
    'stippling' 4:85
    use of mental images 4:83
    use of sketches 4:83, 84
works: contrast in 4:83
    controversial 4:80
    last in oils 4:85
Abbey in the Oakwoods 4:80,
    88-9
Adolf Gottfried Friedrich 4:76
The Arctic Shipwreck 94
Chalk Cliffs on Rügen 4:91

The Cross in the Mountains 4:78,
    80
    symbolism of 4:83
Greifswald Harbour 4:86
The Large Enclosure 4:81
    use of colour in 4:85
*Man and Woman Gazing at the
    Moon* 4:84-5
    detail 4:84
Monk by the Sea 4:80
Moonrise over the Sea 4:93
Morning in the Riesenbirge
    4:82-3
Mother Heide 4:76
Oak Tree in the Snow 4:82-3
painting of his wife *see Woman
    at the Window*
Port by Moonlight 4:76-7
Ruin at Eldena 4:98-9
self-portrait 4:76, 78
The Stages of Life 4:81, 86, 86-7,
    96-7
    details 4:86, 87
    study for 4:87
    use of colour in 4:85
Times of Day: Evening 4:83
    Morning 4:83
*Village Landscape in Morning
    Light* 4:92
*Wanderer Looking over a Sea of
    Fog* 4:90
The Watzmann 4:95
Woman in the Setting Sun 4:84
Woman at the Window 4:80
Frink, Elizabeth 7:135
Fuseli, Henry 4:140-41
The Nightmare 6:70-71

G

Gainsborough, Thomas
influence of Van Dyck 3:82
Landscape with Sand Pit 3:116
Gallen-Kallela, Askeli 9:140
Lemmingkäinen's Mother 9:133
Gauguin, Paul
and Anne Martin 5:49
    painting of 5:49
arrangement of figures 5:53
and Bernard 5:47
and Brittany 5:46
    at Pont-Aven 5:46, 46
business career 5:45, 45
    loses job 5:46
and carving 5:53
Chagall and 6:82
childhood 5:44, 44-5
and colour: changes in use of
    5:50
    revolutionary use of 5:51
commitment to art 5:46

death of 5:49
    number of works sold after
        5:53
in Denmark 5:46
epitaph 5:49
family 5:44, 45, 45
    death of his daughter 5:54
    desertion of 5:46-7
    grandmother 5:44
    and son Clovis 5:46-7
    Tahitian wife 5:50-51
    wife and children 5:45
    with his daughter 5:54
finances 5:48
    in Marquesas 5:49
    near destitution 5:46
    in Pont-Aven 5:47
    in Tahiti 5:48
    windfall 5:48
first takes up painting 5:45,
    50
gallery guide 5:139
Van Gogh and 5:36, 79
    gift to 5:84
    sketch for 5:86-7
    visits 5:47-8
guardian 5:45
goes to sea 5:44-5
impact on modern art 5:53
and the Impressionists 5:45-6
    buys work by 5:45, 50
    exhibiting with 5:46
imprisonment 5:49
influence of Egyptian art
    5:52-3
influence of Japanese prints
    8:84
influence on 20th-century art
    5:53
inspiration 5:52
key dates 5:45
on Le Tambourin 5:101
lessons from Pissarro 5:45
letters, to his wife 5:53
Malevich and 7:51
in Marquesas 5:49, 49
    'The House of Pleasure' 5:49
models, Tahitian 5:52
Munch and 9:112
and the Nabis 9:48, 48-9
on his art 5:53
and Paris 5:47
    exhibition in 5:48
    studio, in Montparnasse
        5:48
at Pont-Aven 5:47
and 'primitive' cultures 5:51
Redon and 9:48
and religious symbolism 5:51,
    52, 54
reputation among
    contemporaries 5:48
Rousseau and 6:15
    and Elysée reception 6:16

Seurat and 5:110
in South America 5:47
    and Panama Canal 5:47, 47,
        71
and South Sea culture 5:50-53
and the stock exchange 5:45
style: development of 5:50-51
    effect of sunlight on 5:50
    fullest flowering of 5:52
subjects: sources of 5:51
and Symbolism, approach to
    9:70
in Tahiti 5:48-9, 66
techniques: in Tahiti paintings
    5:53
tomb 5:49
trademarks 5:52
in West Indies 5:47
    effect of sunlight on style
        5:50
works: expression of emotion
    in 5:50
    most characteristic features
        5:52-3
    most revolutionary 5:51
    period of best 5:48
Arearea 5:51
La Belle Angèle 9:52
Breasts and Red Flowers 5:65
The Day of the God 5:52
Eve and the Serpent 5:53
Harvest in Brittany 5:50
The Market 5:60-61
Martinique Landscape 5:50
Riders on the Beach 10:61
self-portrait 5:43, 51, 80, 84;
    9:49
    final 5:49
    first 5:44
The Spirit of the Dead Watching
    5:50-51
Tahitian Girl with a Flower 5:58
The Tahitian Women on a Beach
    5:59
Vairumati 5:54
Vision after the Sermon 5:51, 52,
    56; 9:69
*Where Do We Come From? What
    Are We? Where Are We Going
    To?* 5:54, 54-5, 62-3
    explanation of 5:55
The White Horse 5:64
The Yellow Christ 5:57
Gentileschi, Artemisia 3:37-8
style 3:37
subjects 3:38
    favourite 3:38, 38
Judith and Holofernes 3:38
self-portrait 3:38
Gentileschi, Orazio 3:141
and Caravaggio 3:36
style 3:36
The Rest on the Flight into Egypt
    3:36-7

Gerard, Francois
Ossian 4:*100-101*
Gerard of the Night Scenes *see*
Honthorst, Gerrit van
Gericault, Théodore 4:141
and Delacroix 4:109
portrait of 4:*108*
The Raft of the Medusa 4:109,
116
Ghiberti, Lorenzo
Commentaries: discovery of
Giotto 1:12
and Florence Cathedral 1:72
Gates of Paradise 1:72
and Linaiuoli Altarpiece 1:47,
51
Ghirlandaio, Domenico 1:140-41
self-portrait 1:*111*
Gilray, James 8:140-41
and Edward Jenner 8:*140*
Giordano, Luca 3:141
Giorgione
Bellini and 1:85
Dürer and 2:14
influence on Venetian art 1:80
landscape by? 1:136
technique 3:21
Giotto di Bondone
achievement of 1:18
acclamation by Dante 1:*14*, 15
appointments in Florence
1:*16*, 17
apprenticeship 1:12-13
Arena Chapel frescoes 1:22-3,
24
details 1:*24-5*
burial place 1:17, *17*
and Basilica of San Francesco
1:13, 39
fresco cycle for 1:13-15
basis of style 1:12
and Campanile, Florence
1:*16*, 17
character 1:15-16
commissions: after the Arena
Chapel frescoes 1:15
from Boniface VIII 1:13-14
from Cardinal Stefaneschi
1:16
for Friars Minor, Padua 1:14
from King of Naples 1:16-17
from Peruzzi 1:16
from Scrovegni 1:22-3
discovery as artist 1:12, *12-13*
enhancing dramatic impact
1:23
family/financial affairs 1:15
in Florence 1:14
and *fresco secco* 1:16
gallery guide 1:139
handling of figures 1:19
ideal setting for style 1:22
influence of Cimabue on 1:12
key dates 1:12

and King of Naples 1:16-17
last known work 1:17
marriage 1:14
memorial to 1:*17*
in Naples 1:16-17
narrative frescoes 1:19, 22
as a 'natural' artist 1:18-19
patrons, secular 1:16-17
first 1:14
wealthiest 1:22
powers of expression 1:20-21,
20-21
devices for effect 1:20
facial 1:22-3
records Halley's Comet 1:40
Rivera and 8:114
and spirit of the mendicant
orders 1:19
success as artist 1:15
technique 1:23
trademarks 1:23
by Uccello 1:*11*
visits Rome 1:13
The Adoration of the Magi 1:40,
41
The Annunciation of St Anna
1:*26*
The Betrayal of Christ 1:22, *29*
detail 1:*21*
The Clares Mourning St Francis
1:*39*
Crucifix, Santa Maria Novella
1:*18*
The Death of St Francis 1:*34-5*
Enrico degli Scrovegni 1:*24*
The Expulsion of Joachim 1:*25*
Figure of Inconstancy 1:*25*
The Flight into Egypt 1:*28*
The Lamentation 1:22
details 1:*20-21, 30-31*
The Last Judgement (detail) 1:*25*
Life of Saint Francis 1:13
Lives of Christ and the Virgin
1:14
Madonna and Child 1:13, *33*
The Massacre of the Innocents
1:*21*
The Meeting at the Golden Gate
1:*27*
detail 1:*20*
mosaic angel 1:*19*
The Nativity 1:*24*
Navicella 1:*15*
The Ognissanti Madonna 1:*32*
The Raising of Drusiana 1:*18-19*
The Raising of Lazarus 1:*18*
St Francis Preaching to the Birds
1:*38*
St Francis Renouncing the World
1:*19*
The Vision of Joachim 1:*22*
details 1:*23*
'God of Wood, The' *see*
Montañes, Juan Martinez

Gogh, Vincent van
in Arles 5:36-7, *79*, 79-83, 104
effect on townspeople 5:79
the Yellow House 5:79, *86*
on art 5:85
and artists' colony 5:80, 82-3
as assistant preacher 5:77
in the asylum at St Rémy 5:*80*,
81
in Auvers 5:81, *81*
and the Bargues technique
5:82
behaviour 5:78
in Belgium 5:77
and Bernard 5:79
and colour: changes his
palette 5:82
exaggerating 5:*83*, 83-4
letter about 5:84
most used 5:84
concentrates on art 5:77-8, 82
and Cormon 5:101
friends in studio of 5:79, 101
cuts off ear lobe 5:80
early life 5:76
effect of urban squalor on 5:77
in England 5:76-7
enrolls at Antwerp academy
5:78
family 5:76
and his brother 5:78-9, 81
death of his father 5:78
quarrels with his father 5:78
finances: asks brother for help
5:78
friendships, in Arles 5:79
gallery guide 5:139
Gauguin and 5:36, 47-8, 79
and artists' colony 5:80, *80*
gift from 5:84
quarrels with 5:80, *80*
sketch for 5:*86-7*
and the 'groupe du petit
boulevard' 5:101
influence of the
Impressionists on 5:79, 82,
100
influence of Japanese art 5:79,
82, 84, *84*; 6:78, 84
and Kee Vos 5:78
key dates 5:77
Klee and 6:46-7
letters to his brother 5:79,
80-81, 84
love affairs 5:78, *78*
and Mauve 5:78, 82
mental health 5:80, *80*, 81, *81*
effect on work 5:84-5
models, mistress as 5:78
in Paris 5:98
at Café Tambourin 5:101
decides to leave 5:79
lives with his brother 5:78-9
studies with Cormon 5:79

and Pissarro 5:79, 81
respect for 5:*100-101*
as a pupil 5:79, 82, 101
sells painting 5:81
Seurat and 5:110
and Sien 5:78, *78*
sketch by Bernard 5:*83*
suicide 5:81
and Symbolism 9:71
and Tanguy 5:101
technique: of applying paint
5:83
drawing 5:82
and *impasto* 5:83
temperament 5:79
Toulouse-Lautrec and 5:79;
8:78
painted by 5:*100*
trademarks 5:85
trains for the ministry 5:77
working methods 5:82
effects on health 5:83
on work-rate 5:84
works: number painted in
asylum 5:81, 85
number painted before
breakdown 5:84:
portraits of peasants 5:78
start of recognition 5:81
The Bedroom at Arles 5:86-7,
90-91
details 5:*87*
Café Terrace at Night 5:85
detail 5:*85*
method of painting 5:83
The Church at Auvers 5:*96*
Cornfield and Cypresses 5:*93*
Miners 5:77
The Painter on his way to Work
5:82-3
Peasant Woman 5:82
Peasant Woman Tying Sheaves
9:*116*
Père Tanguy 5:*88*
The Postman Roulin 5:*89*
The Potato Eaters 5:78, 82
use of colour in 5:82, *82*
The Restaurant de la Sirène 5:*83*
self-portrait 5:*75*, 79, 85, *97*
Sorrow 5:*78*
Starry Night 5: *94-5*
*Stone Steps in the Hospital
Garden*
use of colour in 5:*83*
Sunflowers 5:*92*
use of colour in 5:84
Vincent's Chair 5:*86*
The Yellow House 5:*86*
Goncharova, Natalia 7:46
Malevich and 7:45
and 'Russian Primitive'
movement 7:45
Gardening 7:*46-7*
Gossaert, Jan 2:140

Goya y Lucientes, Francisco de
apprenticeship 4:12
and Art Academy of Parma
competition 4:12-13
and Bayeu 4:12, 13
change in approach to art 4:18
commissions: from Charles III
4:13
from Ferdinand VII 4:41-2
first important 4:13
for S. Antonio de la Florida
4:14
country property 4:16, 17
death of 4:17
and Duchess of Alba 4:14, 15
and Escorial Palace 4:14, 15
family 4:16
in France 4:17
friends 4:16-17
gallery guide 4:139
as graphic artist 4:18, 21
illness 4:13, 16, 16-17, 18-21
imaginative tendencies 4:13
influence of Mengs 4:12, 13
influence of Rembrandt 4:18
influence of Tiepolo 4:12
influence of Velázquez 4:18
and the Inquisition 4:16, 34, 34
in Italy 4:12-13
and Joseph Bonaparte 4:14
key dates 4:12
Klee and 6:45
and Leocadia Weiss 4:16
and lithography 4:17
in Madrid 4:12, 13-14
marriage 4:12, 18
media used 4:21
member of Royal Order of
Spain 4:14
models: Duchess of Alba as?
4:14, 15
on nature 4:20
official recognition 4:13
political views 4:14, 16
posts: at Madrid Academy of
Art 4:13-14
First painter to the King 4:14
royal painter 4:13
resigns as court painter 4:17
as religious painter 4:18
as self-expression 4:21
slow beginnings 4:13
style, late development of
4:18
subjects 4:13
best-known 4:18
'fantasy and invention' 4:13
use of Spanish tradition
4:20
and tapestry manufacture
4:13, 13, 18
technique 4:18, 20, 21
trademarks 4:21
and Wellington 4:16

work: effects of illness on
4:18-21
gloom of later 4:16
'black paintings' 4:16, 17,
20-21
Bulls of Bordeaux 4:17
The Burial of the Sardine 4:32
Caprichos 4:20-21
The Clothed Maja 4:14, 24-5
Inquisition and 4:16
The Colossus 4:29
The Court of the Inquisition
4:34-5
Disasters of War 4:14, 19, 23
Doña Isabel de Porcel 4:26
The Duchess of Alba 4:15
The Duke of Wellington 4:28
The Family of Charles IV 4:14
Josefa Bayeu 4:12
The Madhouse 4:20-21
detail 4:21
La Manola 4:17
The Naked Maja 4:14, 15
Inquisition and 4:16, 34, 34
painting for himself see 'black
paintings'
Proverbios 4:19, 21
*Saturn Devouring One of his
Sons* 4:33
The Second of May, 1808 4:16,
18-19, 42
self-portrait 4:11
detail 4:18
with Dr Arrieta 4:16, 16-17
*The Sleep of Reason Produces
Monsters* 4:17
The Straw Manikin 4:19
The Swing 4:13
Tauromaquia 4:19, 21
The Third of May, 1808 4:16, 22,
22-3, 42
details 4:28
Two Majas on a Balcony 4:27
Goyen, Jan van 3:108, 112
Gozzoli, Benozzo 1:141
draughtsmanship 1:49
and foreshortening/
perspective 1:49
and Fra Angelico 1:48, 53
frescoes in Pisa 1:49
The Journey of the Magi 1:49,49
self-portrait 1:49
'Graveyard painter' *see*
Friedrich, Caspar David
Gris, Juan
Rivera and 8:109, 114
Gross, Baron Antoine Jean
and Delacroix 4:110
Grünewald, Mathis 2:140
The Resurrection 4:85
Guercino, Il 3:141
Guérin, Pierre-Narcisse
and Delacroix 4:109
Guido di Pietro *see* **Fra Angelico**

H

Hamilton, Richard 7:134
Hayes, Colin 7:109
Heem, Jan Davidsz de
Still-life with a Lobster 5:20
Heemskerck, Martin van 2:140
'Hell Brueghel' *see* Brueghel,
Peter the Younger
Herbin, Auguste 7:141
Herbster, Hans
by Holbein 2:77
and Holbein 2:76, 82
Hicks, Edward
The Peaceable Kingdom 5:53
Hilliard, Nicholas 2:141
Elizabeth I 2:87
John and Frances Croker 2:140
*Man Clasping a Hand from a
Cloud* 2:141
*A Woman, known as Mrs
Holland* 10:51
Hiroshige, Utagawe
Ohashi Bridge in the Rain 5:84
Hirschfield, Morris 6:141
Hobbema, Meindart 3:141
The Avenue at Middelharnis
3:111; 10:54
Hockney, David 7:133, 135
Hodler, Ferdinand 9:140
Hogarth, William
and Amigoni 8:16
The Analysis of Beauty 8:17, 21
apprenticeship 8:12
art training 8:13-14
'artistic manifesto' 8:17
attacks on 8:16
and *The Beggar's Opera* 8:14
and Chéron 8:13
in Chiswick 8:15
and Churchill 8:17
commissions 8:16-17, 16, 17
'conversation pieces' 8:14, 21
on depiction of contemporary
life 8:19
elopement 8:14
and English painting 8:12-13
and Engravers' Copyright Act
8:16
and engraving 8:12, 12
employs other engravers 8:17
illustrating literary works
8:13, 13-14
selling by subscription 8:15
on silver plate 8:12
transition from silver to
copper 8:20
and etching 8:20
and 'face painting' 8:15
family 8:12
death of brothers 8:12
in debtors' prison 8:12
wife 8:14-15
and Fielding 8:14

finances: income from
engravings 8:15, 16, 18
from portraits 8:15
and formal painting 8:12-13
and the Foundling Hospital
8:16
in France 8:40
gallery guide 8:139
and Gamble 8:12
graphic shorthand 8:20
Hazlitt on 8:18
hero 8:13
and 'historical' painting 8:12,
12, 21
influence of Coypel 8:20
influence of Dutch genre
works 8:19-20
influence of the theatre 8:14
and Jane Thornhill 8:14, 14-15
key dates 8:13
and line 8:16-17, 17, 20, 21
marriage 8:15
and murals 8:16, 16, 21
narrative series: aim of
campaign with 8:15, 18-19
audience for 8:18
high society satire 8:17
and 'Old-Masters' 8:17
and portraiture 8:14-15, 21
as print seller 8:12, 15
prints pirated 8:15, 16-17
publishes art theory 8:16-17
and religious painting 8:21
reputation established 8:16
and satire 8:14
'The Shakespeare of painting'
8:18-21
style: of early engravings 8:20
refinement of 8:20
sources of 8:19-20
subjects: 'the book of nature'
8:19
'modern moral' 8:19
religious decorative 8:15-16
summing up of his art 8:21
and the theatre 8:14-15
themes 8:14
and Thornhill: at academy of
8:13
lives with 8:15
trademarks 8:21
treatment of his friends 8:17
and Vanderbank 8:13
works: and conveying a moral
8:21
first oil paintings 8:14
in the grand style 8:17
last major series 8:21
London as model 8:36
most successful oils 8:21
sells by auction 8:17
altarpiece for St Mary Redcliffe
8:16
The Bathos 8:17

Beer Street 8:32
 crudity of engraving 8:21
Benjamin Hoadley, Bishop of Winchester 8:29
Calais Gate 8:40
Captain Coram 8:19, 21
The Conquest of Mexico 8:18
The Covent Garden Tragedy 8:15
The Election 8:21
 Chairing the Member 8:34-5
 engraving of a London street 8:36-7
Gin Lane 8:33
 crudity of engraving 8:21
The Good Samaritan 8:16
The Graham Children 8:21, 27
A Harlot's Progress 8:15
 pamphlet on 8:15
 purpose of painting 8:15, 20-21
 third plate 8:18
Hudibras 8:20
Industry and Idleness, crudity of engraving 8:21
 first plate 8:19
 London in 8:36
Lord Grey and Lady Mary West as Children 8:26
The March to Finchley 8:20-21
 detail 8:21
Marriage à la Mode 8:22, 22-3
 The Countess's Suicide 8:23
 details 8:22-3
 The Killing of the Earl 8:23
 The Marriage Contract 8:30
 purpose of painting 8:15, 20-21
 Shortly after the Marriage 8:31
 success of 8:17
Masquerades and Operas see *The Taste of the Town*
Miss Mary Edwards 8:28
The Painter and the Pug 8:11, 16
Pool of Bethesda 8:16, 16
Portrait of John Wilkes 8:17
The Rake's Progress: in the Debtors' Prison 8:25
 The Madhouse 8:37
 purpose of painting 8:15, 20-21
 The Tavern Scene 8:24
Roast Beef of Old England see *Calais Gate*
Servants 8:18-19
shop card 8:12, 12
Sigismunda 8:17
 directions for selling 8:17
 reason for painting 8:17
 subscription ticket 8:15
The Taste of the Town 8:13, 13-14
Tom Thumb 8:14
Hogenberg, Frans
 The Blue Cloak 2:119
Holbein, Hans, the Elder 2:76

Holbein, Hans, the Younger
appointed King's Painter 2:80
apprenticeship 2:76
in Basel 2:76
 buys home in 2:78
 inducements to stay 2:81
basis of reputation 2:82
and book illustration 2:76
in Brussels 2:81
chalk drawings 2:83
character 2:80
 personality clues 2:76
commissions: in Basel 2:78
 from German merchants 2:80-81
 from Henry VIII 2:80
 from Sir Henry Guildford 2:82
 from Oberreid 2:82
death of 2:81
destruction of early religious works 2:83
drawing ability 2:83
in England: and political/ intellectual life 2:77-8
 settles in 2:81
 sitters in 2:78
family 2:77
 illegitimate 2:81
 painting of 2:79
in France 2:77
gallery guide 2:139
and Henry VIII: first meeting with 2:77, 78
 income from 2:80
 paints prospective wives 2:81
and Herbster 2:76
and the Humanists 2:76
 finest works for 2:77
 friends among 2:78, 78
influence of Dürer 2:82
influence on English art 2:81
influence of Grünewald 2:82
influence of Italian artists 2:77
influence of Italian Renaissance on 2:82-3
influence of Leonardo 2:76
influence of Mantegna 2:76
and ink 2:83-4
in Italy 2:76
key dates 2:77
in London 2:77
 second visit 2:78-9
in Lucerne 2:76
mastery of textures 2:84
and mechanical aids 2:84
mistress 2:77
most momentous task 2:80, 80-81
most popular drawings 2:83, 84-5
most prestigious work 2:86
and painters' guild 2:77

patrons: in England 2:77, 78-9
 German 2:80-81:
 German merchants 2:79
 status of 2:79
and portraits 2:82-7
 backgrounds in 2:84-5
 finest 2:78
 method of working 2:84
 realism in 2:83
 speed of execution 2:84
 style for Henry VIII 2:102
and *Praise of Folly* 2:76
as propagandist 2:80, 87
'props' in paintings 2:84
and *sfumato* 2:82
style: change of 2:84, 86
 of early works 2:82
subjects: of early works 2:82
technical brilliance 2:84, 86
and Thomas More 2:77-8
 and his circle 2:83-4
trademarks 2:87
use of inscriptions 2:84-5
use of line 2:86
use of notes 2:84
'vocabulary' of religious work 2:87
and watercolour 2:83
and woodcuts 2:77
 for the Coverdale Bible 2:79
The Ambassadors 2:79, 88, 88-9, 94-5
 details 2:88-9
 symbolic objects in 2:89
Anne of Cleves 2:83; 10:50
Anne Cresacre 2:84
Baptism of St Paul 2:76
Christina of Denmark, Duchess of Milan 2:98
 speed of painting 2:84
Dance of Death 2:77
Family Group 2:79
Family of Thomas More (copy) 2:78
George Gisze 2:79, 86
 detail 2:86
 treatment of textures 2:84
Hans Herbster 2:77
Henry VIII 2:96
 cartoon 2:100
 use of line in 2:86
Jane Seymour 2:97
John More the Younger 2:84
Margaret Wyatt, Lady Lee 2:83
Mary Wotton, Lady Guildford 2:91
The Meyer Madonna 2:90
 influence on 2:82-3
 model for 2:77
The Oberreid Altarpiece 2:82
Portrait of Erasmus 2:78
self-portraits 2: 75, 81
Simon George of Quocoute 2:83, 85

Sir Henry Guildford 2:82
Thomas Boleyn 2:85
Thomas Cromwell 2:79, 80
Sir Thomas More 2:92
The Triumph of Riches (copy) 2:80-81
Tudor Dynasty (copy) 2:80, 80, 86-7
 changes to 2:87
An Unknown Lady 2:85, 99
Unknown Lady 2:99
Unknown Lady with a Squirrel 2:99
 wall painting for Whitehall 2:80, 80-81
William Warham, Archbishop of Canterbury 2:84
Hollar, Wenceslaus
 on Van Dyck's mistress 3:81
 Lucas and Cornelis de Wael (after Van Dyck) 3:79
Hondecoeter, Melchoir
 Bullfinches and Butterflies 3:134
Honthorst, Gerrit van
 and Caravaggio 3:39
 style 3:39
 Christ before the High Priest 3:39
Huet, Paul 4:141
Hunt, William Holman
 and Raphael 9:14
 Rossetti and 9:14
 painting of 9:11

I

Ingres, Jean-Auguste-Dominique 4:112
 Riley and 7:109
 Rivera and 8:114

J

Jawlinsky, Alexei von
 and *Blaue Reiter* group 6:45
 Kandinsky and 7:15
Jordaens, Jacob
 commissions from Charles I 3:81

K

Kahlo, Frida 8:112, 112
 death of 8:113
 and Trotsky 8:113
 Frida and Diego 8:112

Kandinsky, Wassily 7:11
and abstraction 7:15
administrative skills 7:15
aged five or six 7:12
and Anja Chimiakin 7:13
and Arp 7:17
attacked by the press 7:16
and the Bauhaus 6:48; 7:16-17
course taught at 7:37
and life classes 7:17
and mural painting 7:17
reputation at 7:37
and *Blaue Reiter* group 6:45;
7:15, *15*
buys a house 7:15
and colour 7:15, 18-19
characteristics of 7:20
early influences on 7:19
of the Fauves 7:15
of the Impressionists 7:13
potential of 7:19
relationships to shape 7:20
theories about 7:16,
20
'white' 7:37
commitment to painting 7:13
death of 7:17
denunciation of 7:17
description of by friends 7:14
and discipline in drawing 7:14
early drawing lessons 7:12
education 7:12
effect of World War I on 7:16
effect of Russian Revolution
on 7:16
and expressing emotions
7:18-19
family 7:12, *13*
on his mother 7:12
finances: donations for
watercolours 7:17
for holidays 7:17
income from his father 7:14
in Munich 7:13-14
on return to Germany 7:16
salary from Bauhaus 7:17
and form 7:18-19
on the origin of 7:20
and Gabrielle Münter 7:*14*,
15
gallery guide 7:139
and glass paintings 7:19
Gropius and 7:36
and Impressionist painting
7:13
and *Haystacks* (Monet) 7:13,
19
influence of Matisse 7:19
influence of Schönberg 7:14,
14-15
influence on twentieth-
century art 7:18
inspiration from his own
work 7:15

and Institute of Artistic
Culture 7:16
and Jawlensky 7:15
encouragement from 7:15
key dates 7:13
and Klee 6:46; 7:15, 16-17
and landscape 7:15
law studies 7:13
and line 7:15, 19
marriage: first 7:13
second 7:*15*
materials in war years 7:17
and Meyer 7:39
mistress 7:*14*, 15
and Mondrian 7:17
in Moscow 7:16-17, *16-17*
friends in 7:*16-17*
influence of 7:12
at the University 7:13
writing on 7:12
in Munich 7:13-15
at Azbe's art school 7:14
influence of 7:13
organizes exhibitions 7:15
at Royal Academy 7:14
study of avant-garde artists
7:19
and music 7:15-16
art like 7:18
and *Neue Künstlervereinigung,
München* 7:15
in Neuilly 7:17
and Nina Andreewsky 7:*15,*
16
in Odessa 7:12-13, *12-13*
On the Spiritual in Art 7:16, 20
passion for travel 7:15
and People's Commissariat
for Enlightenment 7:16
and Phalanx group 7:*14*, 14
Point and Line to Plane 7:17, 20
principles of art 7:18
principles of geometric
construction 7:17
pupil 7:15
and Russian Academy of
Artistic Sciences 7:16
and the Russian school 7:13
and Schönberg 7:15-16, *16*
in Sèvres 7:15
and spiritual rejuvenation 7:16
and von Stuck 7:14
studios 7:14
and Der Sturm Gallery 7:16
style: close to Klee's 7:17
geometrical 7:20
use of symbols 7:17
subjects/motifs: of early works
7:19
geometrical 7:20
personal hieroglyphs 7:20
re-working 7:19
significance of 7:19
of woodcuts 7:19

and symbols 7:17, *18*
technique: of abstracting
motifs 7:15
learns from Art Nouveau/
Fauves 7:19
trademarks 7:21
and University of Dorpat 7:13
working methods: abstracting
7:19
re-working motifs 7:15
sketches 7:14, 19
works: division of 7:19
early 7:19
first 'abstract' 7:19
output for 1914-21 7:16
painted at Bauhaus 7:20
sold at a loss 7:16
Black Lines I 7:26
coloured woodcuts 7:57
Compositions 7:19-20
Composition IV (Battle) 7:21, *21*
detail 7:*21*
Composition VII, study for
7:*18-19*
Composition VIII 7:28-9
Impressions 7:14, 19
Impression 3 (Concert) 7:*14-15*
Improvisation 19 7:24-5
Improvisation Ravine 7:27
motifs in 7:19
Improvisation 31 (Sea Battle)
7:52
Motley Life, symbolism
in 7:*18*
Red Oval 7:*18-19*
Rows of Signs 7:19
Sky Blue 7:34-5
symbolism in 7:17
Swinging 7:30-31
Train in Murnau 7:22-3
Yellow Painting 7:32-3
Kennington, Eric
Gassed and Wounded 7:72-3
Kersting, Georg Friedrich
and Friedrich 4:79, *79*
paints figures for 4:84
Friedrich in his Studio 4:*82*
Keyser, Thomas de
collaboration with Ruisdael
3:111
Conversation Piece (with
Ruisdael) 3:*109*
Khnopff, Fernand 9:140-41
and the Secessionists 9:102
I Lock the Door Upon Myself
9:70-71
Who Shall Deliver Me? 9:*141*
Kirchner, Ernst Ludwig
and *Die Brücke* 8:138
Klee and 6:49
Kisling, Möise 6:101
by Marevna 8:*108-109*
by Modigliani 6:*101*
and Zborowski 6:102

Klee, Paul 6:*43*
in the army 6:46
and Arp 6:47
and Ball 6:47
and the Bauhaus 6:48; 7:36-7
contribution to 6:47
in Berne 6:44, 48-9
and Blake 6:45
and *Blaue Reiter* group 6:45
exhibits with 6:45
and Braque 6:49
and Breton 6:47
and Cézanne 6:45
on his childhood 6:44
and children's art 6:45, 50
and colour 6:51-2; 7:37
influence of Delaunay 6:45
in last works 6:52
'orchestrating' 6:51
preparation for 6:45
writing on 6:46
death of 6:49
and Delaunay 6:45, 51
at Dusseldorf Academy 6:48
effect of World War I on 6:46
effect of friends' deaths on
6:46
in Egypt 6:47-8
and Ensor 6:45
and Exhibition of Degenerate
Art 6:48, *49*
exhibitions 6:47
retropective 6:49
and the Expressionists 6:47
family 6:44
with his father 6:45
with his sister 6:44
finances, with the Bauhaus
6:46
and form 7:37
gallery guide 6:139
and Van Gogh 6:45
and Goya 6:45
and graphic art 6:45
Gropius and 7:36
growing reputation 6:47-8
illness 6:49
effects on works 6:52
influence of Cubists 6:51
influence of Van Gogh 6:46-7
influence of Mozart 6:44, *45*
in Italy 6:45
joins the Bauhaus 6:46
and Kandinsky 6:45, 46; 7:14
analysing works 7:17
finds job for 7:16-17
key dates 6:44
and Kirchner 6:49
and Knirr 6:44
and life-force 6:50
and Lily Stumpf 6:45
and line 6:47
and Marc 6:45
effect on death on 6:46

marriage 6:44-5
and Matisse 6:45
in Munich 6:44, 45
Pedagogical Sketchbook 6:47
and Picasso 6:49
and planes 6:47
as poet 6:44
and print-making 6:45
and Redon 6:45
and the Secessionists 6:44
   and symbolism/satire 6:44
and simplicity of vision 6:50-51
and von Stuck 6:44
studio, with the Bauhaus 6:46
style, linear 6:45
subjects, 'Egyptian' 6:48
   in last years 6:52
   sources 6:51, 52
teachers 6:44
techniques 6:50
   'doodles' 6:52
   of early works 6:45
   with paint surface 6:52
and texture 6:47, 52
trademarks 6:53
in Tunisia 6:45-6, *46*
   on African sunlight 6:*46*
visitors to 6:49
works: basis of first mature
   6:44
   changes in character of 6:49
   essence of 6:50
   last 6:*51, 52*
   scale of last 6:52
   sense of space in 6:51
world of fantasy 6:52
Ad Parnassum 6:64-5
The City of Churches 6:55
Death and Fire 6:49, *67*
Fire in the Evening 6:51
Fish Magic 6:60-61
   order of relationships in
   6:52
Full Moon 6:58
   organization of 6:51
Landscape with Yellow Birds
   6:53, *53*
   detail 6:*53*
Monument in a Fertile Country
   6:*62-3*
   organization of 6:51
Motif of Hammamet 6:*54*
Rock Flora 6:66
Senecio 6:50
Still Life 6:51, *52*
The Twittering Machine 6:59
The Virgin in the Tree 6:50
With the Eagle 6:56-7
Klimt, Ernst (brother) 9:76
   and Lauferberger 9:76
   in class of 9:*76*
   and Matsch 9:76
   recognition 9:77
   studio 9:76-7

Klimt, Gustav 9:*75*
accused of pornography 9:79
and Alma Mahler 9:79
and artistic freedom 9:77
bohemian life-style 9:77
   in Vienna 9:79-80, 81
commissions: *Bergtheater* 9:77,
   77
   Emperor's silver wedding
   9:76
   Kunsthistorisches museum
   9:*77, 77*
   Lauferberger and 9:76
   most important early 9:77,
   77
   for Stoclet 9:*80-81, 81*
   for Vienna University 9:78,
   78, 79
   while still studying 9:76
and cyclical nature of
   existence 9:82-3
death of 9:81
denounces censorship 9:79
draughtsmanship 9:83
early art training 9:76
easel paintings, importance of
   frames 9:84
and Emilie Flöge 9:79-80
family 9:76
finances: supplementary art
   school 9:76
gallery guide 9:139
greatest achievement 9:*80-81,*
   81
and Impressionists 9:78, 85
influence of Ancient Egypt/
   Greece 9:84
influence of Arts and Crafts
   movement 9:84
influence of Byzantine
   mosaics 9:84
influence of Japanese prints
   9:84-5
influence of Makart 9:84
key dates 9:76
and Kokoschka 9:80
at Kunstgewerbeschule 9:76
and the Künstlerhaus 9:78
and landscape 9:80
   influence of Impressionists
   on 9:85
and Laufberger 9:76
and Matsch 9:76
and mosaic/fresco 9:76
ornamental details 9:83
patrons 9:79
and pattern, abstracting 9:85
and portraiture 9:76, 79
   backgrounds in late 9:84-5
   popularity of female 9:79
prizes/awards 9:77
   for *Burgtheater* 9:77
recognition 9:77
and Schiele 9:80, *80*

and Secession 9:*100,* 101
   rift with 9:80-81
   sets up 9:78
sexuality 9:79, *79*
sources, eclectic approach to
   9:84-5
style: influence of decorative
   training on 9:84
   originality of 9:84
   use of horizon line 9:85
subjects: impassiveness of
   9:83
   subordinate to decoration
   9:83
   use of frontal pose 9:82
   women 9:82
and symbolic detail 9:83
and Symbolist painters 9:78
themes: central obsessions
   9:82
trademarks 9:84
and Wiener Werkstätte 9:81
'working dress' 9:77, *81*
works: erotic opulence of
   9:82-5
Adam and Eve 2:52
*The Beethoven Frieze: The Hostile
   Powers* 9:92
   Pure Joy 9:93
Birch Wood 9:82
The Black Feather Hat 9:82-3
The Bride 9:81, *83*
Danaë 9:98
Emilie Flöge 9:79
Expectation 9:81
   cartoon for 9:84
Fulfilment 9:81, *84-5*
   detail 9:*84*
Goldfish 9:91
Hope I 9:95
Judith I 9:*20,* 82, 86, 90
   details 9:*86, 87*
   source of background 9:*87*
Judith II 9:86
Jurisprudence 9:79
The Kiss 9:82, *99*
*Margaret Stonborough-
   Wittgenstein* 9:97
Medicine 9:78, *78, 79*
   detail 9:*78*
Music I 9:*88-9*
Philosophy 9:78-9
Secession poster 9:79, *101*
Self-Portrait as Genitalia 9:79
Stoclet Frieze 9:80-81, 81
   Tree of Life, working
   drawing 9:*80*
*Water Serpents II (Women
   Friends)* 9:96
Kokoschka, Oscar
   Klimt and 9:80
Kruchenykh, Alexei
   Malevich and 7:46
   Victory over the Sun 7:46

L
La Tour, Georges de 3:39, 141
   Adoration of the Shepherds 3:*38-9*
Lacombe, Georges 5:141
Landseer, Sir Edwin 6:39
   Dignity and Impudence 6:*38*
   Queen Victoria at Osborne 3:*85*
Larionov, Mikhail Fedorovich
   6:141; 7:46
   and 'Russian primitive'
   movement 7:45
   Glass 7:*46*
Laurencin, Marie
   Guillaume Apollinaire 6:*103*
Laurent, Ernest
   Seurat 5:*107*
Lawrence, Sir Thomas 4:111
Le Valentin
   Soldiers Playing Dice 3:*36-7*
Léger, Fernand 6:101
Leonardo da Vinci
   Caravaggio and 3:16
   Dürer and 2:19
   Holbein and 2:76
   and imagination 6:115
   and mechanical aids 2:84
   in Milan 1:111
   recording life of 1:44
   Isabella d'Este (drawing) 1:*81*
   Mona Lisa, Dalí and 6:116
   *Study for the Trivulzio
   Equestrian Monument* 6:*116*
Leoni, Ottavio
   drawing of Caravaggio 3:36
Leotard, Jules 5:132
Leyden, Lucas van 2:141
Liebermann, Max 9:110, 135
Limbourg brothers
   *Les Trés Riches Heures du Duc
   de Berri* 2:*116*
Lipchitz, Jacques 6:101; 8:108
Lippi, Filippino 1:46, 69, 112, 141
   and Botticelli 1:109
   self-portrait 1:*112*
   The Vision of St Bernard 1:*112*
Lippi, Filippo 1:141
   and Botticelli 1:109, 116
   comparison with Fra Angelico
   1:69
   patron of 1:*133*
   The Coronation of the Virgin
   1:*133*
   detail 1:*46*
   The Feast of Herod 1:*117*
   Madonna and Child 1:*46*
   self-portrait 1:*46*
Lissitzky, El 7:140
Lorenzetti, Pietro 1:39
Lotto, Lorenzo
   Triple Portrait of a Jeweller 3:*87*
Luce, Maximilien 5:141
Luthi, Hanny
   Sacré Coeur 6:*20*

M

Magritte, René 6:141
  Miró and 7:78
Makart, Hans
  Klimt and 9:84
  successor to 9:77
Malevich, Kasimir
  and the applied arts 7:48-9
  as architect 7:48-9
    architecton 7:51
    collaboration with Suetin 7:48
    'houses of the future' 7:48-9
  on his art 7:52
  and the Bauhaus 7:49
  beliefs about art 7:49
  and Braque 7:45
  brushwork, in early works 7:50
  and collage 7:50, 51-2
  and colour: in early works 7:50
    in Suprematist works 7:52
  death of 7:49
  education 7:44
  employment during Revolution 7:47
  exhibitions: after the Revolution 7:45, 49
  family 7:44
    daughter 7:44
    his mother 7:44
  and Federation of Leftist Artists 7:47
  and folk art 7:47
  and French Post-Impressionists 7:45
  From Cubism to Suprematism 7:47
  From Impressionism to Suprematism 7:48
  and Futurism/Futurists:
    collaborates with 7:46
    exhibits with 7:46
    and ideas 7:45
    illustrates verse 7:47
  gallery guide 7:139
  and German avant-garde artists 7:49
  and Goncharova 7:45, *46*
  and Holbein 7:48-9
  influence of Braque 7:51
  influence of Cézanne 7:51
  influence of French Impressionists 7:50
  influence of the Futurists 7:45
  influence of Gauguin 7:51
  influence of Mayakovsky 7:45
  influence of Picasso 7:51
  influence of Russian icons 7:51
  and Jack of Diamonds Group 7:45
  jobs pre-Revolution 7:47
  key dates 7:45

and Kiev School of Art 7:*44, 45*
and Kruchenykh 7:46
and Larionov 7:45
last days 7:*49*
and Matyushin 7:47
and Morosov 7:45
in Moscow 7:45
one-man show 7:48
patrons 7:45
and perspective 7:50
and Petrograd State Free Art Workshops 7:47
and Picasso 7:45
principles of art 7:50
reputation post-Revolution 7:49
and the Russian Impressionists 7:45
and Shchukin 7:45
and stage design 7:46, 47
style: after the Revolution 7:49
  'Cubo-Futurist' 7:45, 51-2
  influences on 7:50
  of painting people 7:50
  for peasant life 7:51
  return to figurative painting 7:*48-9, 49*
  of Suprematist paintings 7:52
  transitions in 7:50
  see also Suprematism
subjects: men at work 7:51
  peasant life 7:45
and Suetin 7:48
and Suprematism 7:47-8
  culmination of 7:48
  division of 7:52
  ideas behind 7:52
  origin of style 7:46
  subjects of first works 7:46
teaching 7:47, 49
trademarks 7:53
and *Victory over the Sun* 7:46
  backcloth for 7:46
  influence on career 7:46
in Vitebsk 7:48-9
  and the art school 7:48
working method: metallic sheen 7:51
works: dating 7:50
  earliest known 7:50
  first Suprematist 7:46
'white on white' series 7:48, 52
writes for *Anarchy* 7:47
and 0.10 Exhibition 7:52
architecton 7:51
drawing of his mother 7:44
Eight Red Rectangles 7:59
Girl with a Comb 7:49
The Knife Grinder 7:57
  style of 7:51
On the Boulevard 7:54
Painterly Realism of a Footballer 7:52

pamphlet cover 7:*50-51*
Planits 7:48-9
Portrait of a Member of the Artist's Family 7:55
A Private of the First Division 7:*50*, 52
The Rye Harvest 7:56
  style of 7:51
Self-Portrait 7:48-9
Suprematist Composition 7:64-5
Suprematist Composition: Airplane Flying 7:60
Suprematist Composition: Red Square and Black Square 7:58
Suprematist Composition: White on White 7:67
Suprematist Painting 7:62-3
Suprematist Painting 1916 7:53
  detail 7:*53*
Supremus 7:47
Woman with Buckets and Child, influence on 7:51
The Woodcutter 7:50
Yellow Parallelogram on White 7:66
Mander, Karl/Karel van
  on Bruegel the elder 2:108-109, 117
    effect of the Alps on 2:110
    on his marriage 2:111
  on Caravaggio 3:14
    naturalism of 3:19
  on Holbein 2:80
  Het Schilderboek 2:108
Manet, Edouard 5:*98*
  and Académie des Beaux-Arts 5:98
  Cézanne and 5:13-14
  and the Impressionists 5:99
  in Paris 5:99; 8:82-3
  patron 5:99
  Argenteuil 10:62
  The Luncheon on the Grass 5:98
    reaction to 5:98, 99
  Nana 8:84
  Olympia, Cézanne's parody of 5:18
  The Waitress 5:99
Manfredi, Bartolommeo
  subjects 3:37
  The Chastisement of Cupid 3:37
Mantegna, Andrea
  death of 1:81
  Dürer and 2:14, 19
  Holbein and 2:76
  link with the Bellinis 1:77
  and perspective 1:83
  and spatial clarity 1:82-3
  and *studiolo* of Isabella d'Este 1:79
  Agony in the Garden 1:77
  Bergamo Madonna, The 1:141
  self-portrait 1:77

Marc, Franz 6:46; 7:16
  and *Blaue Reiter* group 6:45; 7:15, *15*
  on painting animals 6:39
  Fighting Forms 6:47
  Red and Blue Horses 6:39
Martin, John 4:141
Martini, Simone 1:39
  The Annunciation 1:53
Masaccio 1:47, 141; 8:114
  The Madonna and Child with St Anne 10:49
Masson, André 6:141; 7:77
Massys, Quentin 2:141
Matisse, Henri
  Kandinsky and 7:19
  and Nice 5:37
  and Redon 9:49
Matout, Louis
  Woman Killed by a Lioness, Rousseau and 6:22
Matsch, Franz
  commissions: *Burgtheater* 9:77, *77*
    for Vienna University 9:78, *78*
    villas 9:77
  Klimt and 9:76
  recognition 9:77
  studio 9:76-7
Matta, Echaurren Roberto 7:141
Mayakovsky Vladimir 7:73
  and Futurism 7:46
  influence of Malevich 7:45
  design for *Mystery Bouffe* 7:45
  on Revolutionary artists' duty 7:48
  A Cloud in Trousers 7:73, *74*
Mengs, Anton Raffael 4:12, 13
Merisi, Michelangelo *see* **Caravaggio**
Meryon, Charles 4:141
Messina, Antonello da 1:80
  Giovanni Bellini and 1:78
  lost masterpiece 1:80
  and oil painting 1:78, 83
  in Venice 1:78, 83
  S. Cassiano Altarpiece 1:80
  Portrait of a Man 1:80
  self-portrait 1:80
Michelangelo 1:*133*
  and Bertoldo 1:*133*
  Blake and 4:50
  Caravaggio and 3:16
  recording the life of 1:44
  The Creator 4:52
  David, Botticelli and 1:113
Millais, John Everett 9:141
  and Raphael 9:14
  Rossetti and 9:14
Millet, Jean-François 8:141
  The Angelus, Dalí and 6:112, 114, 115-16
  The Gleaners 8:53

Miró, Joan 7:*75, 76*
  in America 7:*79,* 80-81
    commissions in 7:80
    and Pierre Matisse Gallery
      7:80
  and Arp 7:78
  and Artigan 7:76-7
  'assassinating painting' 7:79
  and avant-garde 7:77
  in Barcelona 7:76-7
  and ceramics 7:80
  character, fantasy in 7:82
  and collage 7:79
  commissions: for Barcelona
    airport 7:81
    for Cervantes Gardens 7:81
    for Harvard University 7:81
    for Solomon R.
      Guggenheim Museum
      7:81
    for Spanish government
      7:79
    for Terrace Hilton 7:80,
      80-81
    for Unesco 7:81
  and conventional standards
    7:84
  and the Cubists 7:77, 82
  Dalí and 6:110
  and Dalman 7:77
  on detail 7:83
  education 7:76
  and engraving 7:81
  and Ernst 7:78
    collaboration with 7:78
    nearly hanged by 7:78
  and etching 7:81
  exhibitions 7:77, 78
  family 7:76
    birth of his daughter 7:79
    with his wife 7:*80*
  and fascism 7:79
  and the Fauves 7:77, 82
  finances: contract with Viot
    7:78
    in Paris 7:77
  first job 7:76
  and Foundation Maeght 7:81
  and Galerie Maeght 7:81
  and Galerie Surréaliste 7:78
  and Galí 7:76
  gallery guide 7:139
  health, breakdown in 7:76
  in Holland 7:79
  humour 7:82-4
  influence on Art Brut 7:84
  influence on Catalan
    landscape 7:76, *76-7,* 82
  influence of medieval masters
    7:77
  influence on twentieth
    century 7:84
  key dates 7:77
  at La Lonja 7:76

  and lithography 7:80, 81
    from 'Art for Research' 7:*98*
    'The Lizard with Golden
      Feathers' 7:*83*
    from 'Seers' 7:*99*
  in Majorca 7:80, *80*
  materials 7:79, 84
  and monotype 7:81
  and murals 7:80, *80-81,* 94-5
  in Normandy 7:80
  in Paris 7:77-9
    circle of friends 7:77, 78
    life-style in 7:77
  'peintures sauvages' 7:79
  and Picasso 7:77
  and Pilar Juncosa 7:79
  and Pollock 7:84
  and popular crafts 7:81
  and the Post-Impressionists
    7:82
  and poster art 7:79, *79, 83, 91*
  prizes: for engraving 7:81
    from Guggenheim
      Foundation 7:81
  and Romanesque art 7:82
  and *Romeo and Juliet* 7:78
  and Sant Lluch circle 7:76-7
  and sculpture 7:82-3
  and 17th-century Dutch
    interiors 7:79
  and Spanish Civil War 7:*79*
    anticipation in paintings
      7:79
  and stained glass 7:81
  studios: in Paris 7:77, 78
    specially built 7:81
  style: development of 7:83
    for figures 7:83
  subjects: distortion of 7:84-5
    imaginary 7:77
    nightmares 7:84
    treatment during war years
      7:84
    Woman 7:83
  and the Surrealists 7:77, 78
    alienation from 7:79
    influence of 7:82-3
  symbols: of escape 7:83
    favourite 7:82-3
    recurring 7:83
  trademarks 7:85
  and Vermeer 7:79
  and Viot 7:78
  working methods 7:77, 83
    for 'dream paintings' 7:77-8
    on *The Farm* 7:82
  works: early sketches 7:76
    'for the public' 7:81
    output 8:81
    secretive about 7:78
  on World War II 7:80
  Aidez Espagne 7:*79, 91*
  'Art for Research' (lithograph)
    7:*98*

  The Barcelona Suite 7:80
    images in 7:84
  *The Beautiful Bird Revealing the
    Unknown to a Pair of Lovers*
    7:82
  Blue III 7:96-7
  cover for *Minotaure* 7:78
  Dog Barking at the Moon 7:82-3
    symbolism in 7:*82-3, 83*
  Dutch Interior I 7:79, 85
    detail 7:*85*
  The Farm, working method
    7:82
  Harlequin's Carnival 7:88-9
    humour of 7:84
  Inverted Personages 7:92
  Kitchen Garden with a Donkey
    7:86-7
  lithograph from 'Art for
    Research' 7:*98*
  lithograph from 'Seers' 7:*98*
  Mural Painting: Barcelona 7:*94-5*
  Portrait of Mistress Mills in 1750
    7:*90*
  The Reaper 7:79
  self-portrait, Picasso and 7:77
  Still-Life with an Old Shoe,
    symbolism in 7:79-80
  Terrace Plaza mural 7:80, *80-81*
  Wall of the Moon 7:81
  Wall of the Sun 7:81
  *Woman and Birds in the
    Moonlight* 7:*93*
Modigliani, Amedeo 6:101, *102*
  and art discussions 6:103
  girlfriend 6:101, 103
  by Marevna 8:*108-109*
  in Paris 6:103
  Rivera and 8:109
  and Zborowski 6:102
  Moïse Kisling 6:*101*
  Portrait of Blaise Cendrars 6:*78*
Moholy-Nagy, Laszlo
  and the Bauhaus 7:37-8
Monaco, Lorenzo
  and Fra Angelico 1:46-7
Mondrian, Piet 7:141
  Kandinsky and 7:17
  Broadway Boogie Woogie 7:*116,
    141*
  Flowering Apple Tree 7:*52*
Monet, Claude 5:98
  Courbet and 8:48
  influence on Van Gogh 5:79
  and landscape 5:99
  and Manet 5:13
  by Renoir 5:*98*
  Riley and 7:111
  techniques 5:18
  Haystacks, Kandinsky and
    7:13, 19
    light in 7:*20*
Montañes, Juan Martinez
  Crucifix 3:46

Moreau, Gustave 9:141
  exhibitions 9:69
  and Huysmans 9:69
  Redon and 9:50
  works: ideas behind 9:69
  The Apparition 9:69
  The Unicorns 6:84
Morgunov, Alexei
  and Jack of Diamonds group
    7:45
Morris, William 8:141; 9:36
  beliefs for art 9:37
  commissions: for Queen
    Victoria 9:37
  crafts mastered 9:34, 36
  family, with Burne-Jones 9:36
  'grinds' 9:36
  influence of Ruskin 9:34-5
  and Kelmscott Press 9:37, *37*
  manuscript collection 9:37
  marriage 9:16, 36
  and Morris & Co 9:34-7
  nickname 9:34
  and the Pre-Raphaelite
    Brotherhood 9:34
  Rossetti and 9:16, 34
    influence of 9:20
    paints under 9:34
    quarrel with 9:35
    wife sits for 9:16, *16*
  and socialism 9:37
  temperament 9:34
  Chrysanthemum 9:34-5
  Kelmscott Chaucer 9:37
  Kelmscott Manor bedroom
    9:37
  Queen Guenevere 9:36
Motherwell, Robert 7:140-41
Munch, Edvard
  affairs, first 9:112
  and art for the masses 9:116
  bedside reading 9:114
  in Berlin: artist/writer coteries
    9:111
    escapes from 9:134-5
  and Bonnat 9:*109*
    disagreement with 9:109
    enrolls with 9:109
  childhood, writing on 9:108
  and Clot 9:112, 116
  and colour: criticism of use of
    9:114
    symbolic use of 9:110
  commissions: from Dr Linde
    9:112
    major 9:112
    for Oslo University 9:113
    from Reinhardt 9:112, *134-5*
  and Dagny Przybyszewski
    9:112, 134, *134*
  death of 9:113
  and Dehmel 9:134
  and *Die Brücke* 9:117
  and etching 9:115

exhibitions: in Berlin 9:110, *110-11*, 111, 132
  of complete works 9:116
  first one-man 9:109
  tours with 9:110
  at Verein Berliner Künstler 9:135
family 9:108, *108, 109*
  with his 'children' *9:112-13, 113*
feelings of persecution 9:113
finances: income from exhibitions 9:110
  problems over 9:112
final projects 9:113
and form, simplification of 9:110
gallery guide 9:139
and graphic art 9:115
health 9:108, *112*, 113
influence of Krohg 9:109
influence of Symbolists 9:110
international recognition 9:110
and Japanese prints 9:112
key dates 9:108
last years 9:118
launch of career 9:135
life-style 9:112, 117
  remoteness of 9:112-13
and lithography 9:116
models *9:134*
and new printing techniques 9:112
on his art 9:114
on his creativity 9:113
in Oslo: and writers/painters in 9:109, 110
and paint: use of 9:109
in Paris 9:109
  influence on 9:109
  meets Gauguin and followers 9:112
  studies in 9:109
on Péladan 9:70-71
prizes/awards 9:113
and Przybyszewski 9:111, 133
scholarship 9:109
sexuality 9:111-12
and Strindberg 9:111, 133
studio in Oslo 9:109
style: naturalist phase 9:114
subjects: change in 9:113
  defending his approach to 9:114
  during Symbolist phase 9:115
  female sexual power 9:111
  femme fatale 9:110
  images of the soul 9:114-17
  key images 9:115
  in later works 9:117
  love/death 9:111

terms of his will 9:113
and Thaulow 9:109
themes, of public projects 9:117
trademarks 9:117
travels 9:112, 113
and tricks of the light 9:114
and Tulla Larsen 9:112
  painting of *9:112*
  shot by 9:112, 113
and Verein Berliner Künstler 9:110
and woodcuts 9:116
working methods 9:114-15
  with prints 9:116
works: criticism of 9:113, 132
  directness in 9:114
  first important 9:114
  lose emotional intensity 9:117
  Nazi reaction to 9:113
  obsessions in later 9:117
  in Paris 9:116
  reluctance to part with 9:116
  for the theatre 9:112, 135
Anxiety 9:123
Attraction 9:118
Bathing Men 9:115
The Dance of Life 9:111, 118, *118-19, 124-5*
  details 9: *118, 119*
  preliminary sketch 9:*119*
The Dead Mother 6:69
Dr Jacobson 9:115
Family Evening 9:108-9
Frieze of Life: formulates scheme for 9:111
  key images 9:115
  meaning of 9:111-12
  paintings in the series 9:111
  theme of 9:111
Girls on the Jetty 9:*114-15*
Hans Jaeger 9:110
Jealousy 9:111, *114*
  model for 9:112
The Lonely Ones 9:*130-31*
Madonna 9:111; 10:64
Nude by the Wicker Chair 9:*117*
  detail 9:*117*
  obsessions in 9:117
Puberty 9:*121*
  obsessions in 9:117
Reinhardt frieze 9:*134-5*
The Scream 9:111, *122*
  effect on emotions 9:114
  in *La Revue Blanche* 9:69
  self-parody 9:*112*
· self-portrait 9:*107*
The Sick Child 9:*120*
  criticism of 9:114
  influence on 9:109
Stanislaw Przybyszewski 9:*133*
Stéphane Mallarmé 9:*68*, 111
The Sun 9:*126-7*

Tulla Larsen 9:*112*
The Vampire 9:111
Winter in Kragerø 9:*128*
Workers Returning Home 9:*129*
  obsessions in 9:117
Murillo, Bartolomé Esteban 3:141
  and the people 3:71
  Birth of the Virgin 3:*140*
Mytens, Daniel
  and Earl of Arundel 3:83-4

N

Nabi aux belles icônes see Denis, Maurice
'notary, the' see **Seurat, Georges-Pierre**
Notti, Gherardo delle see Honthorst, Gerrit van

O

Olbrich, Joseph Maria
  and first secessionist exhibition 9:101
  Secessionist building 9:*100-101*,102
Orazco, José Clemente 8:111, 141
  Las Soldaderas 8:*134-5*
  The Trench 8:*111*
Oriagna, Andrea
  Strozzi Altarpiece 1:*17*
Overbeck, Friedrich 4:141

P

Pacheco, Francisco
  cultural interests 3:44-5
  and Montañes 3:46
  and Rubens 3:47
  and Velázquez 3:44-5, 46, 50
  The Art of Painting 3:50
  St John on Patmos (after Velázquez) 3:*44*
Pacher, Michael 2:141
Palmer, Samuel 4:49, 141
Pareja, Juan de 3:48, 53
  by Velázquez 3:*48*, 64
  The Baptism of Christ 3:*48*
  The Calling of St Matthew 3:*49*
  self-portrait 3:*49*
Pen, Jehuda
  and Chagall 6:76, *76*
Pforr, Franz 4:141

Phillips, Ammi
  Harriet Leavens 6:*20*
Picasso, Pablo 6:*103*
  and Antibes 5:37
  in Barcelona 6:132, 135
  by Casas 6:*132*
  and circus 5:132
  Dalí and 6:108, 109
  and La Lonja 7:76
  Malevich and 7:45, 51
  Miró and 7:77
  painting method 6:51
  in Paris 6:102-103
  Rivera and 8:109
  and Rousseau 6:16, *16*
  subjects in early 1900s 6:135
  visits to Klee 6:49
  Bread and Compotier with Fruit on a Table 5:*20*
  Guernica 7:*103*
Piero della Francesca 1:*78*
  Riley and 7:110
  Rivera and 7:114
  Legend of the True Cross 1:*22-3*
Piranesi, Giambattista 4:141
  and the Gothic Revival 4:99-100
  Carceri d'Invenzione 4:*98, 99, 141*
Pisanello, Antonio
  Portrait of a Princess of the d'Este Family 9:*52*
Pisano, Andrea 1:17
Pisano, Giovanni
  pulpit of San Andrea 1:*40*
Pissarro, Camille 5:98
  Cézanne and 5:14, *15*, 15-16
  friends 5:99
  Gauguin and 5:45
  Van Gogh and 5:79, 81
  patrons 5:99
  on Renoir 5:100
    respect for 5:100-101
  techniques 5:18
  The Pilot's Jetty, Le Havre 5:*114*
  self-portrait 5:*98*
Pollaiuolo, Antonio
  Dürer and 2:19
Pollaiuolo, Piero del
  commission from Merchants' Guild 1:109
Pollaiuolo brothers
  in Rome 1:111
Pollock, Jackson
  influence of Miró 7:84
  Convergence 7:*116*
Popova, Lyubov Sergeevna 7:141
Poussin, Nicolas
  The Annunciation 1:53
Puvis de Chavannes, Pierre 5:110, 9:141
  Seurat and 5:111
  The Poor Fisherman 9:70-71

R

Raphael, Sanzio
  Blake and 4:50
  Caravaggio and 3:16
  Dalí and 6:116
  the Pre-Raphaelites and 9:14
  tapestry cartoons: influence
    on Flemish artists 2:112
    sent to Brussels 2:112
Redon, Odilon 9:49
  Bernard and 9:49
  Bonnard on 9:48
  and Camille Falte 9:47, 47
  charcoal drawings 9:46
  childhood home 9:44, 45
  and Clavaud 9:46
    portrait of 9:46-7
    subjects introduced by 9:45
    on his teaching 9:46
  and colour 9:48
    bolder use of 9:49
    influence of Gauguin on
      9:48
    writing on 9:51
  commissions 9:49
  and Decadent movement 9:47
  and Delacroix: copies *The Lion
    Hunt* 9: 45
    inspiration from 9:50
  and Durand-Ruel 9:49
  effects of personal tragedies
    on 9:48 48-9
  and etching 9:46
  exhibitions: at last
    Impressionist 9:48
    at Salon d'Automne 9:49, 72
    with Société des Artistes
      Indépendants 9:47-8
    with Les Vingt 9:48
  family 9:44-5
    death of first son 9:48, 48
    disputes in 9:48
    fears for his son 9:49
  and Fantin-Latour 9:46
  first art teacher 9:44, 45
  and Flaubert 9:45
  formal training 9:45-6
    at Ecole des Beaux-Arts 9:46
  gallery guide 9:139
  and Gauguin 9:48
  and Gérôme 9:46
  and Gorin 9:44, 45
  help with his career 9:47
  and Hennequin 9:47
  and Huysmans 9:47, 69
  images: power of 9:50
    joyful/optimistic 9:48
    strange/horrific 9:46, 47
  and Impressionists, criticism
    of 9:44
  influence of Clavaud 9:45
  inspiration of Bresdin 9:45, 46
  inspiration of Moreau 9:50

key dates 9:44
Klee and 6:45
and line, in monochrome 9:50
and lithography 9:46-7
  first album 9:46-7, 47
and Madame de Rayssac 9:46,
  46
marriage 9:47, 47
Matisse and 9:49
mentor 9:45
models, his wife as 9:51
motifs, symbol of
  contemplation 9:51-2
and the Nabis 9:48, 48-9, 49
and Naturalists, criticism of
  9:44
on his drawings 9:47
in Paris 9:46
  studies in 9:46
patrons 9:49
and Poe 9:45
prizes/awards 9:49
religious crisis 9:48-9
reputation 'consecrated' 9:47
and romantic art concepts 9:45
roots of his art 9:50
and Seurat 9:48
severs links with past 9:49
solitary life 9:45, 46
  end of 9:47
  writing on 9:50
subjects: of charcoal drawings
  9:46
  of early paintings 9:48
  of etchings 9:46
  favourite device 9:51, 51
  mythological 9:51
  religious 9:51
  new themes 9:49
  transition to optimistic
    9:50-51
support of younger artists 9:49
and Symbolism/Symbolists
  9:47, 50
  champion of 9:48
and texture, in monochromes
  9:50
and tone, in monochromes
  9:50
trademarks 9:53
unorthodox approach to art
  9:44
and Vollard 9:49
works: 'blacks' 9:48, 50
  collectors of 9:49
  decorative panels/screens
    9.49
  flights of fantasy 9:50-52
  use of flowers in 9:52
  flower pieces 9:49, 52
  ideas behind 9:50
  in last years 9:49
  most abstract 9:52
  objectivity of 9:52

transition to colour 9:50-51
  virtuosity in late 9:52
Birth of Venus 9:62
  objectivity in 9:52
Bouquet of Flowers 9:64
Bouquet in a Turquoise Vase 9:65
Camille Falte 9:47
Closed Eyes 9:51, 51
Dans la Rêve: Germination 9:47
*Death: My irony surpasses all
  others* 9:47, 50
The Evocation of the Butterflies
  9:67
Head of Christ and Snake 9:57
Head of a Martyr on a Platter
  9:50
Homage to Leonardo da Vinci
  9:60-61
In Dream 9:46-7, 47
Mystery 9:56
Ophelia among the Flowers
  9:58-9
  imagery in 9:52
Orpheus 9:54
Pandora, objectivity in 9:52
Pegasus Triumphant 9:50-51, 51
Portrait of Arï Redon 9:48
Portrait of Violette Heymann
  9:53
  detail 9:53
  use of flowers in 9:52
Red Sphinx 9:66
Roger and Angelica 9:63
St Sebastian 9:51, 55
self-portrait 9:43
Les Songes: Portrait of Clavaud
  9:46-7
*Wild Flowers in a Long-necked
  Vase* 9:51
Rembrandt van Rijn 4:18; 9:46
Reni, Guido
  and Caravaggio 3:31
  Commissions: from
    San'Onofrio 3:105
  The Archangel Michael 3:105
Renoir, Auguste 5:98
  and Cagnes 5:37
  on Cézanne's eccentricity 5:14
  critical approval of 5:100
  influence on Van Gogh 5:79
  and Manet 5:13
  patron 5:99
  Rivera and 8:114
  techniques 5:18
  Portrait of Monet 5:98
Reymerswaele, Marinus van
  Two Tax Gatherers 2:133
Reynolds, Joshua
  influence of Van Dyck on
    3:82
Ribera, Jusepe de 3:141
  brushwork 3:38
  and Caravaggio 3:38
  Velázquez and 3:47-8

Riley, Bridget
  and American Abstract
    Expressionist Exhibition
    7:109
  and architecture 7:113
  art training, first experiences
    7:108-109
  at Cheltenham Ladies'
    College 7:108-109
  and colour: Ancient Egyptian
    7:110-11, 112
    broadens her palette 7:111
    influence of Van Gogh 7:109
    influence of Seurat 7:110
    introduction of 7:115
    mixing 7:112, 115
    monochrome palette
      7:110-11
    new inspiration 7:112-13
    standards for selecting
      7:116-17
    visual/emotional response
      to 7:112
  critical acclaim 7:111-12
  and 'The Developing Process
    Exhibition' 7:109
  elements: effect of colour on
    7:115
    in monochrome works
      7:114-15
    use of simple 7:114-15
  in Egypt 7:110-11, 112
  exhibitions 7:111
  family 7:108, 108
    during the war years 7:108
    nurses her father 7:109
    on her mother 7:108
  finances, wins bursary 7:111
  first art teacher 7:109
  gallery guide 7:139
  and Gallery One 7:111
  at Goldsmiths' College 7:109
  and Hayes 7:109
  at Hornsey College of Art
    7:110
  influence of Egyptian painting
    7:110-11, 114, 116-7
  influence of Futurists 7:110
  influence of Ingres 7:109
  influence of Italian
    Renaissance 7:110
  influence of Piero della
    Francesca 7:110
  influence of Seurat 7:109, 110
  inspiration 7:111, 114
    from childhood 7:108, 108,
      114
  in Italy 7:110
  key dates 7:107
  and Monet 7:111
  and the National Gallery 7:113
  and Op Art 7:110
  and perception 7:111
  prizes 7:111, 136

and Rabin 7:109
and 'Responsive Eye
    Exhibition' 7:111
at Royal College of Art 7:109
    contemporaries at 7:109
and Sausmarez 7:110
and Sedgley 7:111
studios 7:112
and Stuyvesant Foundation
    7:111
and the 'Swinging Sixties'
    7:135
and theatre design 7:112-13,
    113
trademarks 7:117
use of assistants 7:115
working methods 7:112, 114,
    115
works: developing 7:115
    experiencing full effect
        7:116
    first optical 7:110
    giving titles to 7:116
    of the late 60s/70s 7:112
    precision in 7:115-16
    technical foundations 7:111
Blaze I 7:120
Cataract 3 7:115
Colour Moves 7:112, 113, 112-13
Continuum 7:111
Current 7:123
Deny I 7:116-17
Gather 7:130
Hidden Squares 7:114-15
hospital murals 7:113
Little Diamonds 7:124
Paean 7:118-19
    studies for 7:118
Pink Landscape 7:114
    influence on 7:110
Portrait of her Mother 7:108
Rill 7:126-7
Rose Return 7:131
Shiver 7:121
SPACE 7:111
Static I 7:122
Streak 2 7:128-9
Tonal landscape study, France
    7:109
Where 7:115
Zing I 7:125

Rivera, Diego
and Academy of San Carlos
    8:108, 109
in America 8:112-13
and Anahuacalli 8:113
and Angeline Beloff 8:109
and Anti-Imperialist League
    of the Americas 8:111
aptitude for art 8:108
and art for the masses 8:114-17
and Breton 8:113
and Classicism 8:114
and colour, heightened 8:117

commissions: during the
    1940s 8:113
    for Detroit Art Institute
        8:117, 126-7
    for Edsel B. Ford 8:112
    first major mural 8:115
    for Hotel del Prado 8:113
    for Ministry of Public
        Education 8:111, 115
    for National Palace 8:116
    for National Preparatory
        School 8:110
    for National School of
        Agriculture 8:111, 116,
        116-17
    for Palace of Cortez 8:116
    for the Rockefeller Center
        8:113, 113
and compressed space 8:117
criticized by Reverdy 8:109-10
and Cubism/Cubists 8:109
    first experiments in 8:114
and Delaunay 8:109, 114
earliest memory 8:108
exhibitions 8:109, 112
family 8:108, 110
finds a role for his art 8:114-17
and Frida Kahlo 8:112
gallery guide 8:139
and Giotto 8:114
and Gris 8:109, 114
health: cancer diagnosed 8:113
    effect of dieting on 8:113
    suffers serious injury 8:111
homes as museums 8:113
and Ingres 8:114
influence of Cézanne 8:114
influence of composition 8:114
influence of El Greco 8:109
influence of Pre-Columbian
    art 8:110
influence of Renaissance 8:110
in Italy 8:110
    influence of murals 8:114
key dates 8:106
and latest developments in art
    8:114
and Lhote 8:109
and Lipchitz 8:109
in Madrid 8:109
and Marevna 8:110
    portrait by 8:108-109
marriage: first wife 8:110-11
    second wife 8:112, 112
    third wife 8:113
and Masaccio 8:114
and Mexican Communist
    Party 8:111-12
at military college 8:108
and Modigliani 8:109
motifs: in Cubist works
    8:114
    Mexican 8:114
    sources of 8:119

and mural painting: strain of
    8:111
    studies in Italy 8:110
and Pani 8:110
in Paris 8:108-109, 109
patrons 8:110
and Picasso 8:109
and Piero della Francesca 8:114
and politics 8:110-12
and Pre-Columbian art 8:114
and Rebull 8:114
and Renoir 8:114
and role of art for society 8:110
in Russia 8:111, 111, 113
scholarships: to Academy of
    San Carlos 8:108, 109
    to study in Europe 8:109
sources of inspiration 8:115
style: of dress 8:108
    influence on 8:114
    version of Cubism 8:114
subjects: inspiration of
    machinery 8:116-17
trademarks 8:117
and Trotsky 8:112, 113, 113
and Workers' and Farmers'
    Bloc 8:111
works: at Academy of San
    Carlos 8:114
    first mural 8:110
    last scandal over 8:113
    most harmonious/
        integrated 8:115-16,
        116-17
in Yucatán 8:110, 111, 115
Agrarian Leader Zapata 8:113
The Artist's Studio 8:115
Battle of the Aztecs and the
    Spaniards 8:111
    Crossing the Barranca
        8:114-15
The Corrido of the Agrarian
    Revolution, theme of 8:115
The Corrido of the Proletarian
    Revolution, theme 8:115
Creation 8:110
Detroit Industry 8:126-7
    preparatory work for 8:112
    themes for 8:117
Dream of a Sunday Afternoon in
    the Alameda 8:128-9
    scandal over 8:113
La Era 8:109
Flower Seller 8:123
The Grinder 8:122
History of Medicine in Mexico:
    The People's Demand for Better
    Health 8:130-31
    use of colour/space in 8:117
The History of Mexico 8:116,
    118, 118-19, 124-5
    details 8:118-19
    starts work on 8:112
The Liberation of the Peon 8:135

The Making of a Fresco Showing
    the Building of a City 8:8
Man at the Crossroads Looking
    with Hope and High Vision to
    the Choosing of a New and
    Better Future: fate of 8:113,
    113
    smaller version of 8:112-13
mural for National Palace
    8:112-13
Our Bread 8:120
The Peasant 8:115
Portrait of his Wife 8:110-11
Protest 8:121
The Village Schoolteacher 8:135
Zapatista Landscape – The
    Guerilla 8:114
Robbia, Luca della,
    and Florence Cathedral 1:72
Rodchenko, Alexander,
    Mikhailovich 7:141
    principles of 7:49
Rops, Félicien 9:141
Rossetti, Dante Gabriel
    and academic drawing 9:13,
        13
    and Alexa Wilding 9:16
    art training, lack of 9:18
    and backgrounds 9:19
    and Brown 9:13
    and Burne-Jones 9:16
    death of 9:17
    deciding on a career 9:13-14
    description of 9:13, 17
    draughtsmanship 9:18, 20
    and drawing 9:20
    education 9:13
    effect of criticism on 9:15
    and Elizabeth Siddal 9:15
        drawings of 9:20
        effect of death of 9:16
    and exhibiting 9:15
    family 9:12
        birth of daughter 9:16
        photograph by Carroll 9:17
    and Fanny Cornforth 9:16, 21
        ends relationship with 9:17
        sells paintings of 9:16
    finances: in the 1860s 9:16
    friends: at Oxford 9:16
        at Royal Academy 9:14
    health: effect of alcohol/drugs
        on 9:17
        influence on later works
            9:21
        physical collapse 9:16-17
        suffers a stroke 9:17
    homes in London 9:15, 15,
        16-17, 17, 39
    and Hunt 9:14
        painted by 9:11
    gallery guide 9:139
    as illustrator 9:20
    Sir Galahad 9:19

and Janey Morris 9:21, 36
joins Artists' Rifle Corps 9:42
key dates 9:12
and landscape 9:19
love of drawing 9:13
marriage 9:17
  death of wife 9:16
  meets future wife 9:15
menagerie 9:16, 17
and Millais 9:14
mistress 9:15, 15-16
models: Elizabeth Siddal as
  9:14
  favourites in later years 9:21
  in later works 9:16
  Pre-Raphaelite practice
    with 9:19
  'stunners' 9:15
and Morris 9:16, 34
  end of friendship with 9:36
  influence on talent 9:20
  paints with 9:34
  quarrel with 9:35
and Morris & Co 9:34-6
and paint: application of 9:20
and perspective 9:18
as poet 9:13-14, 17
and Raphael 9:14
reputation as an eccentric 9:17
at the Royal Academy 9:13
and Ruskin 9:14
  influence of 9:15
at Sass's Art School 9:13
and stained glass 9:20
subjects: femme fatale 9:21
  in last years 9:20-21
  modern-day morality 9:18
  romantic dreamworld
    9:18-21
techniques 9:18
  unusual 9:20
and texture 9:20
tomb 9:17
trademarks 9:21
and water-colour 9:15, 19
  selling 9:15
  technique with 9:19-20
and women 9:15
works: detail in 9:19
  first major 9:14
  painted to help Elizabeth
    Siddal 9:19
  for Oxford University 9:16,
    20
  unfinished look to 9:20
  use of titles 9:21
The Annunciation 9:25
  technical limitations 9:18-19
Astarte Syriaca 4:52; 9:33
Beata Beatrix 9:30
The Beloved 9:8
The Blue Bower 9:15
  model for 9:15
The Blue Closet 9:18

The Bower Meadow 9:32
Elizabeth Siddal 9:14
The First Anniversary of the
  Death of Beatrice 9:22, 22-3,
  26-7
  details 9:22-23
  early version of 9:23
  inspiration for 9:22
Found 9:18
The Girlhood of Mary Virgin
  9:14-15, 24
  limitations in 9:18
  painting technique on 9:20
  purchaser 9:15
Janey and the Wombat 9:16
Monna Vanna 9:31
Paolo and Francesca da Rimini
  9:19
Preparation for the Passover in
  the Holy Family 9:19
Proserpine 9:21
  detail 9:21
self-portrait 9:12
Sir Galahad 9:19
The Tune of Seven Towers 9:29
Wedding of St George and
  Princess Sabra 9:20, 28
Rousseau, Henri
  and academic painting 6:19
  and Academy teaching 6:13-14
  and Apollinaire 6:16, 17
  arrested: for fraud 6:16-17
    painting as evidence 6:17
    for stealing 6:12-13
  artistic and literary evenings
    6:15-16
  and artistic recognition 6:16
  the avant-garde and 6:15, 19
  begins drawing/painting 6:13
  and Clémence Boitard 6:13
  advice from Clément 6:13
  and colour 6:21
    mood set by 6:21
    use of tones 6:21
  commissions: from Jarry 6:15
    for portraits 6:16
  in Customs House 6:13
    retirement from 6:15
  death of 6:17
  description of 6:12
    by himself 6:19
  drawings 6:19
  enlists in army 6:13
  exhibits with Blaue Reiter 7:15
  and Exposition Universelle
    6:14-15
    influence of 6:14, 14-15
    A Visit to the Exhibition of
      1889 6:14
  family 6:12
    deaths of children 6:13
    sends his children away
      6:15
  and figure painting 6:20

finances: begging letters 6:16
  in last years 6:17
  pension 6:15
  supplementing 6:15
gallery guide 6:139
and Gauguin 6:15
  hoaxed by 6:16
and Gérôme 6:13
  influence of 6:21
and his own academy 6:16
and illumination 6:20
influence of Delacroix 6:21
and the Jardin des Plantes
  6:12-13, 18-19, 19
and Jarry 6:15
key dates 6:13
and landscape 6:19
  inspiration for 6:18
last love 6:17
and Legion of Honour 6:16
marriage 6:13
  death of first wife 6:14
  death of second wife 6:17
  portrait of first wife? 6:14
  portrait of second wife? 6:26
and Mexico 6:13, 19
and music 6:12
  income from 6:15
  'Clémence' 6:16
on nature 6:18
  inspiration from 6:12-13,
    18-21
need for love/companionship
  6:13
and other artists 6:13
in Paris 6:13
and perspective 6:20
portraits: backgrounds for 6:21
  difficulty with 6:20
  method of painting 6:20
'primitive mentality proved'
  6:17
and proportion 6:20
public debut 6:14
publicist 6:15, 15
and Salon des Artistes
  Indépendants 6:14
scrapbook 6:15
as source of amusement 6:16
style: in jungle pictures 6:19
  paradox of 6:19
subjects: animals 6:21, 39, 39
  bouquets 6:18-19
  of early drawings 6:18
  of landscapes 6:18
  sources 6:19, 21, 22
the Sunday painter 6:18-19
as teacher 6:16
and technical aspects of art
  6:20
tomb 6:17
  epitaph on 6:17, 17
trademarks 6:21
use of vegetation 6:20

working methods 6:18
  Apollinaire on 6:18
  with colour 6:21
  matching colours 6:20
  for portraits 6:20
  use of pantograph 6:21
works: the avant-garde and
  6:15
  criticism of first 6:14
  destroyed by Jarry 6:15
  flower paintings 6:18-19
  mockery of 6:14
  nature studies 6:18
  portrait-landscapes 6:11,
    14, 15
  Toulouse-Lautrec and 6:14
The Artillerymen 6:8-9
Boy on the Rocks 6:27
The Dream 6:34-5
Exotic Landscape 6:39
The Football Players 6:32
The Merry Jesters 6:30
  photo with 6:16
The Muse Inspiring the Poet 6:17
Myself: Portrait-Lansdscape 6:11
  criticism of 6:15
Negro Attacked by a Jaguar 6:19
The Painter and His Model
  6:18-19
Père Juniet's Cart 6:33
Portrait of a Woman 6:14, 26
The Sleeping Gypsy 6:22, 22-3
  details 6:22, 23
    sources for 6:22, 23
The Snake Charmer 6:31
Surprised! (Tropical Storm with
  a Tiger) 5:53; 6:24-5
The Toll House 6:13
Tropical Forest with Monkeys
  6:21
  detail 6:21
The Vase of Flowers 6:18
War 6:15
Rowlandson, Thomas 8:141
Roy, Pierre 6:141
Rubens, Peter Paul
  chief assistant 3:77
  commissions 3:77, 80
  description of Charles I 3:80
  and the Escorial 3:46, 47
  in Madrid 3:46
  and tapestry design 3:77
  tribute to Bruegel 2:113, 113
  use of form 3:85
  and Van Dyck 3:77
  on Velázquez 3:47
The Emperor Theodosius Refused
  Entry into Milan Cathedral
  3:78
The Hippopotamus Hunt 3:116
A Knight of the Golden Fleece
  3:85
self-portrait 3:47
Stage of Welcome 3:106

Ruisdael, Jacob van 3:*107*
in Amsterdam 3:*110*, 111
artistic background 3:108
baptism of 3:111
and Castle of Bentheim
3:*108-109, 112-113*, 114
collaboration with Keyser
3:111
death of 3:111
as doctor of medicine
3:109-110, *110-11*
draughtsmanship 3:114-15,
114-15
early influences in 3:108
early training 3:108, 109
family 3:108, 110, *110*
finances, from his father 3:111
gallery guide 3:139
and Guild of St Luke, Haarlem
3:136
influence of Everdingen 3:114
influence of Vroom 3:*108-109*
key dates 3:108
and landscape 3:112-14,
116-17
approach to 3:113-14
constructs more complex
3:114
inventiveness in 3:114
qualities of 3:112-14
winter 3:117
and light/shade 3:116-17
and the open market 3:111
patrons 3:111
de Graeff 3:111
publishes etching 3:111
pupil 3:111
and S. van Ruisdael 3:108
search for inspiration
3:*108-109*
style, treatment of water 3:116
subjects 3:113
of early works 3:114
enlarges repertoire 3:116
and Sweerts 3:111
trademarks 3:117
travels 3:110
to new landscapes 3:114
use of high view-point 3:116
wills 3:111
works: earliest dated 3:109
most popular 3:114
output 3:109
*Blasted Elm with a View of
Edmond aan Zee* 3:9
The Castle at Bentheim 3:*109*
Conversation Piece (with
Keyser) 3:*109*
Le Coup de Soleil 3:112, 117, *131*
*Dune Landscape with Plank
Fence* 3:*120*
*An Extensive Landscape with a
Ruined Castle and a Church*
3:112, 116, *129*

The Great Oak 3:*114*, 121; 10:*58*
*Hilly Wooded Landscape with
Castle* 3:114, *116-127*
detail 3:*117*
*The Interior of the Old Church at
Amsterdam* 3:114
The Jewish Cemetery 3:112,
118-19, *112*
details 3:*118-19*
preliminary drawing 3:*119*
*Landscape with the Ruins of the
Castle of Egmond* 3:*112-13*
*Panoramic View of the Amstel
River Looking Towards
Amsterdam* 3:*112-13*
A Pool Surrounded by Trees
3:*112*
Shore at Egmond-aan-Zee
3:*113*
*The Shore of the Zuider Zee near
Naarden* 3:*114-15*
*Sun-dappled Trees at the Edge of
a Stream* 3:*115*
*Sunlit Grain Field see Lé Coup de
Soleil*
*A Sunlit Grain Field on the
Banks of a Coast* 3:*125*
Three Half-timbered Houses
3:*115*
*Two Watermills and an Open
Sluice* 3:*124*
Vessels in a Breeze 3:*123*
*View of Haarlem with the
Bleaching Grounds* 3:*130*
A Village in Winter 3:*113*
A Waterfall 3:*127*
*A Windmill and Cottages
near a High Footbridge*
3:*114-15*
*The Windmill at Wijk by
Duurstede* 3:*126*
Winter Landscape 3:*112*, 128
Runge, Philipp Otto 4:141
Ruskin, John 8:141
on Blake 4:53
on Caravaggio 3:18, 39
on Fra Angelico 1:50
and medieval art 9:35
Morris and 9:34-5
and 'rediscovery of Botticelli'
1:17
Rossetti and 9:*14*, 15
Edinburgh Lectures, Morris
and 9:34
Ruysdael, Jacob Salonomsz
moves to Amsterdam 3:111
*Landscape with Waterfall by a
Cottage* 3:*110*
Ruysdael, Salomon van
and landscape 3:108
River Landscape 3:*110*
Rysselberghe, Theo van 5:*110*,
141
Seurat and 5:110

S

Sassetta, Stephano di Giovanni
Francis and the Pope 1:*37*
*St Francis Renounces his Earthly
Father* 1:*37*
*The Whim of the Young St
Francis to Become a Soldier*
1:*36*
Schongauer, Martin 2:12, 141
Scorel, Jan van 2:141
Scott, William Bell 9:20
Iron and Coal 9:*116*
Sedgley, Peter 7:111
SPACE 7:111
Serusier, Paul 5:141; 9:49
Seurat, Georges-Pierre
approach to work 5:109, 111
centre of controversy 5:110-11
characteristics 5:108
and circus 5:114, 130
and colour 5:112-14, *113*
death of 5:111
description of 5:108
drawings 5:114
at Ecole des Beaux-Arts 5:108
family 5:108
birth of his son 5:111
secret 5:111
wife/heiress 5:111, *111*
Fénéon and 5:110
defended by 5:109
finances: calculating expenses
5:111
and prices for work 5:111
regular allowance 5:108
hero 5:111
and the Impressionists:
exhibits with 5:110
subjects 5:114
and Indépendants exhibitions
5:111
key dates 5:109
by Laurent 5:*107*
and line 5:114
of emotions 5:*113*
military service 5:108-109
and painting theories 5:112
in Paris 5:109, 110
and the Paris Salon 5:109
personality 5:*108*
and pointillism: first
experiment 5:113
and Puvis de Chavannes 5:111
Riley and 7:109
and Rysselberghe 5:*110*
and Signac 5:109-110
book on painting theory
5:*109*
as socializer 5:111
and Société des Artistes
Indépendants 5:109-110
studies 5:108
of treatises 5:112

studios 5:109, 110
subjects 5:*112*, 114
technique: beginning a canvas
5:112
in drawings 5:114
Pointillist method 5:109, 114
for vibrancy of colours 5:113
tomb 5:*111*
and Toorop 5:*110*
trademarks 5:115
use of individual figures 5:114
and Les Vingt 5:*110*
working method: daily
routine 5:112
on *La Grande Jatte* 5:110
yearly routine 5:111
works: characteristics 5:112
first major 5:109
most famous see *La Grande
Jatte*
painted borders to 5:113
second major canvas 5:110
Seurat on 5:111
At the 'Concert Européen' 5:*113*
Bathing at Asnières 5:109,
118-19
The Bec du Hoc, Grandcamp
5:*120*
Boats at Grandcamp 5:*121*
The Bridge at Courbevoie 7:*109*
Le Chahut 5:*128*
*The Channel at Gravelines,
Evening* 5:*127*
The Circus 5:111, *129*
working sketch 5:*113*
The Eiffel Tower 5:*113*
The Grande Jatte 5:110, 116-17,
122-3, 135
detail 5:*117*
The Harbour at Gravelines 5:*126*
The Models 5:*112-113*
study for 5:*114*
La Parade 5:*124-5*
Paul Signac 5:*109*
Port-en-Bessin 5:*115*
detail 5:*115*
The Stone Breaker 5:*112*
Study for The Models 5:*114*
Woman Powdering Herself 5:*111*
'Shakespeare of painting'
see **Hogarth, William**
Signac, Paul 5:141
and Seurat 5:109-110, 114
book on painting theories
5:*109*
drawn by 5:*109*
on his death 5:111
on his drawings 5:114
Félix Fénéon 5:*109*
Signorelli, Luca 1:141
Siqueiros, David Alfaro 8:111,
141
self-portrait 8:*111*
Porfiriato 8:*132*

Snyders, Frans 3:76-7
Soutine, Chaim 6:101, *101*, 103
  by Marevna 8:108-9
  and Zborowski 6:102
Stäel, Nicolas de 7:141
Steen, Jan
  Hogarth and 8:19
  The Cat's Dancing Lesson 7:84
  The Dissolute Household 8:20
Stubbs, George
  and animals 6:38
  Green Monkey 2:21
  Lion and Lioness 6:38-9
Stuck, Franz von 9:141
  Kandinsky and 7:14
  and Klee 6:44
Suetin, Nikolai 7:48
  china design 7:48
  Malevich and 7:48
  and Suprematism 7:48
'Swiftest of Painters' *see* **Cranach, Lucas**

T

Tanguy, Yves 6:141
Tanning, Dorothea 6:141
Tatlin, Vladimir 7:49, 141
Teniers, David
  Hogarth and 8:19
Terborch, Gerard
  Ratification of the Treaty of Munster 3:136
Terbruggen, Hendrick 3:141
  and Caravaggio 3:39
Thornhill, Sir James
  Hogarth and 8:13, *13*, 15
  ceiling, Greenwich Naval College 8:13
Tiepolo, Giambattista 4:12
Tintoretto
  The Discovery of the Body of St Mark 10:52
Tissot, James
  Amateur Circus 5:131
Titian Vecellio
  Bellini and 1:85
  challenges Bellini's supremacy 1:81
  influence on Van Dyck 3:79, 80, 82
  influence on Velázquez 3:51
  influence on Venetian art 1:80
  technique 3:21
  Velázquez and 3:51
  The Birth of Venus 1:118
  Pope Paul III 3:52
  Salome 9:20
Toorop, Jan
  The Three Brides 5:110
Torrigiano, Pietro 2:100

Toulouse-Lautrec, Henri de
5:*110*; 8:76
  academic training 8:82
  and Anquetin 8:78
  and Bernard 8:78
  and Bonnard 8:79
  and Bonnat 8:77, 80
  and Bourges 8:78
  and Bruant 8:79
    poster for 8:84, *91*
  childhood 8:76-7, *77*
  and the circus 5:132, *132*
  and colour: in later works 8:84
    number used in lithographs 8:82
  commissions: for the Moulin Rouge 8:79
  and Cormon 8:77, 82
  and *crachis* 8:84, *85*
  death of 8:81
  description of 8:76
  double photograph of 8:*79*
  and drawing 8:82
  and dressing up 8:101
  drinking 8:79, 80-81
    committed for alcoholism 8:81
  early art training 8:77
  in England 8:80, 104
    Goupil exhibits works for 8:80
    one-man 8:80
    at Salon des Indépendants 8:78
  exhibitions: and Les Vingt 8:78
  family 8:76
    portrait of his mother 8:*77*
    tensions in 8:80-81
  finances: allowance from home 8:78
    private income reduced 8:80
  gallery guide 8:139
  Van Gogh and 5:79, 101; 8:78
  and La Goulue 8:100
  and Grenier 8:78
  grown height 8:76
  health: weakness of the bones 8:76
    contracts syphilis 8:79
    failing 8:80
  on himself 8:76
  influence of Degas 8:84
  influence of Japanese prints 8:84
  and Joyant 8:80
  key dates 8:77
  and lithography 8:*82*
  matures as an artist 8:84
  and the Mirliton 8:79
  and Misia Natanson 8:79
  mistress 8:78, *78*
  models 8:80, *80*
  and the Moulin Rouge 8:98
    poster for 8:*78-9*

  and music-hall 8:82-4
  nickname 8:76
  and paint: *peinture à l'essence* 8:83
    use of in later works 8:84
  in Paris: and the brothels 8:80, *80*
    discovers Montmartre 8:77-8
    life-style in 8:78-9
    lodgings in 8:78, *80*
    studies in 8:77
  and portraits, aim of 8:83
  and poster art 8:78-9, *79*, 84
    number made 8:84
  and Princeteau 8:77
  and printmaking 8:84
  and Rousseau 5:14
  sexuality 8:79-80
  Seurat and 5:110
  subjects: brothels 8:80
    capturing essence of 8:84
    favourite 8:82-3
  studio 8:78
    in a brothel 8:80
  style: developing a new 8:80
    finding his own 8:78
    influence of Japanese prints on 8:84
  and the theatre 8:79
  trademarks 8:85
  and Viaud 8:81
  and Les Vingt 8:78
  and Vuillard 8:79, *81*
  working methods 8:79
    development of major images by 5:*141*; 8:83
    use of photographs 8:83
    for posters 8:84
    use of sketches 8:83
    for *Yvette Guilbert Taking a Curtain Call* 8:83
  works: decline in quality 8:84
    destroyed 8:80
    magazine illustration 8:79
    one of earliest 8:76
    period of most brilliant 8:79
    in private clinic 8:81
  and Zidler 8:100
  Aristide Bruant at the Ambassadeurs 8:*91*
  At the Circus Fernando 8:*88-9*
  At the Moulin Rouge 8:86, *86-7*, 95
    details 8:*86*, 87
  The Dance at the Moulin Rouge 8:*92-3*
  Le Divan Japonais 8:*85*
    detail 8:*85*
  Doctor Bourges 8:*79*
  Dr Gabriel Tapié de Céleyran 8:*86*
  Emile Bernard 5:*47*
  The Female Clown, Cha-U-Kao 8:*97*

  La Goulue entering the Moulin Rouge 8:*94*
  Jane Avril at the Jardin de Paris 8:*90*
  Moulin Rouge: La Goulue 8:*79*, *82*
    study for 8:*83*
  Oscar Wilde 8:*81*
  The Private Room at the Rat Mort
    use of paint in 8:*83*
  Promenade en Mail Coach à Nice 8:*76*
  The Salon at the Rue Des Moulins 8:*96*
  self-portrait 8:*75*, 83
  Van Gogh at the Tambourin 5:*100*
  Yvette Guilbert Taking a Curtain Call, method of painting 8:83
Turner, J. M. W.
  Light and Colour: the Morning after the Deluge 7:*20*

U

Uccello, Paolo
  Dalí and 6:116
Utrillo, Maurice 8:*78*

V

Valadon, Suzanne 8:78, *78*
  The Blue Room 8:78
Valdes Leal, Juan de 3:141
Vallotton, Felix 5:141
Van Dyck, Anthony
  and Anguissola 3:*80*
  in Antwerp 8:79, 81
  apprenticeship 3:76
  and backgrounds 3:82, 83
  collaboration with Rubens 3:76-7
  commissions: best in Italy 3:*80*
    from the Church 3:79
    for Duke of Buckingham 3:77
    for Earl of Arundel 3:77, *77*
    for the Oratorio del Rosario 3:*80*
  description of 3:78, 81
  early success 3:77-8
  engaged by Rubens 3:77
  in England 3:81, 84
  family 3:76
    daughter 3:81
    death of sister 3:79
    illegitimate daughter 3:81

finances: under Charles I 3:80
  from James I 3:78
friends, in Italy 3:79
gallery guide 3:139
in Genoa 3:77, 78-9
  portraits painted in 3:82-3
influence on English
  portraiture 3:82-5
influence of Italian art on
  3:77-8, 83-4
  Venetian artists 3:79, 80, 82
influence of Rubens 3:76, 78,
  78, 79
influence of Titian 3:79, 80, 82
influence of Veronese 3:79,
  80
in Italy 3:80, 80
key dates 3:76
and landscape 3:79
  in portraits 3:82
last years 3:81
and line 3:84-5
in London 3:80-81
marriage 3:81
mistress 3:78, 81
most productive period 3:79
and painters' guild 3:76
in Palermo 3:80
in Paris 3:81
patrons: Archduchess Isabella
  3:79
  Charles I 3:79-80
portraits: first half-length 3:82
  of Henrietta Maria 3:85
posts: Court Painter 3:79
  Painter to Charles I 3:80-81
and 'props' 3:84
sex appeal of 3:81
sitters: female 3:85
  flattery of 3:83, 85
sketchbooks, of Italy 3:79, 80,
  80
studio: in England 3:84
  first 3:76
style: changes 3:82
  changes in for portraits 3:84
  of early portraits 3:78, 82
  influence of Rubens on 3:78
subjects 3:79
and tapestry design 3:78
trademarks 3:84
and watercolour 3:79
Character studies 3:84-5
Charles I on Horseback with
  Seigneur de St Antoine 3:92
Charles I in Three Positions 3:86,
  94-5
  details 3:86, 87
  inspiration for 3:87
Christ Crowned with Thorns 3:88
Cupid and Psyche 3:98
The Emperor Theodosius Refused
  Entry into Milan Cathedral
  3:79

Five Children of Charles I 3:96-7
  preparatory sketch 3:83
François Langlois 3:82-3
Henrietta Maria 3:87, 101
Lady Elizabeth Thimbleby and
  Dorothy, Viscountess Andover
  3:99
The Lomellini Family 3:82, 83
Lord John and Lord Bernard
  Stuart 3:84
Louis and Rupert of Bavaria
  3:102-103
Lucas and Cornelis de Wael
  (copy, Hollar) 3:79
Marchessa Elena Grimaldi 3:78,
  82, 83
Margaret Lemon 3:78
Marie de Raet 3:91
Mary Ruthven 3:81
Nicholas Lanier 3:80
Philippe le Roy, Seigneur de
  Ravels 3:90
Prince William of Orange and
  Princess Mary Stuart 3:83
Queen Henrietta Maria with her
  Dwarf Sir Jeffrey Hudson
  3:93
The Rest on the Flight into Egypt
  3:89
Rinaldo and Armida 3:79, 81
self-portrait 3:75, 76
Sketches of a Head 3:84-5
Thomas Howard, 2nd Earl of
  Arundel and his Wife 3:77
Vasarély, Victor 7:141
Velázquez, Diego Rodríguez
  de Silva y
  and Accademia di San Luca
  3:49
  apprenticeship 3:44-5
  bodegones 3:50-51
  and characterization 3:52-3
  commissions, from Philip IV
  3:46
  Dalí and 6:116
  death of 3:49
  and the Escorial 3:46, 47
  family 3:44, 45
    illegitimate son 3:49
    wife and child? 3:45
  gallery guide 3:139
  Goya and 4:18
  grandchildren 3:48
  influence of Renaissance
  masters 3:48
  influence of Titian 3:51
  in Italy 3:46, 47-9
  key dates 3:44
  as Knight of the Order of
  Santiago 3:49
  in Madrid 3:45, 45-7 as maestro
  pintor de ymagineria 3:45
  marriage 3:45
  medal of merit 3:48

models, wife as? 3:45, 45
most fruitful period 3:48-9
and Philip IV 3:46-7
and Pope Innocent X 3:48
posts 3:46, 47, 49
practice at portraits 3:50
pupils 3:53
pupil, outstanding 3:48
and Ribera 3:47-8
in Rome 3:46
  as Ambassador to 3:49
  royal favours 3:46-7
and Rubens 3:47, 47
sitters, and 'inner life' of
  3:50-53
speed of working 3:50
studio 3:53
style, subtlety of 3:50
subjects: change in 3:51-2
  early 3:50
  low-life 3:50-51
  for Philip IV 3:48
technique: changes in 3:51
  'freeness' of 3:52, 53
trademarks 3:53
working methods 3:53
works 3:50
workshop 3:46
The Adoration of the Magi 3:45
  detail 3:45
The Artist's Family 3:48
Bacchus and his Companions
  10:53
Boar Hunt 3:68-9
The Buffoon Juan de Calabazas
  3:52
  detail 3:53
The Court Fool 'El Primo' 3:60
The Court Fool Sebastián de
  Morra 3:61
The Expulsion of the Moriscos
  3:46
The Forge of Vulcan 3:48
Gaspar de Guzman, Count of
  Olivares 3:68
The Immaculate Conception 3:56
  technique for 3:51
The Infanta Margarita in Blue
  3:67
Innocent X 3:53
Isabel of Bourbon (with Jan
  Brueghel) 3:69
Joseph's Coat 3:48
Juan de Pareja 3:64
Las Meninas 3:49, 53, 54, 54, 66
Luis de Góngora 3:45, 46
Old Woman Frying Eggs 3:50
Philip IV 3:46, 51, 68
Pope Innocent X 3:65
Prince Balthasar Carlos 3:70
Prince Philip Prosper 3:53
The Rokeby Venus 3:50, 62-3
  damaged by Suffragette
  9:105, 106

St John the Evangelist on the
  Island of Patmos 3:50
  copy of 3:44
The Spinners 3:51
Study for a Head 3:51
The Surrender of Breda 3:48,
  52-3, 58-9
Villa Medici 3:47
The Waterseller of Seville 3:51, 57
Velde, Esias van de
  and landscape 3:108, 112
Vermeer, Johannes 6:109; 7:79
Veronese, Paolo
  influence on Van Dyck 3:79, 80
Verrocchio, Andrea del 1:137
  commission from the Medici
  1:137
  Colleoni Monument 1:111
  Doubting Thomas 1:137
Vinci, Leonardo da see Leonardo
  da Vinci
Vorobëv-Stebelska, Marevna
  Rivera and 8:110
  Homage to the Friends of
  Montparnasse 8:108-109
  self-portrait 8:108-109
Vroom, Cornelis 3:108-109
  Landscape with a River by a
  Wood 3:108-109
Vuillard, Edouard 5:141
  and the Nabis 9:49
  Toulouse-Lautrec and 8:79
  portrait of Toulouse-
  Lautrec 5:141; 8:81
  and La Revue Blanche 8:79

W

Wallis, Henry
  The Death of Chatterton
  4:100-101
Webber, John
  Princess Poedua 5:68
Whistler, James McNeill
  Courbet and 8:48
  The Bathing Posts 10:59
Wolgemut, Michael 2:36, 38, 141
  and Dürer 2:12, 36, 37
  and Nuremberg Chronicle
  2:36
  The Creation 2:39

Z

Zborowski
  by Marevna 8:108-109
  and Soutine 6:102
Zurburan, Francisco 2:141

A GLOSSARY IN PICTURES

Masaccio's 'Relief'

During the Renaissance, Masaccio was particularly admired for his skill in creating the illusion of relief – the illusion that his forms were solid and three-dimensional. Masaccio achieved this effect by a skilful use of light and shade.

In the Sant'Ambrogio Madonna shown here, the light is coming from a point high up on the left of the picture. That side of the Virgin's face is brightly lit while on the right it is cast into shadow. The light falls most brightly on the prominent parts of her face – her cheekbones, nose and chin, defining the structure of her face with remarkable subtlety and precision.

In painting the Christ Child, Masaccio has paid similar attention to detail. The light falls brightly on his forehead while his podgy cheeks cast his lower face and neck into deep shadow to strongly convey the sense of underlying form.

Scala

The Madonna and Child with St Anne (detail) *1424-25*
Uffizi, Florence

Holbein's Portraiture

In the Renaissance, portraits had a number of different functions. This portrait of Anne of Cleves was commissioned by Henry VIII during negotiations for their marriage. Henry had not yet seen the Lady Anne, who was then living in Germany. So Holbein's task was to produce for the king a clear and straightforward likeness of his prospective wife. This is reflected in the relative simplicity of the portrait. It is not designed to commemorate the sitter, and gives little indication of her interests or personality.

Unlike most of Holbein's sitters, the Lady Anne is shown full-face. Her pose is very simple and static, and her face expressionless. Since her face is rather bland, it is overshadowed by her ornate costume. Henry seems to have been satisfied with Anne's appearance, and arranged to marry her. However, he was less happy when he saw her in the flesh, and dubbed her 'the Flander's mare', and ended the marriage.

This particular portrait is unusual in that it is painted on parchment, which made it easier to transport. The parchment base of this work helps to account for its unusual refinement and delicacy of execution.

Réunion des Musées Nationaux

Portrait of Anne of Cleves *1539*
25⅝" × 19" Louvre, Paris

Hilliard's Miniature

Many of Hilliard's miniatures carry meanings which remain obscure to the modern viewer. These 'hidden' meanings were usually highly personal and may often have been fully understood only by the sitter, or the owner of the miniature. They could be expressed by means of inscriptions, or by using complex visual symbols. Alternatively, they might be expressed in the details of the sitter's costume, as in this portrait of a lady, known as Mrs Holland.

Here, the sitter's costume carries a number of embroidered devices, which Hilliard has painted in meticulous detail. The front panel of her dress is adorned with repeated forms of bees and stags, interspersed with intricate floral emblems. Although the meaning of these motifs has not been deciphered, the animals are almost certainly symbolic. The floral designs may have formed part of the lady's family crest, and could provide a clue to her identity.

In *Young Man among Roses* the unknown sitter wears the black and white of Elizabeth I, perhaps indicating a link with the Queen. This 'hidden' meaning is underlined by the roses, which were one of the Queen's personal emblems.

A Woman, known as Mrs Holland *1593*
2¼″ × 1⅕″ Victoria and Albert Museum, London

Tintoretto's Mannerism

A recurrent feature of Mannerist art was the use of an asymmetrical composition. High Renaissance artists tended to develop their compositions symmetrically around a central axis, making the centre of the painting the focus of attention. Mannerist artists often rejected this convention and moved the focus of their works to one side.

Tintoretto developed this type of composition in a particularly dramatic way. In this picture, the ghostly figure of St Mark provides the focal point of the drama. He is placed on the extreme left of the composition, where our attention is drawn to him by his commanding gesture and by Tintoretto's skilful use of perspective. Whereas Renaissance artists usually placed the vanishing points of their perspective in the centre of the picture, Tintoretto has placed the vanishing point on the left, behind the Saint's outstretched hand. The burial vault in which the figures stand plunges into depth at an angle to the view creating a strangely disorientating effect. Tintoretto has further reversed the Renaissance conventions of composition by placing the donor in the centre of the picture, where he kneels with outstretched arms.

Scala

The Discovery of the Body of St Mark *c.1562*
159½″ × 159½″ Brera, Milan

Velázquez's Naturalism

Velázquez approached classical subjects in an original and highly distinctive way. Unlike Titian, for example, whom he greatly admired, Velázquez painted classical themes with a high degree of naturalism, often reinterpreting them as scenes from contemporary life.

The antique and the modern worlds meet in this unusual painting. Velázquez shows the wine-god Bacchus in the company of a group of peasants, one of whom he crowns with a wreath. These are not the remote, idealised figures of antique art, but contemporary figures who are painted in a highly individualized way. Velázquez has painted the peasants with a naturalism and directness that recall his early *bodegones*, emphasizing their coarse features, rough clothes and undignified poses. Bacchus too is a sensual and vivid figure with an individuality unusual in a classical prototype.

Velázquez has interpreted the subject as if it were a genre scene. Bacchus is not the remote god of antiquity, but a human being, sharing the joys of wine with his fellows. The enigmatic figure of the beggar who hovers in the background reinforces the realistic quality of the scene.

Scala

Bacchus and his Companions: *1628-29*
65″ × 88½″ Prado, Madrid

Hobbema's Perspective

Meindert Hobbema (1638-1709) was not only a pupil but also a close friend and companion of Jacob van Ruisdael, the late 17th-century Dutch landscape painter. Hobbema's most famous work *The Avenue at Middelharnis* (1689), is a perfect example of his wonderful gift for composition and his ability to depict the natural perspective in a landscape.

The system of perspective generally employed by artists is a version of the *Costruzione Legittima*. This was developed from the early 15th century when architects and theorists attempted to form a picture plane so that all lines that recede into a vanishing point on the horizon converge, giving a distinct impression of distance – just as the decreasing height and converging lines of the trees leads the viewer along the avenue into the picture below.

Hobbema's work was very undervalued by his contemporaries and it was not until a hundred or so years later that English collectors were excited by his talent; his paintings became popular and influenced English landscape artists who were painting at this time, Thomas Gainsborough being most obviously in his debt.

The Avenue at Middelharnis *1689*
40¾" × 55½" National Gallery, London

Canaletto's Capriccio

During the second part of his career, Canaletto painted a large number of *capriccios* or 'caprices' – imaginary views which enjoyed great popularity in the 18th century. *Capriccios* were usually based on identifiable sites or buildings which were accurately drawn but placed in bizarre combinations or altered in a startling or fantastic way. They combined familiar places with an element of fantasy and wit.

This painting of the *Horses of San Marco in the Piazzetta* is a particularly good example of a *capriccio*. In Canaletto's time, the bronze horses were placed on the front façade of San Marco, in front of the central window. But Canaletto has put them onto elaborate imaginary pedestals in the Piazzeta, in front of the Doge's Palace.

Canaletto has also altered the lay-out of the Piazzeta. The Doge's Palace and the corner of San Marco on the left are accurately drawn but the details on the right are largely invented. The colonnaded building is a free adaptation of the existing building on that site – Sansovino's Library – while the column of St Mark with its winged lion is, in reality, on the other side of the Piazzetta.

The Horses of San Marco in the Piazzetta *1743*
42½" × 51" Royal Collection

Fragonard's Rococo

Bathing women were very popular subjects in 18th-century French art, whether the figures represented a mythological story or, as here, were painted for their own sake. Fragonard's handling of this work is so lively, free and bold that the flesh, draperies and foliage all seem to melt into the same frothy substance. Although this painting would have probably been commissioned for a particular room, where the other decorations would have set it off superbly, all Fragonard's canvases have such a lightness and freshness that they make splendid pictures in their own right.

The frivolous Rococo style of decorating and painting at which Fragonard excelled was at its height during the middle years of the 18th century and was particularly popular at the French court, Madame de Pompadour (Louis XV's mistress) being an enthusiastic patron. The Revolution of 1789, however, brought a complete reversal of artistic taste and values with patrons turning to the austere 'Republican' art of Jacques-Louis David. During the Reign of Terror, Fragonard fled to his native town of Grasse, only returning to Paris because of great poverty. He died in Paris in 1806, almost forgotten.

Scala

The Bathers *c.1765-70*
25½″ × 32″ Louvre, Paris

Courbet's Realism

Courbet maintained that painting could only consist of the representation of real and existing things, and that abstract objects should not be considered as subjects for artists. His own work underlined this belief. Not only did he use oversized canvases, but he also refused to conform to traditional styles which incorporated idealistic and classical backgrounds. He painted his peasants against real and recognizable scenery – often compiled from several sources. His style of painting was bold, and he pioneered a technique of applying paint with a small trowel to give a strong positive feel to his work.

Many of his paintings depicted working people with their tools, as in *The Sleeping Spinner* where the distaff and the unspun wool are highlighted very clearly. Courbet was not afraid to depict the ordinary, sometimes even unattractive, features of his models – such as the beginnings of a double chin on the sleeper in the picture below. His realism was carried to the extreme when Courbet, who did not often take in pupils, was persuaded to hold teaching classes and instead of allowing his students to paint nudes, flowers and fruit he once produced a real-life bull!

The Sleeping Spinner *1853*
35¾" × 45¼" Musée Fabre, Montpellier

Ruisdael's Staffage

This painting is signed and – unusually for Ruisdael's work – dated, but according to old sources, it once also bore the signature (now no longer visible) of Ruisdael's friend, Nicolaes Berchem, who is credited with painting the figures.

This kind of collaboration was common in 17th-century Dutch art. Called staffage, it was the practice of adding small, not strictly necessary, figures to a landscape to give it some animation, and some painters specialized in this work. For example, in *An Extensive Landscape with a Ruined Castle and a Church*, painted by Ruisdael between 1665 and 1670, the figures in the left foreground are thought to have been painted by Adriaen van de Velde. And during the 1650s, Ruisdael travelled around the border region between the Netherlands and Germany, accompanied by Berchem, who added the finishing touches to the inspired landscapes of Ruisdael.

In contrast, artists outside Holland were less specialized; for example, Italian landscape painters Canaletto and Guardi were both responsible for their own staffage.

The Great Oak *1652*
33½″ × 41″ On loan to Birmingham City Art Gallery

Whistler's Aesthetism

Many of Whistler's works, especially those of his later years, seem to be painted in a very sketchy way, with little regard for detail. Consequently, they often look unfinished. Contemporary critics savagely attacked this aspect of Whistler's technique; they did not see that Whistler was not concerned with surface finish but with less conventional values.

The summary nature of Whistler's late works is well-illustrated by this panel of the Brittany coast. The sky is painted in patches of pink and blue which merge together in an undefined way. The boats are shown as smudges of colour through which we can see the colour of the sky. The waves are painted as thin trails of pink and white and around these we can see the artist's brush-strokes in the dark expanse of the sea.

By leaving aside detail, Whistler allows us to focus more fully on the delicate colour harmonies and the balance of tiny shapes across the wide stretch of sea. This emphasis on the aesthetic aspect makes Whistler's painting an important landmark in the development of abstract art.

The Bathing Posts *1893*
6½″ × 9½″ Hunterian Museum and Art Gallery, Glasgow

Degas' Impressionism

Techniques of composition based on camera 'snapshots' were employed by many artists from the Impressionist period onwards, but Degas was particularly fond of them. He often used the technique to suggest a brief moment in time, creating the impression that the viewer sees just a momentary glimpse of the subject.

This technique is especially apt for depicting the rapid bustle and varied movements of the dance class shown in *The Rehearsal*. The dancer in the right foreground is cut off by the picture frame as she leans forward to have her dress adjusted. This creates the impression that she has momentarily left the scene; but the tension in the girl's clasped hands and the intent expression of her waiting companion suggest that she will shortly move across to join the rehearsal. Degas adds to this impression of a momentary view by including the feet of an unseen dancer at the top of the picture. The girl is hurrying down the staircase and will soon move into the picture space.

Degas combines these cut-off views with the rest of the composition in a very skilful way. For the dancers in the centre of the picture strike an arabesque and, although they seem carefully balanced, this too is a momentary pose. A moment later, the whole scene will be rearranged.

The Rehearsal *1877*
26¾" × 40½" Burrell Collection, Glasgow Art Gallery
and Museum

Gauguin's Post-Impressionism

Gauguin began his artistic career by painting in the natural colours and uncomplicated style of the Impressionists, but after his visit to the West Indies in 1887 he changed to using bright, bold colours and large areas of unbroken paint. Early on he sometimes outlined the colours with dark lines.

After moving to Tahiti he was able to let his imagination run riot, something he had been unable to do while influenced by the Impressionists, and he painted religious and symbolic pictures. His use of colour was intensely personal – used to express how he felt about something or to convey a mood about the subject he was painting. In *Riders on the Beach*, the unnatural colour of the sand contrasts with the natural colours of the riders and their mounts to create a dreamlike quality to an everyday scene. His choice of shades of pinks and blues dominate the picture and produce an unexpected air of peace and tranquility.

Gauguin's poverty meant that he rarely applied his paint heavily and frequently the texture of the coarse canvas shows through clearly, adding to the unreal, almost abstract, use of colour. His non-naturalistic use of colour and his appreciation of the simple and primitive in art has made Gauguin one of the major influences on the development of 20th-century art.

Colorphoto Hinz

Riders on the Beach *1902*
29½" × 36½" Stavros Niarchos Collection, Athens

Manet's Plein-air

Unlike earlier artists – who used sketches done out of doors as source material, but who in general painted in the studio – the Impressionists painted *en plein air* (in the open air) to capture the varying effects of light on their canvases. In natural, outdoor light, objects look quite different from the way they appear in the artificial light of the studio. Particularly in sunlight, colours appear harsh and contours are sharp: we do not often see the gentle gradations of light and shade that make an object seem soft and rounded. Manet worked mainly in the studio, but when he painted out-of-doors he tried to show the effects of light exactly as he saw them.

In *Argenteuil* Manet was working in full sunlight. To capture the dazzling effect of the sun he painted the scene in patches of bright colour set side-by-side, with few intermediate tones between them. The overall effect is rather harsh: the stark contrast between the flesh tones of the woman's face and the black of her hat is accentuated by the brilliant white ribbon. In modelling the face, Manet has replaced the soft, gradual shading of conventional studio light with shadows that are sharp and irregular.

Lauros-Giraudon

Argenteuil *1874*
58″ × 52″ Musée des Beaux-Arts, Tournai

Boccioni's Futurism

Like other Futurists, Boccioni was fascinated by the idea of velocity, or speed, which he described as 'that new absolute . . . which the truly modern temperament cannot disregard'. During the course of his career, he was constantly searching for ways of capturing the sensation of speed and the way in which it appears to dissolve the objects that we see. His forms became gradually more fragmented and less distinct as he developed this idea. In later works, such as the one shown here, they take on a flexible, 'elastic' quality. The central object of the painting is the form of a horse and rider, just distinguishable among the fragments of posts, railings and pylons. Their shapes are broken up into Cubist-like facets which stretch and spread, their surfaces drawn out and distorted by their speed. The sensation of speed is enhanced by the way in which the horse and rider become merged with the background.

Boccioni was not just concerned with the speed of movement from place to place, but with the rapid 'universal dynamism' of objects. The expanding facets of the horse and rider also suggest the swift vibration within the forms themselves.

Elasticity *1912*
39″ × 39″ Brera, Milan

Munch's Symbolism

The image of the 'femme fatale' occurs frequently in Munch's paintings and lithographs. Although it was a common theme in Symbolist art, Munch's treatment of the subject reflects a particularly personal attitude to women, and to physical intimacy, as bringers both of love and of death.

This lithograph is one of the most powerful of Munch's images of women. The woman is highly sensual with her rounded breasts and curved hips, and is shown at the height of sexual ecstasy, with eyes closed and lips parted. For Munch, this sensuality had a strong religious quality, made clear in the woman's halo, and in the inclusion of the foetus, recalling traditional images of the Madonna and Child.

Yet the image of the woman in love is also strongly associated with death. Although Munch includes symbols of life in the lithograph, in the foetus and the sperm in the decorative border, the foetus is wizened and death-like, and casts an air of evil and foreboding over the scene. The woman's swooning is both the swoon of ecstasy and the swoon of death.

Madonna (Lithograph) *1895-1902*
23¾″ × 17½″ Oslo, Munch Museum

Index of Masterpieces

A

Abbey in the Oakwoods (Friedrich) 4:80, *88-9*

Abundance (drawing, Botticelli) 1:*114*

Acrobat, The (Chagall) 6:*92*

Ad Parnassum (Klee) 6:*64-5*

Adoration of the Magi, The (Botticelli) 1:*109, 110*

Adoration of the Magi, The (Botticelli) 1:*115*

Adoration of the Magi, The (Dürer) 2:*28-9*; 4:*85*
Italian influence on 2:19

Adoration of the Magi (Fra Angelico) 1:*51*

Adoration of the Magi (Giotto) 1:*41*
Halley's comet in 1:40, *41*

Adoration of the Magi (Velázquez) 3:*45*
detail 3:*45*

Adoration of the Shepherds (La Tour) 3:*38-9*

Adoration of the Trinity, The (Dürer) 2:*31*

After Dinner at Ornans (Courbet):
prize for 8:46
purchaser 8:46

Agnes Frey (sketch, Dürer) 2:*15*

Agony in the Garden (Bellini) 1:*88-9*

Agony in the Garden (Mantegna) 1:*77*

Agrarian Leader Zapata (Rivera) 8:*133*

Aidez Espagne (Miró) 7:79, *91*

Altarpiece of the Holy Kinship
see Torgau Altarpiece

altarpiece for St Mary Redcliffe (Hogarth) 8:16

Amateur Circus (Tissot) 5:*131*

Ambassadors, The (Holbein) 2:79, 88, *88-9, 94-5*
details 2:*88-9*
symbolic objects in 2:*89*

Ancient of Days, The (Blake) 4:*56*

angel (mosaic, Giotto?) 1:*19*

Angelus, The (Millet), Dalí and 6:*112, 114, 115-16*

Animated Still-life (Dalí) 6:*130-31*

Annah the Javanese (Gauguin) 5:*49*

Anne of Cleves (Holbein) 2:*83*; 10:*50*

Anne Cresacre (drawing, Holbein) 2:*84*

Annunciation, The (Botticelli) 1:*129*

Annunciation, The (Fra Angelico) 1:*47, 51, 56-7, 62-3*

Annunciation (illumination, Fra Angelico) 1:*50*

Annunciation, The (Martini) 1:*53*

Annunciation, The (Poussin) 1:*53*

Annunciation, The (Rossetti) 9:*25*
technical limitations 9:*78-9*

Annunciation of St Anna, The (Giotto) 1:*26*

Anxiety (Munch) 9:*123*

Apocalypse, The (woodcuts, Dürer) 2:18, 39
The Four Horsemen 2: *18*
Northern traditions in 2:19

Apocalypse of St John, The (woodcut, Dürer) 2:*14*

Apotheosis of Homer, The (Dalí) 6:*128-9*

Apparition, The (Moreau) 9:*69*

Apples and Oranges (Cézanne) 5:*22, 22-3, 30-31*

Archangel Michael, The (Reni) 3:*105*

architecton (Malevich) 7:*51*

Architectonic Angelus of Millet, The (Dalí) 6:*114*

Arctic Shipwreck, The (Friedrich) 4:*94*

Arena Chapel, Padua 1:14-15, 15, 24
architect of? 1:17
decorative plan 1:*25*
frescoes in 1:*22-3*
details 1:*18, 24-5*

Arearea (Gauguin) 5:*51*

Argenteuil (Manet) 10:*62*

Aristide Bruant at the Ambassadeurs (Toulouse-Lautrec) 8:*91*

'Art for Research' (lithograph, Miró) 7:*98*

Artillerymen, The (Rousseau) 6:*8-9*

Artist's Family, The (Velázquez) 3:*48*

Artist's Father, The (Dalí) 6:*109*

Artist's Studio, The (Rivera) 8:*115*

Astarte Syriaca (Rossetti) 4:*52*; 9:*33*

At the Ambassadeurs (Degas) 8:*84*

At the Circus Fernando (Toulouse-Lautrec) 8:*88-9*

At the 'Concert Européen' (Seurat) 5:*113*

At the Moulin Rouge (Toulouse-Lautrec) 8:86, *86-7, 95*

'Atomicus' (Dalí/Halsman) 6:*111*

Attraction (lithograph, Munch) 19:*118*

Avenue at Middelharnis, The (Hobbema) 3:*111*; 10:*54*

B

Bacchus (Caravaggio) 3:*18*

Bacchus and his Companions (Velázquez) 10:*53*

Baptism of Christ, The (Bellini) 1:*83, 85*

Baptism of St Paul (Holbein the Elder) 2:*76*

Barcelona Suite (lithograph, Miró) 7:*80*
images in 7:*84*

Bardi Altarpiece, The (Botticelli) 1:*126*

Barque of Dante, The (Delacroix) 4:*110, 120-21*

Basilica of St Francis of Assisi 1:*39*
Cimabue and 1:13
problems of authenticating frescoes 1:14-15

Basilica del Santo, high altar (detail) 1:*77*

Bathers, The (Courbet) 8:*52, 53*
buyer of 8:48
ugliness of 8:50

Bathers, The (Fragonard) 10:*56*

Bathing at Asnières (Seurat) 5:*109, 118-19*

Bathing Men (Munch) 8:*115*

Bathing Posts, The (Whistler), 10:*59*

Bathos, The (engraving, Hogarth) 8:*17*

Battle of the Aztecs and the Spaniards (Rivera) 8:*116*
Crossing the Barranca 8:*114-15*

Beata Beatrix (Rossetti) 9:*30*

Beautiful Bird Revealing the Unknown to a Pair of Lovers, The (Miró) 7:*82*

Bec du Hoc, Grandcamp, The (Seurat) 5:*120*

Bedroom at Arles, The (Van Gogh) 5:*86, 86-7, 90-91*
details 5:*87*

Beethoven Frieze, The (Klimt): *The Hostile Powers* 9:*92*
Pure Joy 9:*23*

Beheading of John the Baptist (Caravaggio) 3:*16, 16, 18-19*
detail 3:*16*
sense of violence in 3:*18*

Belle Angèle, La (Gauguin) 9:*52*

Beloved, The (Rossetti) 9:*8*

Benjamin Hoadly, Bishop of Winchester (Hogarth) 8:*29*

Bergamo Madonna, The (Mantegna) 1:*141*

Betrayal of Christ, The (Giotto) 1:*22, 29*
detail 1:*21*

Biblical Message (Chagall) 6:*81*

Big Fish Eat Little Fish (engraving, Bruegel) 2:*111, 111*

Birch Wood (Klimt) 9:*82*

Birth of Mary (Dürer), Rossetti and 9:*22*

Birth of Venus, The (Botticelli) 1:*115, 117, 118-19, 122-3*
details 1:*118, 119*

Birth of Venus (Redon) 9:*62*
objectivity in 9:*52*

Birth of Venus, The (Titian) 1:*118*

Birth of the Virgin, The (Murillo)

Black Feather Hat, The (Klimt) 9:*82-3*

Black Lines I (Kandinsky) 7:*26*

Blasted Elm with a View of Edmond aan Zee (Ruisdael) 3:*9*

Blaze I (Riley) 7:*120*

Blue III (Miró) 7:*96-7*

Blue Bower, The (Rossetti) 9:*15*
model for 9:*15*

Blue Cloak, The (engraving, Hogenberg) 2:*119*

Blue Closet, The (Rossetti) 9:*18*

Blue Room, The (Valadon) 8:*78*

Boar Hunt (Velázquez) 3:*68-9*

Boats at Grandcamp (Seurat) 5:*121*

Body of Abel Found by Adam and Eve, The (Blake) 4:*54, 54-5, 62-3*
details 4:*55*
study for 4:*54*

Bonjour Monsieur Courbet (Courbet) *see Meeting, The*

Book of Job, The (Blake) 4:*49, 53*
Satan Smiting Job with Sore Boils 4:*53, 53*

Bouquet of Flowers (Redon) 9:*64*

Bouquet with Flying Lovers (Chagall) 6:*96*

Bower Meadow, The (Rossetti) 9:*32*

Boy in a Red Waistcoat (Cézanne) 5:*25*
auction of 5:*17*

Boy on the Rocks (Rousseau) 6:*27*

Brasserie Andler (etching, Courbet) 8:*47*

Bread and Compotier with Fruit on a Table (Picasso) 5:*20*

Breasts with Red Flowers (Gauguin) 5:*65*

Bride, The (Klimt) 9:*81, 83*

Bridge at Courbevoie, The (Seurat) 7:*109*

Broadway Boogie Woogie (Mondrian) 7:*116, 141*

Buffoon Juan de Calabazas, The (Velázquez) 3:*52*
detail 3:*53*

Bullfinches and Butterflies (Hondecoeter) 3:*134*

Bulls of Bordeaux (lithograph, Goya) 4:*17*

Burial at Ornans (Courbet) 8:*46, 56-7*
criticism of 8:*47*
method of painting 8:*50*
real subject of 8:*74*
shallow picture space 8:*53*
starts painting 8:*47*

Burial of the Sardine, The (Goya) 4:*32*

Bust of Charles I (copy, Bernini) 3:*87*

C

Café Terrace at Night (Van Gogh) 5:*85*
detail 5:*85*
method of painting 5:*83*

Calais Gate (Hogarth) 8:*40*

Calling of St Matthew, The (Caravaggio) 3:*20-21*
detail 3:*20*
use of light in 3:*21*

Calling of St Matthew (Pareja) 3:*49*

Camille Falte (Redon) 9:*47*

Campanile, Florence, Giotto and 1:*16, 17*

Campo Santo, Pisa, frescoes in 1:*49*

Canterbury Pilgrims (Blake) 4:*48, 48-9*

Canute (drawing, Blake) 4:*51*

Capella della Madonna di San Brizio, Orvieto, vault decorations 1:*48*

Caprichos (etchings, Goya) 4:*20-21*

Captain Coram (Hogarth) 8:*19*

Carceri d'Invenzione (Piranesi) 4:*98, 99*

Card Players, The (Cézanne) 5:*26-7*

Cardinal Wolsey (anon) 2:*101*

Carnival and Lent (Bruegel), influences on 2:*115-16*

Castle at Bentheim, The (Ruisdael) 3:*109*

Cataract 3 (Riley) 7:*115*

Cathedral Church, Wittenberg (engraving, Cranach) 2:*46*

Cat's Dancing Lesson, The (Steen) 7:*84*

ceiling, Greenwich Naval College (Thornhill) 8:*13*

Célèbes (Ernst) 8:*136*

Chahut, Le (Seurat) 5:*128*

Chalk Cliffs on Rügen (Friedrich) 4:*91*

Channel at Gravelines, The (Seurat) 5:*127*

Chapter House, Wells Cathedral 1:*42*

Charles I on Horseback with Seigneur de St Antoine (Van Dyck) 3:*92*

Charles I in Three Positions (Van Dyck) 3:*86, 94-5*
details 3:*86, 87*
inspiration for 3:*87*

Chastisement of Cupid, The (Manfredi) 3:*37*

Château at Medan (Cézanne) 5:*18, 21*
detail 5:*21*

Château Noir, Le (Cézanne) 5:*9*

Christ Before the High Priest (Honthorst) 3:*39*

Christ on the Cross (Bellini workshop) 1:*76*

Christ Crowned with Thorns (Van Dyck) 3:*88*

Christ of St John of the Cross (Dalí) 6:*126-7*

Christ with Two Angels (Bellini) 1:*77*

Christina of Denmark, Duchess of Milan (Holbein) 2:*98*
speed of painting 2:*84*

Chrysanthemum (Morris) 9:*34-5*

Church at Auvers, The (Van Gogh) 5:*96*

Circus, The (Seurat) 5:*111, 129*
working sketch for 5:*113*

City of Churches, The (Klee) 6:*55*

City of Paris, The (Delaunay) 6:*78-9*

Clares Mourning St Francis, The (Giotto) 1:*39*

Cliffs at Etretat After the Storm (Courbet) 5:*114; 8:*65*

Closed Eyes (Redon) 9:*51, 51*

Clothed Maja (Goya) 4:*14, 24-5*
Inquisition and 4:*16*

Colleoni Monument (Verrocchio) 1:*111*

Colossus, The (Goya) 4:*29*

Colour Moves (Riley) 7:*112, 112-13, 113*

Comedy of Death, The (engraving, Bresdin) 9:*45*

Composition IV (Battle) (Kandinsky) 7:*21, 21*
detail 7:*21*

Composition VII (Kandinsky), study for 7:*18-19*

Composition VIII (Kandinsky) 7:*9, 28-9*

Conquest of Mexico, The (Hogarth) 8:*18*

Contarelli Chapel: Caravaggio paints for 3:*4*
reasons for rejection 3:*19*

Continuum (Riley) 7:*111*

Convergence: Number 10 (Pollock) 7:*116*

Conversation Piece (Ruisdael, with Keyser) 3:*109*

Conversion of St Paul, The (Bruegel) 2:*128-9*

Conversion of St Paul (Caravaggio) 3:*30*
use of light in 3:*21*

Corn Harvest, The (Bruegel) 2:*125*

Cornfield and Cypresses (Van Gogh) 5:*93*

Coronation of the Virgin, The (Bellini) 1:*79*

Coronation of the Virgin (Fra Angelico) 1:*47, 61*

Coronation of the Virgin (Filippo Lippi) 1:*133*
detail 1:*46*

Corrido of the Agrarian Revolution, The (Rivera), theme of 8:*115*

Corrido of the Proletarian Revolution, The (Rivera), theme of 8:*115*

Coup de Soleil, Le (Ruisdael) 3:*112, 117, 131*

Court Fool 'El Primo', The (Velázquez) 3:*60*

Court Fool Sebastián de Morra, The (Velázquez) 3:*61*

Court of the Inquisition, The (Goya) 4:*34-5*

Covent Garden Tragedy, The (Hogarth) 8:*15*

Crab (sketch, Dürer) 2:*14*

Creation, The (mural, Rivera) 8:*110*

Creator, The (Michelangelo) 4:*52*

Cross in the Mountains, The (Friedrich) 4:*78, 80*
symbolism of 4:*83*

Crucifix (sculpture, Montañes) 3:46
Crucifix, Santa Maria Novella (Giotto) 1:18
Crucifixion (Cranach) 2:50, 50
Crucifixion (Cranach the Younger) 2:49
Crucifixion of St Peter, The (Caravaggio) 3:31
Creation, The (woodcut, Wolgemut) 2:39
Cupid and Psyche (Van Dyck) 3:98
Current (Riley) 7:123

D

Danaë (Klimt) 9:98
Dance of Albion, The (Blake) see Glad Day
Dance of Death (woodcuts, Holbein) 2:77
Dance of Life, The (Munch) 9:111, 118, 118-19, 124-5
  details 9:118, 119
  preliminary sketch 9:119
Dance at the Moulin Rouge, The (Toulouse-Lautrec) 8:92-3
Dans le Rêve: Germination (lithograph, Redon) 9:47
David (Michelangelo), Botticelli and 1:113
David with the Head of Goliath (Caravaggio) 3:35
Day of the God, The (Gauguin) 5:52
Dead Christ Supported by Four Angels (Bellini) 1:82-3
Dead Mother, The (Munch) 6:69
Death: My irony surpasses all others (lithograph, Redon) 9:47, 50
Death of Chatterton, The (Wallis) 4:100-101
Death and Fire (Klee) 6:46, 67
Death of Sardanapalus, The (Delacroix) 4:111, 124-5
  preliminary sketches 4:114
Death of St Francis, The (Giotto) 1:34-5
Death of the Virgin (Caravaggio) 3:34
  rejection of 3:17
  replacement for 3:36-7
  rumours about 3:21
Deny (Riley) 7:116-17
Deposition from the Cross, The (Fra Angelico) 1:47, 54, 54-5, 58-9
  details 1:54-5
  principles in 1:51
  rhetorical gestures in 1:55

Detroit Industry (Rivera) 8:126-7
  preliminary work for 8:112
  themes for 8:117
Dignity and Impudence (Landseer) 6:38
Disasters of War (etchings, Goya) 4:14, 19, 23
Discovery of the Body of St Mark, The (Tintoretto) 10:52
Dismal Sport (Dalí) 6:113
Dissolute Household, The (Steen) 8:20
Divan Japonais, Le (poster, Toulouse-Lautrec) 8:85
Divine Comedy (Blake) 4:49, 53
  Beatrice Addressing Dante 4:64
  The Inscription over Hell Gate 4:65
  The Simoniac Pope 4:61
Doctor Bourges (Toulouse-Lautrec) 8:79
Dr Jacobson (Munch) 9:115
Dr Johannes Cuspinian and his Wife Anna (Cranach) 2:45
Dog Barking at the Moon (Miró) 7:82-3, 83
Doge Leonardo Loredan, The (Bellini) 1:85, 96
Doge's Palace: decorations in Great Hall 1:77, 78, 81
Don Quixote (Coypel) 8:20
Doña Isabel de Porcel (Goya) 4:26
Drawing of his Mother (Malevich) 7:44
Dream, The (Rousseau) 6:34-5
Dream of a Sunday Afternoon in the Alameda (Rivera) 8:128-9
  scandal over 8:113
Duchess of Alba (Goya) 4:15
Duke of Wellington, The (Goya) 4:28
Dune Landscape with Plank Fence (Ruisdael) 3:120
Dutch Interior I (Miró) 7:79, 85

E

Eiffel Tower, The (Seurat) 5:113
Eight Red Rectangles (Malevich) 7:59
Elasticity (Boccioni) 10:63
Election, The (engravings, Hogarth) 8:21
  Chairing the Member 8:34-5
Electors of Saxony, The (triptych, Cranach) 2:46
Elizabeth I (Hilliard) 2:87
Elisabeth Salter (Delacroix) 4:109
Elizabeth Siddal (drawing, Rossetti) 9:14

Elsbeth Binsenstock (Holbein) 2:79
embroidery design (Böhm) 9:102
Emile Bernard (Toulouse-Lautrec) 5:47
Emilie Flöge (Klimt) 9:94
Emperor Theodosius Refused Entry into Milan Cathedral, The (Rubens) 3:78
Emperor Theodosius Refused Entry into Milan Cathedral (Van Dyck) 3:79
Engraving of a London Street (Hogarth) 8:36-7
Enrico degli Scrovegni (Giotto) 1:24
Entombment of Christ, The (Caravaggio) 3:19-20, 32
Equestrienne (Chagall) 6:93
Era, La (Rivera) 8:109
Eve (Dürer) 2:52
Eve and the Serpent (carving, Gauguin) 5:53
Evocation of the Butterflies, The (Redon) 9:67
Execution of the Doge Marino Faliero, The (Delacroix) 4:123
  use of colour in 4:117
Exotic Landscape (Rousseau) 6:39
Expectation (Klimt) 9:81
  cartoon for 9:84
Expulsion of Joachim, The (Giotto) 1:25
Expulsion of Heliodorus from the Temple, The (Delacroix) 4:113
Expulsion of the Moriscos, The (Velázquez) 3:46
Extensive Landscape with a Ruined Castle and a Church, An (Ruisdael) 3:112, 116, 129

F

Fall of Icarus, The (Bruegel) 2:120-21
  influences in 2:115
Fall of Man, The (engraving, Dürer) 2:19, 20
  detail 2:21
Family of Charles IV, The (Goya) 4:14
Family Evening (Munch) 9:108-109
Family Group (Holbein) 2:79
Family of Thomas More (copy, Holbein) 2:78
Farm, The (Miró), working method 7:82
Feast of the Gods, The (Bellini) 1:85
Feast of Herod, The (Filippo Lippi) 1:117

Feast of the Rose Garlands, The (Dürer) 2:22, 22-3, 30
  details 2:22, 23
  people in 2:23
  preparatory study for 2:23
  symbolism in 2:23
February (Limbourg Brothers) 2:116
Fee, The (Cranach) 2:65
Female Clown, Cha-U-Kao, The (Toulouse-Lautrec) 8:97
First Anniversary of the Death of Beatrice (Rossetti) 9:22, 22-3, 26-7
  details 9:22, 23
  early version of 9:23
  inspiration for 9:22
Five Children of Charles I (Van Dyck) 3:96-7
  preparatory sketch 3:83
Flight into Egypt, The (Fra Angelico) 1:66
Flight into Egypt, The (Giotto) 1:28
Florence Cathedral 1:72, 134
Flower Seller (Rivera) 8:123
Flowering Apple Tree (Mondrian) 7:52
Flowers in a Turquoise Vase (Redon) 9:65
Football Match, The (Malevich) 7:61
Forge of Vulcan, The (Velázquez) 3:48
Fortitude (Botticelli) 1:109, 109
Found (Rossetti) 9:18
Fountain of the Four Rivers (sculpture, Bernini) 3:136
Four Apostles, The (Dürer) 2:17, 34-5
  inscription on 2:17
Francis I (Clouet) 2:87
Francis and the Pope (Sassetta) 1:37
François Langlois (Van Dyck) 3:82-3
Frari Altarpiece (Bellini) 1:93
Frédérick Chopin (Delacroix) 4:112
Frederick the Wise (Cranach) 2:71
Frederick the Wise, Elector of Saxony (Dürer) 2:15
Frida and Diego, 1931 (Kahlo) 8:112
Friedrich in his Studio (Kersting) 4:82
Frieze of Life (Munch): key images 9:115
  paintings in the series 9:111
  formulates scheme for 9:111
  meaning of 9:111-12
  theme of 9:111, 113
Fulfilment (Klimt) 9:81, 84-5
  detail 9:84
Full Moon (Klee) 6:58

G

Garden of Earthly Delights, The (Bosch) 6:*116*
Garden of Eden, The (Cranach) 2:*62-3*
Gardening (Goncharova) 7:*46-7*
Gaspar de Guzman, Count of Olivares (Velázquez) 3:*68*
Gassed and Wounded (Kennington) 7:*72-3*
Gather (Riley) 7:*130*
George Gisze (Holbein) 2:*79, 86*
  detail 2:*86*
  treatment of textures in 2:*84*
George Sand (Delacroix) 4:*113*
Ghost of a Flea, The (Blake) 4:*47*
Ghost of Vermeer of Delft, Which Can Be Used As A Table, The (Dalí) 6:*115*
Giaour and the Pasha, The (Delacroix) 4:*114*
Gin Lane (Hogarth) 8:*33*
  crudity of engraving 8:*21*
Giorlamo Tedesco (drawing, Dürer) 2:*23*
Gipsy Fortune Teller, The (Caravaggio) 3:*24*
Girl at the Piano (detail, Cézanne) 5:*13*
Girl Seated Seen from the Rear (Dalí) 6:*118*
Girl with a Comb (Malevich) 7:*49*
Girlhood of Mary Virgin, The (Rossetti) 9:*14-15, 24*
  purchaser 9:*15*
  painting technique in 9:*20*
  technical limitations in 9:*18*
Girls on the Jetty (Munch) 9:*114-15*
Glad Day (Blake) 4:*60*
Glass (Larionov) 7:*46*
Gleaners, The (Millet) 8:*53*
God Judging Adam (Blake) 4:*47, 57*
Golden Age, The (Cranach) 2:*52-3*
  detail 2:*53*
Golden Stairs, The (Burne-Jones) 1:*117*
Goldfish (Klimt) 9:*91*
Good and Evil Angels, The (Blake) 4:*8*
Good Samaritan, The (Hogarth) 8:*16*
Goulue at the Moulin Rouge, La (Toulouse-Lautrec) 8:*94*
Graham Children, The (Hogarth) 8:*21, 27*
Grande Jatte, La (Seurat) 5:*109, 116-17, 122-3, 135*
  detail 5:*117*
  oil studies for 5:*116, 117*
  sketches for 5:*116*
Grandmaster Alof de Wignacourt (Caravaggio) 3:*16, 17*

Great Bathers, The (Cézanne) 5:*21, 32*
Great Oak, The (Ruisdael) 3:*114, 121;* 10:*58*
Great Pine, The (Cézanne) 5:*28*
Green Monkey (Stubbs) 2:*21*
Greifswald Harbour (Friedrich) 4:*86*
Grinder, The (Rivera) 8:*122*
Guernica (Picasso) 7:*103*
Guillaume Apollinaire (Laurencin) 6:*103*

H

Hammock, The (Courbet) 8:*50-51*
Hands of an Apostle (drawing, Dürer) 2:*18*
Hans Jaeger (Munch) 9:*110*
Harbour at Gravelines, The (Seurat) 5:*126*
Harlequin (Cézanne) 5:*19*
Harlequin's Carnival (Miró) 7:*88-9*
  humour of 7:*84*
Harlot's Progress, A (Hogarth) 8:*15*
  pamphlet on 8:*15*
  purpose of paintings 8:*15, 20-21*
  success of 8:*15*
  third plate 8:*18*
Harriet Leavens (Phillips) 6:*20*
Harvest, The (engraving, Bruegel) 2:*134*
Harvest in Brittany (Gauguin) 5:*50*
Haymaking (Bruegel) 2:*124*
Haystacks (Monet): Kandinsky and 7:*13, 19*
  light in 7:*20*
Head of Christ and Snake (Redon) 9:*57*
Head of a Martyr on a Platter (Redon) 9:*50*
Henrietta Maria (Van Dyck) 3:*87, 101*
Henry VIII (Holbein) 2:*96*
  cartoon for 2:*100*
  use of line in 2:*86*
Heron, The (Dürer) 2:*18*
Hidden Squares (Riley) 7:*114-15*
Hilly Landscape with Cattle (Ruisdael) 3:*114, 116-17*
Hippopotamus Hunt, The (Rubens) 4:*116*
History of Medicine in Mexico: The People's Demand for Better Health (Rivera) 8:*130-31*
  use of colour and space in 8:*117*

History of Mexico, The: from the Conquest to the Future (Rivera) 8:*112, 116, 118, 118-19, 124-5*
  starts work on 8:*112*
Homage to Cézanne (Denis) 9:*48-9*
Homage to the Friends of Montparnasse (Marevna) 8:*108-9*
Homage to Leonardo da Vinci (Redon) 9:*60-61*
Hope I (Klimt) 9:*95*
Horse Attacked by a Tiger (watercolour, Delacroix) 4:*115*
Horses Emerging from the Sea (Delacroix) 4:*129*
Horses of San Marco in the Piazzetta, The (Canaletto) 10:*55*
Hours of Anne of Brittany, The (Bourdichon) 2:*21*
Hudibras (Hogarth) 8:*20*
Hunters in the Snow (Bruegel) 2:*112, 126*

I

I Lock the Door Upon Myself (Khnopff) 9:*70-71*
I and the Village (Chagall) 6:*85, 85*
  detail 6:*85*
  influence of Cubism 6:*83*
Immaculate Conception, The (Velázquez) 3:*56*
  model for 3:*45*
  technique in 3:*51*
Impression of Africa (Dalí) 6:*116*
Impression 3 (Concert) (Kandinsky) 7:*14-15*
Improvisation 19 (Kandinsky) 7:*24-5*
Improvisation Ravine (Kandinsky) 7:*19, 27*
Improvisation 31 (Sea Battle) (Kandinsky) 7:*52*
In Dream (lithograph, Redon) 9:*46-7, 47*
Inconstancy (Giotto) 1:*25*
Industry and Idleness (Hogarth):
  crudity of engraving 8:*21*
  first plate 8:*19*
  London in 8:*36*
Infanta Margarita, The (Velázquez) 3:*54*
Infanta Margarita in Blue, The (Velázquez) 3:*67*
Innocent X (Velázquez) 3:*53*
Interior of the Old Church at Amsterdam, The (drawing, Ruisdael) 3:*14*
Inverted Personages (Miró) 7:*92*

Iron and Coal (Scott) 9:*116*
Isabel of Bourbon (Velázquez/Jan Brueghel) 3:*69*
Island of the Dead, The (Böcklin) 9:*70*

J

Jacob Muffel (Dürer) 2:*19*
Jane Avril at the Jardin de Paris (Toulouse-Lautrec) 8:*90*
Jane Seymour (Holbein) 2:*97*
Janey and the Wombat (drawing, Rossetti) 9:*16*
Jealousy (Munch) 9:*111, 114*
  model for 9:*112*
Jenny le Guillou (Delacroix) 4:*110*
Jerusalem (Blake) 4:*49, 66-9, 67*
  title page 4:*51*
Jewish Cemetery, The (Ruisdael) 3:*112, 118-19, 122*
  details 3:*118-19*
  preliminary drawing 3:*119*
Jewish Wedding, The (Delacroix) 4:*127*
Johannes Cuspinian (Cranach) 2:*50*
John and Frances Croker (Hilliard) 2:*140*
John Frederick the Magnanimous, Elector of Saxony (Cranach) 2:*46*
John More the Younger (drawing, Holbein) 2:*85*
John the Steadfast, Elector of Saxony (Cranach) 2:*46*
Josefa Bayeu (Goya) 4:*12*
Joseph's Coat (Velázquez) 3:*48*
Journey of the Magi, The (Gozzoli) 1:*49, 49*
Juan de Pareja (Velázquez) 3:*64*
Judgement of Paris, The (Cranach) 2:*51, 54, 54-5, 64*
  details 2:*54, 55*
  original sketch for 2:*54*
Judith I (Klimt) 9:*20, 82, 86, 90*
  details 9:*86, 87*
  source of background 9:*87*
Judith II (Klimt) 9:*86*
Judith Beheading Holofernes (Caravaggio) 3:*27*
  sense of violence in 3:*18*
Judith with the Head of Holofernes (Cranach) 2:*59*
Judith and Holofernes (A. Gentileschi) 3:*38*
Jurisprudence (Klimt) 9:*79*

K

Kill, The (Courbet) 8:51
King Sebert (copy, Blake) 4:45
Kiss, The (Klimt) 9:82, 99
Kitchen Garden with a Donkey (Miró) 7:86-7
Knife Grinder, The (Malevich) 7:57
style of 7:51
Knight, Death and the Devil, The (engraving, Dürer) 2:20, 32
Knight of the Golden Fleece (Rubens) 3:85

L

Lady and the Unicorn (tapestries) 6:36-7
Lady Elizabeth Thimbleby and Dorothy Viscountess Andover (Van Dyck) 3:99
Lake at Annecy (Cézanne) 5:29
Lamentation, The (Botticelli) 1:130
Lamentation, The (Giotto) 1:22, 30-31
details 1:20-21
Lamentation over the Dead Christ, The (Fra Angelico) 1:54-5
Landscape with a River by a Wood (Vroom) 3:108-109
Landscape with the Ruins of the Castle of Egmond (Ruisdael) 3:112-13
Landscape with Sandpit (Gainsborough) 3:116
Landscape with Waterfall by a Cottage (J. S. Ruisdael) 3:110
Landscape with Yellow Birds (Klee) 6:53, 53
detail 6:53
Large Enclosure, The (Friedrich) 4:81
use of colour in 4:85
Large Piece of Turf, The (Dürer) 2:27
Las Meninas (Velázquez) 3:49, 53, 54, 54, 66
details 3:54, 55
Last Day in the Old House, The (Braithwaite Martineau) 8:20
Last of England, The (Brown) 9:16
Last Judgement (unfinished, Fra Angelico) 1:49
Last Judgement, The (detail, Giotto) 1:25
Laying-out of Christ, The (Carpaccio) 1:84
Legend of the True Cross (Piero della Francesca) 1:22-3
Liberation of the Peon, The (Rivera) 8:135

Liberation of St Peter, The (Caracciolo) 3:37
Liberty Leading the People (Delacroix) 4:112, 126
Life of Saint Francis (cycle, Giotto) 1:13
detail 1:19
Light and Colour: The Morning after the Deluge (Turner) 7:20
Linaiuoli Altarpiece (Fra Angelico) 1:45, 47, 51
description of 1:51
designer of frame 1:47, 51
principles in 1:51
Lion Hunt, The (Delacroix) 9:44-5
detail 4:114-15
Redon copies 9:45
Lion and Lioness (Stubbs) 6:38-9
Little Diamonds (Riley) 7:124
Lives of Christ and the Virgin (Giotto) 1:14
Lomellini Family, The (Van Dyck) 3:82, 83
Lonely Ones, The (Munch) 9:130-31
Lord Grey and Lady Mary West as Children (Hogarth) 8:26
Lord John and Lord Bernard Stuart (Van Dyck) 3:84
Louis and Rupert of Bavaria (Van Dyck) 3:102-103
Lucas and Cornelis de Wael (Hollar, after Van Dyck) 3:79
Lucretia (Cranach) 2:51
Luis de Góngora (Velázquez) 3:45, 46
Luncheon on the Grass (Manet) 5:98
reaction to 5:98, 99
Lutanist, The (Sorgh) 7:84
Luther Altarpiece (Cranach) 2:71

M

Madame Cézanne in a Red Armchair (Cézanne) 5:24
Madhouse, The (Goya) 4:20-21
detail 4:21
Madonna (Munch) 9:111; 10:64
Madonna of the Book, The (Botticelli) 1:116-17
detail 1:116
Madonna and Child (Jacopo Bellini) 1:78
Madonna and Child, The (Giotto) 1:13, 33
Madonna and Child (Filippo Lippi) 1:46
Madonna and Child between St Catherine and St Mary Magdalene (Bellini) 1:94-5

Madonna and Child with St Anne (Masaccio) 10:49
Madonna di Loreto, The (Caravaggio) 3:33
Madonna of the Magnificat (Botticelli) 1:128
Madonna of the Meadow, The (Bellini) 1:81, 86-7, 98
Madonna dei Palafrenieri (detail, Caravaggio) 3:15
Madonna of Port Lligat, The (Dalí) 6:114-15, 116
Making of a Fresco Showing the Building of a City, The (Rivera) 8:8
Man at the Crossroads Looking with Hope and High Vision to the Choosing of a New and Better Future (Rivera): fate of 8:113, 113
smaller version of 8:113, 113
Man Clasping a Hand from a Cloud (Hilliard) 2:141
Man and Woman Gazing at the Moon (Friedrich) 4:84-5
detail 4:84
Manola, La (Goya) 4:17
March to Finchley, The (Hogarth) 8:20-21
detail 8:21
Margaret Lemon (Van Dyck) 3:78
Margaret Stonborough-Wittgenstein (Klimt) 9:97
Margaret Wyatt, Lady Lee (Holbein) 2:83
Marie de Raet (Van Dyck) 3:91
Market, The (Gauguin) 5:60-61
Marriage à la Mode (Hogarth): *The Countess's Suicide* 8:23
The Killing of the Earl 8:23
The Marriage Contract 8:22, 22-3, 30
details 8:22-3
purpose of painting 8:15, 20-21
Shortly After the Marriage 8:31
Mars and Venus (Botticelli) 1:114-15, 115
Martinique Landscape (Gauguin) 5:50
Martyrdom of St Catherine (Cranach) 2:46, 51, 51
Martyrdom of St John the Evangelist, The (Fra Angelico) 1:51
Martyrdom of St Matthew (Caravaggio), uncertainty in painting 3:14
Mary Ruthven (Van Dyck) 3:81
Mary Wotton, Lady Guildford (Holbein) 2:91
Masquerades and Operas (Hogarth) see *The Taste of the Town*

Massacre of Chios, The (Delacroix) 4:110, 118, 118, 122, 135
details 4:118-19
Massacre of the Innocents (Bruegel) 2:113, 127
Massacre of the Innocents (Fra Angelico) 1:67
Massacre of the Innocents, The (Giotto) 1:21
Medicine (Klimt) 9:78, 78, 79
detail 9:78
Medusa (Caravaggio) 3:19
Meeting, The (Courbet) 8:58
Meeting at the Golden Gate, The (Giotto) 1:27
detail 1:20
Melencolia I (engraving, Dürer) 2:16, 20, 33
Merry Jesters, The (Rousseau) 6:16, 30
Metamorphosis of Narcissus, The (Dalí) 6:122-3
technique in 6:115
Meyer Madonna, The (Holbein) 2:90
influence in 2:82-3
model for 2:77
Milton (Blake) 4:49
Miners (Van Gogh) 5:77
Misanthrope, The (Bruegel) 2:115
medium for 2:116
Miss Mary Edwards (Hogarth) 8:28
Models, The (Seurat) 5:112-13
study for 5:114
Modern Olympia, A (Cézanne) 5:18, 18
Moïse Kisling (Modigliani) 6:101
Monk by the Sea (Friedrich) 4:80
Monkey (sketch, Hans Cranach) 2:48-9
Monna Vanna (Rossetti) 9:31
Mont Sainte-Victoire (Cézanne) 5:18-19, 33
Monument in a Fertile Country (Klee) 6:62-3
organization of 6:51
Moonrise over the Sea (Friedrich) 4:93
Morning in the Riesengebirge (Friedrich) 4:82-3
Mother Heide (Friedrich) 4:76
Motif of Hammamet (Klee) 6:54
Motley Life (Kandinsky), symbols in 7:18
Moulin Rouge: La Goulue (poster, Toulouse-Lautrec) 8:79, 82
study for 8:83
Mural Painting: Barcelona (Miró) 7:94-5
Murano Altarpiece, The (Bellini) 1:8
Muse Inspiring the Poet, The (Rousseau) 6:17

Music I (Klimt) 9:*88-9*
Musicians, The (Caravaggio) 3:*14*
My Fiancée with Black Gloves (Chagall) 6:*82*
Myself: Portrait-Landscape (Rousseau) 6:*11, 14-15*
 criticism of 6:15
Mystery (Redon) 9:*56*
Mystic Nativity, The (Botticelli) 1:*117, 131*

N

Naked Maja, The (Goya) 4:*14, 15*
 Inquisition and 4:*16, 34, 34*
Nana (Manet) 8:*84*
Nativity, The (Giotto) 1:*24*
Navicella (Giotto) 1:*15*
Nebuchadnezzar (Blake) 4:*52, 59*
Negro Attacked by a Jaguar (Rousseau) 6:*19*
Netherlandish Proverbs (Bruegel) 2:*118-19, 122-3*
 details 2:*118, 119*
 influences in 2:115
 source of 2:*119*
Newton (Blake) 4:*51-2, 58*
Nicholas Lanier (Van Dyck) 3:*80*
Nightmare, The (Fuseli) 6:*70-71*
Noli Me Tangere (Fra Angelico) 1:*60*
Nude in the Bath (Bonnard) 5:*140*
Nude by the Wicker Chair (Munch) 9:*117*
 detail 9:*117*
 obsessions in 9:117
Nüremberg Woman (drawing, Dürer) 2:*37*

O

Oak Tree in the Snow (Friedrich) 4:*82-3*
Oberreid Altarpiece, The (Holbein) 2:*82*
Ognissanti Madonna, The (Giotto) 1:*32*
Ohashi Bridge in the Rain (Hiroshige) 5:*84*
Old Woman Frying Eggs (Velázquez) 3:*50*
Olympia (Manet), Cézanne's parody of 5:*18*
On the Boulevard (Malevich) 7:*54*
Ophelia among the Flowers (Redon) 9:*58-9*
 imagery in 9:52
Orpheus (Redon) 9:*54*

Oscar Wilde (Toulouse-Lautrec) 8:*81*
Ossian (Gérard) 4:*100-101*
Our Bread (Rivera) 8:*120*
Over Vitebsk (Chagall) 6:*88-9*

P

Paean (Riley) 7:*118-19*
 studies for 7:*118*
Painter and his Model, The (Rousseau) 6:*18-19*
Painter and the Pug (Hogarth) 8:*11, 16*
Painter on the Way to Work, The (Van Gogh) 5:*82-3*
Painterly Realism of a Footballer (Malevich) 7:*52*
Painter's Studio, The (Courbet) 8:*48, 54, 54-5, 60-61*
 details 8:*55*
Palladio's Corridor of Thalia (Dalí) 6:*116*
Pandora (Redon), objectivity in 9:52
Panoramic View of the Amstel River Looking Towards Amsterdam (Ruisdael) 3:*112-13*
Paolo and Francesca da Rimini (Rossetti) 9:*19*
Parable of the Blind, The (Bruegel) 2:*111, 117*
 detail 2:*116*
 influence on 2:115
 medium for 2:116
Parade, La (Seurat) 5:*124-5*
Passion scenes from the Maestà (Duccio) 1:*23*
Paul Alexis Reading to Emile Zola (Cézanne) 5:*14*
Paul Signac (drawing, Seurat) 5:*109*
Peaceable Kingdom, The (Hicks) 5:*53*
Peasant, The (Rivera) 8:*115*
Peasant Dance, The (Bruegel) 2:*117, 131*; 8:*53*
Peasant Wedding (Bruegel the Younger) 2:*132-3*
Peasant Woman (drawing, Van Gogh) 5:*82*
Peasant Woman Tying Sheaves (Van Gogh) 9:*116*
Peasants of Flagey Returning from the Fair, Ornans, The (Courbet) 8:*50*
 unsettling elements in 8:50
Pegasus Triumphant (Redon) 9:*50-51*
Pembroke Family, The (Van Dyck) 3:*84*

Penance of St Jerome, The (Cranach) 2:*56*
Père Juniet's Cart (Rousseau) 6:*33*
Père Tanguy (Van Gogh) 5:*88*
Persistence of Memory, The (Dalí) 6:*120-21*
Pesaro Altarpiece (Giovanni Bellini) 1:*78, 79*
Phantom Chariot, The (Dalí) 6:*114*
Philip IV (Velázquez) 3:*51, 68*
Philippe le Roy, Seigneur de Ravels (Van Dyck) 3:*90*
Philosophy (Klimt) 9:*78-9*
Pietà (Bellini) 1:*87*
Pilgrimage of the Soul, The (Bellini) 1:*83*
Pilot's Jetty, Le Havre, The (Pissarro) 5:*114*
Pink Landscape (Riley) 7:*114*
 influence on 7:110
Pity (Blake) 4:*50-51*
Planits (Malevich) 7:*48-9*
Poet Reclining, The (Chagall) 6:*82-3*
Pool of Bethesda (mural, Hogarth) 8:*16, 16*
Pool Surrounded by Trees, A (Ruisdael) 3:*112*
Poor Fisherman, The (Puvis de Chavennes) 9:*70-71*
Pope I (Bacon) 3:*52*
Pope Innocent X (Velázquez) 3:*65*
Pope Paul III (Titian) 3:*52*
Porfiriato (Sequeiros) 8:*132*
Port-en-Bessin (Seurat) 5:*115*
 detail 5:*115*
Port by Moonlight (Friedrich) 4:*76-7*
Port of Naples, The (detail, Bruegel) 2:*108-109*
Portrait of
 Alfred Bruyas (Courbet) 8:*48*
 Ambroise Vollard (Cézanne) 5:*17*
 Arï Redon (Redon) 9:*48*
 Baudelaire (Courbet) 8:*46*
 Delacroix (Géricault) 4:*108*
 Elsbeth Tucher (Dürer) 2:*25*
 Erasmus (Holbein) 2:*78*
 Hans Herbster (Holbein) 2:*77*
 John Wilkes (engraving, Hogarth) 8:*17*
 a Man (Messina) 1:*80*
 a Member of the Artist's Family (Malevich) 7:*55*
 Michael Wolgemut (Dürer) 2:*37*
 Marchesa Elena Grimaldi (Van Dyck) 3:*78, 82, 83*
 Mistress Mills in 1750 (Miró) 7:*90*
 Mme Cézanne (detail, Cézanne) 5:*15*
 Monet (Renoir) 5:*98*
 her Mother (Riley) 7:*108*

 a Princess of the d'Este Family (Pisanello) 9:*52*
 Rossetti (Holman Hunt) 9:*11*
 Thomas Cromwell (Holbein) 2:*80*
 Violette Heymann (Redon) 9:*53*
 detail 9:*53*
 use of flowers in 9:52
 his Wife (Rivera) 8:*110-11*
 a Woman (Rousseau) 6:*14, 26*
 a Young Man (Botticelli) 1:*124*
Postman Roulin, The (Van Gogh) 5:*89*
Potato Eaters, The (Van Gogh) 5:*78, 78*
 use of colour in 5:*82, 82*
Premonition of Civil War (Dalí) 4:*20*
Preparation for the Passover in the Holy Family, The (Rossetti) 9:*19*
Primavera (Botticelli) 1:*109, 115, 116, 120-21*
Prince Balthasar Carlos (Velázquez) 3:*70*
Prince Philip Prosper (Velázquez) 3:*53*
Prince William of Orange and Princess Mary Stuart (Van Dyck) 3:*83*
Princess Poedua (Webber) 5:*68*
Private of the First Division, A (Malevich) 7:*50, 52*
Private Room at the Rat Mort, The (Toulouse-Lautrec) use of paint in 8:*83*
Promenade en Mail Coach à Nice (Toulouse-Lautrec) 8:*76*
Proserpine (Rossetti) 9:*21*
 detail 9:*21*
Protest (Rivera) 8:*121*
Proudhon and his Children (Courbet) 8:*66*
Proverbios (etchings, Goya) 4:*19, 21*
Puberty (Munch) 9:*121*
 obsession in 9:117
Punishment of the Rebels (Botticelli) 1:*110, 111*

Q

Queen Guenevere (Morris) 9:*36*
Queen Henrietta Maria with her Dwarf Sir Jeffrey Hudson (Van Dyck) 3:*93*
Queen Victoria at Osborne (Landseer) 3:*85*

R

Raft of the Medusa, The (Géricault) 4:109, *116*

Raising of Drusiana, The (Giotto) 1:*18-19*

Raising of Lazarus (Caravaggio), models for 2:21

Raising of Lazarus, The (Giotto) 1:*18*

Rake's Progress, The (Hogarth): *In the Debtor's Prison* 8:25
The Madhouse 8:37
purpose of painting 8:15, 20-21
The Tavern Scene 8:24

Ratification of the Treaty of Munster (Terborch) 3:*136*

Reaper, The (Miró) 7:79

Reckless Sleeper, The (Magritte) 6:68-9

Reclining Water Nymph (Cranach) 2:66-7

Red and Blue Horses (Marc) 6:39

Red Oval (Kandinsky) 7:18-19

Red Sphinx (Redon) 9:66

Rehearsal, The (Degas) 10:60

Reinhardt frieze (Munch) 9:*134-5*

Resurrection, The (Grünewald) 4:85

Rest on the Flight into Egypt (Caravaggio) 3:25

Rest on the Flight into Egypt, The (Cima da Coneglione) 1:84

Rest on the Flight into Egypt, The (Cranach) 2:57

Rest on the Flight into Egypt, The (Gentileschi) 3:36-7

Rest on the Flight into Egypt, The (Van Dyck) 3:89

Restaurant de la Sirène, The (Van Gogh) 5:83

Riders on the Beach (Gauguin) 10:61

Rill (Riley) 7:126-7

Rinaldo and Armida (Van Dyck) 3:79, 81

River Landscape (S, van Ruysdael) 3:110

Roast Beef of Old England (Hogarth) *see Calais Gate*

Rock Flora (Klee) 6:66

Roger and Angelica (Redon) 9:63

Rokeby Venus, The (Velázquez) 3:50, 62-3
damaged by Suffragette 9:105, *106*

Rose Return (Riley) 7:131

Rows of Signs (Kandinsky) 7:19

Ruin at Eldena (Friedrich) 4:98-9

Rye Harvest, The (Malevich) 7:56
style of 7:51

S

Sacré Coeur (Lüthi) 6:20

Sacrifice of Abraham, The (Caravaggio) 3:26
sense of violence in 3:18

Saint Augustine (Botticelli) 1:*113*

St Francis (Giovanni Bellini) 1:79, 84, *90*

St Francis Preaching to the Birds (Giotto) 1:*38*

St Francis Receiving Stigmata (illumination) 1:*38, 39*

St Francis Renounces His Earthly Father (Sassetta) 1:*37*

St Francis Renouncing the World (Giotto) 1:*19*

St Jerome in his Study (engraving, Dürer) 2:20

St John the Evangelist on the Island of Patmos (Velázquez) 3:50

St John on Patmos (drawing, Pacheco after Velázquez) 3:44

St Lawrence Distributing Alms (Fra Angelico) 1:65

St Lawrence Receiving the Treasures of the Church (Fra Angelico) 1:64

St Mark Preaching to the Alexandrians (Gentile Bellini) 1:*80-81*

St Peter Preaching (Fra Angelico) 1:51

St Sebastian (Redon) 9:51, 55

St Stephen (woodcut, Cranach) 2:50, *50*

St Stephen and St Lawrence (Frescoes, Fra Angelico) 1:48, *48)*

Salome (illustration, Beardsley) 9:87

Salome (Titian) 9:20

Salon at the Rue Des Moulins, The (Toulouse-Lautrec) 8:96

San Barnarba Altarpiece (Botticelli) 1:*127*

S. Cassiano Altarpiece (Messina) 1:80

San Giobbe Altarpiece (Bellini) 1:79, 81, 85, 92
Venetian touches in 1:85

San Marco Altarpiece (Fra Angelico) 1:51

San Zaccaria Altarpiece (Bellini) 1:97

Sante Croce, Florence:
Altarpiece 1:36
Giotto frescoes in 1:16, *16*
detail 1:*18-19*

Santo reliefs (detail, Donatello) 1:77

Satan, Sin and Death (Blake) 4:51

Saturn Devouring One of his Sons (Goya) 4:33

Scenes from the life of St Francis (Anon) 1:*36*

Scenes from the life of St Nicholas (Fra Angelico) 1:*50-51*

Schéhérazade (costume design, Bakst) 6:77

Scream, The (Munch) 9:111, *122*
effect on emotions 9:114
in *La Revue Blanche* 9:69

Second of May 1808, The (Goya) 4:16, *18-19*, 42
contemporary engraving 4:22

'Seers' (lithograph, Miró) 7:99

self-parody (Munch) 9:*112*

Self-portrait of
Botticelli 1:*107*
Bruegel 12:*115*
Caravaggio 3:*11*
as Bacchus 3:*13*
Courbet 8:43
see also Self-portrait with Black Dog; Self-portrait in Prison
Cranach 2:43, 53
H. Cranach 2:*48*
Delacroix 4:*107*
Dürer 2:*11*, 12, 13, 14, 22, 24
silverpoint 2:12
Friedrich 4:*78*
in sepia 4:76
A. Gentileschi 3:*38*
Ghirlandaio 1:*111*
Gauguin 5:43, *51*, 80, 84; 9:49
final 5:49
first 5:44
Goya 4:*11*
detail 4:*18*
with Dr Arrieta 4:16, *16-17*
Gozzoli 1:49
Holbein 2:75, *81*
Filippino Lippi 1:*112*
Filippo Lippi 1:46
Malevich 6:48-9
Mantegna 1:77
Antonello Messina 1:*80*
Miró, Picasso and 6:77
Munch 9:*107*
Pareja 3:49
Pissarro 5:98
Redon 9:43
Rossetti 9:*12*
Rubens 3:47
Siqueiros 8:*111*
Toulouse-Lautrec 8:*75*
cartoon 8:83
Van Dyck 3:75
as Paris 3:76
Van Gogh 5:75, 79, 85, 97
Velázquez 3:49
with a Black Dog (Courbet) 8:45
as Genitalia (caricature, Klimt) 9:79
in Prison (Courbet) 8:49
with Seven Fingers (Chagall) 6:86

Senecio (Klee) 6:*50*

Servants (Hogarth) 8:*18-19*

Seven Works of Mercy (Caravaggio) 3:37

Shiver (Riley) 7:*121*

Shore at Egmond-aan-Zee (Ruisdael) 3:113

Shore of the Zuider Zee near Naarden, The (Ruisdael) 3:*114-15*

Sick Child, The (Munch) 9:*120*
criticism of 9:114
influence of 9:109

Sigismunda (Hogarth) 8:*17*
directions for selling 8:17
reason for painting 8:17

Simon George of Quocoute (Holbein) 2:*83*
preliminary drawing 2:85

sinopie, by Fra Angelico 1:51, 52

Sir Galahad (illustration, Rossetti) 9:*19*

Sir Henry Guildford (Holbein) 2:*82*

Sir Thomas More (Holbein) 2:*83*, 92

Sistine Chapel: before painting of ceiling 1:*110*
painting of the 1:110-11

Sketches of a Head (Van Dyck) 3:*84-5*

Sky Blue (Kandinsky) 7:34-5
symbols in 7:17

Sleep of Reason Produces Monsters, The (etching, Goya) 4:*17*

Sleepers, The (Courbet) 8:64

Sleeping Gypsy, The (Rousseau) 6:22, *22-3*, *28-9*
details 6:*22*, *23*
sources for 6:22, 23

Sleeping Spinner, The (Courbet) 10:57
purchaser 8:48

Smeralda Bandinelli (Botticelli) 1:*115*

Snake Charmer, The (Rousseau) 6:31

Sofonisba Anguissola (sketch, Van Dyck) 3:80

Soldaderas, Las (Orozco) 8:*134-5*

Soldiers Playing Dice (Le Valentin) 3:36-7

Solitude (Chagall) 6:*94-5*
mood of 6:80

Songes, Les: Portrait of Clavaud (lithograph, Redon) 9:46-7

Songs of Experience (Blake) 4:47, 50, 51

Songs of Innocence (Blake) 4:47, 50
colour quality in 4:50-51
influence on 4:50

Sorrow (drawing, Van Gogh) 5:78

Spain (Dalí) 6:*117*
detail 6:*117*

Spinners, The (Velázquez) 3:*51*

Spirit of the Dead Watching, The (Gauguin) 5:*50-51*

Spirits of Fountain Court, The (Blake) 4:*49*

Stag Hunt, The (Cranach) 2:*60-61*

Stage of Welcome (Rubens) 3:*106*

Stages of Life, The (Friedrich) 4:*81*, 86, *86-7, 96-7*
details 4:*86, 87*
study for 4:*87*
use of colour in 4:*85*

Stanislaw Przybyszewski (Munch) 9:*133*

Starry Night (Van Gogh) 5:*94-5*

Static I (Riley) 7:*122*

Stéphane Mallarmé (Munch) 9:*68, 111*

Still-life (Caravaggio) 3:*18, 21*

Still-life (Klee) 6:*51*, 52

Still-life (Zeuxis) 3:*21*

Still-life with Apples and Pomegranate (Courbet) 8:*51*

Still-life with Basket of Apples (Cézanne) 5:*22*

Still-life with a Lobster (de Heem) 5:*20*

Still-life with an Old Shoe (Miró), symbolism in 7:*79-80*

Still-life with Onions (Cézanne) 5:*19*

Stoclet Frieze (Klimt) 9:*80*
Tree of Life, working drawing 9:*80*

Stone Breaker, The (Seurat) 5:*112*

Stonebreakers, The (copy after Courbet) 8:*52*

Stone Steps in the Hospital Garden (Van Gogh) 5:*83*

Straw Manikin, The (tapestry cartoon, Goya) 4:*19*

Streak 2 (Riley) 7:*128-9*

Strozzi Altarpiece (Orcagna) 1:*17*

Studio, The (Courbet), method of painting 8:*50*

Study for a Head (drawing, Velázquez) 3:*51*

Study for the Models (Seurat) 5:*114*

Study for the Trivulzio Equestrian Monument (Leonardo) 6:*116*

Sun, The (Munch) 9:*126-7*

Sun-dappled Trees at the Edge of a Stream (drawing, Ruisdael) 3:*115*

Sunflowers (Van Gogh) 5:*92*
use of colour in 5:*84*

Sunlit Grain Field (Ruisdael see *Coup de Soleil, Le*

Sunlight Grain Field on the Banks of a Coast, A (Ruisdael) 3:*125*

Sunset on Lake Geneva (Courbet) 8:*51*

Supper at Emmaus, The (Caravaggio) 3:*19, 22, 22-3, 28-9*
details 3:*22-3*

Suprematist Composition (Malevich) 7: *64-5*

Suprematist Composition: Airplane Flying (Malevich) 7:*60*

Suprematist Composition: Red Square and Black Square (Malevich) 7:*58*

Suprematist Composition: White on White (Malevich) 7:*67*

Suprematist Painting 1916 (Malevich) 7:*53, 62-3*
detail 7:*53*

Surprised! (Tropical Storm with a Tiger) (Rousseau) 5:*53*; 6:*24-5*

Surrender of Breda, The (Velázquez) 3:*48, 52-3, 58-9*

Swing, The (tapestry, Goya) 4:*13*

Swinging (Kandinsky) 7:*30-31*

T

Tahitian Girl with a Flower (Gauguin) 5:*58*

Taking of Constantinople, The (Delacroix) 4:*128*

Taste of the Town, The (Hogarth) 8:*13*, 13-14

Tauromaquia (etchings, Goya) 4:*19*, 21

Temptation of St Anthony, The (detail, Bosch) 4:*20*

Temptation of St Anthony, The (engraving, Bruegel) 2:*114*

Temptation of St Anthony, The (Dalí) 6:*124-5*

Temptation of St Anthony, The (Ernst) 6:*140*

Terrace Plaza Mural (Miró) 7:*80, 80-81*

Third of May 1808, The (Goya) 4:*16, 22, 22-3, 30-31, 42*
details 4:*23*

Thomas Boleyn (drawing, Holbein) 2:*85*

Thomas Coram (Hogarth) 8:*19*, 21

Thomas Howard, 2nd Earl of Arundel and his Wife (Van Dyck) 3:*77*

Thoth (sculpture, Egyptian) 6:*52*

Three Brides, The (Toorop) 5:*110*

Three Candles, The (Chagall) 6:*97*

Three Half-Timbered Houses (drawing, Ruisdael) 3:*115*

Times of Day (Friedrich): *Evening* 4:*83*
Morning 4:*83*

To Russia, Asses and Others (Chagall) 6:*87*

Toll House, The (Rousseau) 6:*13*

Tom Thumb (engraving, Hogarth) 8:*14*

Tonal landscape study, France (Riley) 7:*109*

Train in Murnau (Kandinsky) 7:*22-3*

Transfiguration (Bellini) 1:*79, 84, 91*

Trellis, The (Courbet) 8:*63*

Trench, The (mural, Orozco) 8:*111*

Triadic Ballet (sketch, Schlemmer) 7:*36, 37*

Triple Portrait of a Jeweller (Lotto) 3:*87*

Triumph of Riches, The (copy, Holbein) 2:*80-81*

Triumphal Arch of Maximilian 2:*38*
Dürer collaboration on 2:*16*

Triumphal Procession (woodcut, Dürer) 2:*38-9*

Tropical Forest with Monkeys (Rousseau) 6:*21*
detail 6:*21*

Tropical Storm with a Tiger (Rousseau) *see Surprised! Tropical Storm with a Tiger*
triptychs, of San Pietro Martire 1:*46*

Tudor Dynasty (copy, Holbein) 2:*80*, 80, *86-7*
changes to 2:*87*

Tulla Larsen (Munch) 9:*112*

Tune of the Seven Towers, The (Rossetti) 9:*29*

Turn in the Road, The (Cézanne) 5:*19*, 20

Twelve Tribes of Israel (stained glass, Chagall) 6:*80*
Benjamin 6:*99*
Joseph 6:*98*

Twittering Machine, The (Klee) 6:*59*

Two Gentlemen of Verona (Holman Hunt), model for Sylvia 9:*14*

Two Majas on a Balcony (Goya) 4:*27*

Two Majesties (Gérôme), Rousseau and 6:*23*

Two Monkeys (Bruegel) 2:*115*

Two Tahitian Women on a Beach (Gauguin) 5:*59*

Two Tax Gatherers (Van Reymerswaele) 2:*133*

Two Watermills and an Open Sluice (Ruisdael) 3:*124*

U

Unicorns, The (Moreau) 6:*84*

Unknown Lady (Holbein) 2:*99*

Unknown Lady (drawing, Holbein) 2:*85*

Unknown Lady with a Squirrel (Holbein) 2:*93*

V

Vairumati (Gauguin) 5:*54*

Vampire, The (Munch) 9:*111*

Vase of Flowers, The (Rousseau) 6:*18*

Venus and Cupid as the Honey Thief (Cranach) 2:*9*

Venus and the Graces (Botticelli) 1:*114*

'Venus pudica' (sculpture) 1:*119*

Vessels in a Breeze (Ruisdael) 3:*123*

Victorious Cupid (Caravaggio) 3:*13, 19*

View of Arco (Dürer) 2:*23*

View of Cairo (Gentile Bellini) 1:*79*

View of Haarlem with the Bleaching Grounds (Ruisdael) 3:*130*

Villa Medici (oil sketch, Velázquez) 3:*47*

Village Landscape in Morning Light (Friedrich) 4:*92*

Village Market, The (Bruegel the Younger) 2:*134-5*

Village Schoolteacher, The (Rivera) 8:*135*

Village in Winter, A (Ruisdael) 3:*113*

Vincent's Chair (Van Gogh) 5:*86*

Virgin and Child (Bellini) 1:*82*

Virgin and Child with a Cake (Cranach) 2:*52*

Virgin and Child with St John the Baptist and a Female Saint (Bellini) 1:*84*
detail 1:*85*

Virgin and Child with Saints Dominic, John the Baptist, Peter Martyr and Thomas Aquinas (detail, Fra Angelico) 1:*52-3*

Virgin of the Grapes, The (Cranach) 2:*58*

Virgin with the Pear (Dürer) 2:*19*

Virgin in the Tree, The (etching, Klee) 6:*50*

Vision After the Sermon (Gauguin) 5:*51, 52, 56*; 9:*69*

Vision of Joachim, The (Giotto) 1:*22*
details 1:*23*

Vision of St Bernard (Filippino Lippi) 1:*112*

W

Waitress, The (Manet) 5:99

Wall of the Moon (Miró) 7:81

Wall of the Sun (Miró) 7:81

Wanderer Looking over a Sea of Fog (Friedrich) 4:90

War (Rousseau) 6:15

Water Serpents II (Women Friends) (Klimt) 9:96

Waterfall, A (Ruisdael) 3:127

Water-mill at Gillingham (Constable) 3:116

Waterseller of Seville, The (Velázquez) 3:51, 57

Watzmann, The (Friedrich) 4:95

Wedding Dance in the Open Air (Bruegel) 2:114

Wedding Feast, The (Bruegel) 2:130

Wedding of St George and Princess Sabra (Rossetti) 9:20, 28

Wehlsch Pirg (Dürer) 2:14-15

Where (Riley) 7:115

Where Do We Come From? What Are We? Where Are We Going To? (Gauguin) 5:54, 54-5, 62-3
details 5:55

Whim of the Young St Francis to become a Soldier, The (Sassetta) 1:36

White Crucifixion (Chagall) 6:84
mood of 6:80

White Horse, The (Gauguin) 5:64

Who Shall Deliver Me? (Khnoppf) 9:141

Wild Flowers in a Long-necked Vase (Redon) 9:51

William Warham, Archbishop of Canterbury (drawing, Holbein) 2:84

Windmill and Cottages near a High Footbridge, A (drawing, Ruisdael) 3:114-15

Windmill at Wijk bij Duurstede, The (Ruisdael) 3:112, 128

Windsor drawings, (Holbein) 2:84, 84-5

Winnowers, The (Courbet) 8:59

Winter in Kragerø (Munch) 9:128

Winter Scene, Skaters (Avercamp) 2:116

With the Eagles (Klee) 6:56-7

Woman with Buckets and Child (Malevich), influences on 7:51

Woman with a Coffee Pot (Cézanne) 5:20

Woman Killed by a Lioness (Matout), Rousseau and 6:22

Woman, known as Mrs Holland, A (Hilliard) 10:51

Woman Powdering Herself (Seurat) 5:111

Woman in the Setting Sun (Friedrich) 4:84

Woman at the Window (Friedrich) 4:80

Woman at the Window at Figueras (Dalí) 6:119

Women of Algiers (Delacroix) 4:116-17

Women and Birds in the Moonlight (Miró) 7:93

Woodcutter, The (Malevich) 7:50

Woodpecker tapestry (Morris) 9:37

Workers Returning Home (Munch) 9:117, 129

Y

Yellow Christ, The (Gauguin) 5:57

Yellow House, The (Van Gogh) 5:86

Yellow Painting (Kandinsky) 7:32-2

Yellow Parallelogram on White (Malevich) 7:66

Young Ladies on the Banks of the Seine (Courbet) 8:62

Young Man with a Medal (Botticelli) 1:125

Young Woman with a Mirror (Bellini) 1:81, 85, 99

Yvette Guilbert Taking a Curtain Call (Toulouse-Lautrec), method of painting 8:83

Z

Zapatista Landscape – The Guerilla (Rivera) 8:114

Zing I (Riley) 7:125

Glossary

absorbent ground The surface of a canvas which has been treated with chalk to enable it to absorb the oil from paint, so leaving a matt finish.

Abstract Art Art that does not try to represent the appearance of objects, real or imaginary. An old tradition in the decorative arts and in Islamic art – according to the Koran, the human figure may not be depicted – abstract art emerged in Western art in the early 20th century in works by artists such as Mondrian, Kandinsky and Malevich.

Abstract Expressionism School of almost automatic painting developed in New York in the 1940s, marked by spontaneous expression through abstract forms. Jackson Pollock was its most famous exponent.

Academic Art Formal, usually **Classical** art inspired by, or devoted to, the axioms of the Academies that flourished in France, England and other countries from the 17th to 19th centuries. See also **Classical Art, Romantic Art.**

academy figure Depiction of a nude figure used for teaching purposes and not as a work of art.

acrylic paint Quick-drying synthetic paint first exploited by artists in the late 1940s. Because it can be used as a thin wash or as a very thick **impasto**, acrylic paint can be used like both traditional **watercolours** and **oil paints.**

Action Painting This term was used first

in 1952 to describe splashing and dribbling paint on canvas, designed to allow the unconscious mind to produce a work of art.

Aestheticism Theory that the beauty of a work of art justifies its existence – often summarized as 'art for art's sake'. Ideas taken up in the 19th century by the Aesthetic Movement.

after In imitation of the style of, as in 'after Raphael'.

altarpiece Screen, painting or wall behind a church altar.

American Abstract Artists' Group Founded in New York in 1939 to promote abstract art in America. Founder members included Diller, Bolotowsky and Greene.

Anamorphosis Painting or drawing of an object distorted in such a way that the image is only lifelike when seen from a particular angle or by a special mirror. The skull in the foreground of *The Ambassadors* (1533) by Holbein is a famous example.

Archaic Art Art of Greece from about 650 BC. This era is usually said to end in 480 BC when the Persians sacked Athens. Followed by the **Classical** era.

Armory Show International Exhibition of Modern Art in New York held in 1913, which showed modern works by, among others, Duchamp, the **Symbolists, Impressionists** and **Post-**

Impressionists, and challenged the **Representational** tradition in the USA.

Art Deco Decorative style popular in 1920s and 1930s. Geometric shapes, smooth lines and streamlining were features of this style.

Art Nouveau Style that flourished from about 1890 to World War 1. Characteristics included asymmetry and flowing lines.

Ashcan School A group, led by Robert Henri, of 19th-20th century American **Realist** painters interested in depicting the sordid side of city life, especially New York.

attribution Term used when assigning a work to an artist when the authorship cannot be definitely stated.

Barbizon School A mid-19th century group of landscape painters who depicted realistic peasant life. The group worked from the village of Barbizon in the Forest of Fontainebleau, and its chief members were Millet, Theodore Rousseau and Diaz.

Baroque The style that emerged from 16th century **Mannerism** and lasted, with many modifications, well into the 18th century. It was concentrated in the High Baroque in Rome from 1620-80, where Bernini united the arts of architecture, painting and sculpture in his work. The blend of light, colour, **illusionism** and movement was intended to overwhelm the spectator by a direct emotional appeal. The Baroque had little appeal in northern Europe but was used to glorify the French monarchy at Versailles. In the 18th century many south German palaces and abbeys emulated this form of Baroque.

Bauhaus Influential German school of architecture and design founded by the architect Walter Gropius at Weimar, Germany, in 1919.

Biedermeier Style predominant in Germany and Austria from 1815 to 1848, emphasizing a solid, totally unheroic bourgeois comfort.

Biomorphic form Abstract form derived from organic shapes.

bon dieuserie (French: good Goddery). Over-sentimental religious art from France and Belgium.

bust Painting or sculpture showing only the head and shoulders of a sitter.

camera obscura (Latin: dark chamber) Device used as an aid to accuracy in drawing, consisting of an arrangement of lenses in a darkened tent or box, invented in the 16th century. Much used by Vermeer and by Canaletto.

capriccio (Italian: caprice) Any fantasy, but usually an imaginary landscape consisting of identifiable buildings in bizarre combinations.

caricature Drawing of a person with exaggerated features which make the person appear ridiculous.

cartoon A full-size drawing used to transfer a design to the painting surface, now mainly referring to humorous drawings or animated films.

chiaroscuro (Italian: light-dark) Term used to describe dramatic effects of shade and light in painting, as in the works of Caravaggio and his followers.

Cinquencento (Italian: five hundred) The 16th century, used especially in relation to Italian art.

Classic, Classical Term describing the ordered harmony associated with the art of Ancient Greece and Rome, long considered the ideal art forms. It is also used in a wider sense as the antithesis of **Romanticism,** denoting an art that adheres to accepted canons of beauty and –

in most cases – to a particular type of subject matter, rather than relying on personal inspiration. See also **Academic Art, Romantic Art.**

collage (French: sticking) A picture built up from pieces of paper, cloth or other matter stuck onto a canvas.

Colour Field Painting Description for some of the work of the **Abstract Expressionists,** especially Newman and Rothko, who were interested in the effects created by large areas of colour.

composition Arrangement of objects or figures in a picture to please the eye and make an effective whole.

continuous narrative or **representation** One picture showing several scenes of a complete story, such as the martyrdom of a saint or the life of Christ.

contrapposto Pose in which one part of the body is twisted in the opposite direction from the rest of the body. Much used by Michelangelo.

Constructivism A Russian **abstract** movement headed by Vladimir Tatlin. Materials used included wire, glass and sheet metal.

conversation piece Group portrait with the subjects in an informal, usually domestic, setting. Particularly popular with 18th-century English artists.

craquelure (French: cracking) Fine cracks on the surface of an old painting.

Cubism Movement that revolutionized 20th-century painting and sculpture by rejecting the **naturalistic** tradition. Inspired by Cézanne's last works, Picasso and Braque abandoned attempts to represent things as they actually appear in favour of a more intellectual approach to form and colour, as seen in their superimposed and interlocking geometric planes. First seen in Paris in 1907, it attracted much opposition. Painters like Malevich and Mondrian took Cubism to its **abstract** conclusion. See also **Abstract Art, Orphism.**

Dada (French: hobbyhorse) A nihilistic precursor of **Surrealism** invented in Zurich in 1915, it set out to be anti-art and irrational. One of its most famous products was Marcel Duchamp's *Mona Lisa* with a moustache, and a typical event was a lecture given by 38 lecturers

simultaneously. It had died out by 1923. See also **Surrealism.**

decorative arts Arts in which decoration is applied to a functional object – for example, hand-painting on fine porcelain – as opposed to the fine arts of painting and sculpture.

diptych A picture in two, normally hinged, parts, usually of a religious nature such as an **altarpiece.** Similarly, a triptych is a three-part picture, and a polyptych has more than three parts.

distemper Powdered colour mixed with **size** to make an inexpensive, impermanent paint **medium.**

drôlerie Humorous picture, or the grotesque drawings in the margins of medieval manuscripts.

Dugento (Italian: two hundred) The 13th century, usually used in relation to Italian art.

eclecticism The practice of selecting different styles or features from various artists and combining them.

engraving Term denoting both the process of cutting a design into wood or metal and the print taken from the plate or block so cut. The former refers properly to only two processes of printmaking – metal engraving or line engraving, and wood engraving. The latter is a **relief** method in which negative parts of the design are cut away from a block of hardwood, leaving raised lines for inking. Metal engraving, with hard, clear lines, is an **intaglio** process in which the design is cut into a smooth metal plate with an engraving tool, and paper is pressed into the ink furrows. Metal engraving was both an independent art form and the main method of reproductive printing from the 16th to 19th centuries.

etching The process of biting out a design in a metal plate with acid, also the resulting print.

Expressionism A quality of expressive emphasis and distortion that may be found in art of any period. More specifically it is a term used for northern European, 20th-century art, deriving from Van Gogh, especially German art. The *Brucke* and the *Blaue Reiter* are two principal subgroups, major artists being Beckman, Ensor and Nolde.

fancy picture Idealized rural **genre** picture, most notably in 18th-century England. Thomas Gainsborough was an exponent.

Fauvists (French: 'wild beast') A group of artists associated with Matisse from 1905 to 1907, noted for their luminous use of colour. See also **Cubism.**

fête champêtre Genre painting set in an idealized garden or parkland. Giorgione's *Fête Champêtre* is the best-known Renaissance example. The genre's popularity continued until the 18th century with Antoine Watteau's fêtes galantes.

Figurative Art Art representing figures or other recognizable objects. Also known as Representational Art. See also **Abstract Art.**

fine arts See **decorative arts.**

Fontainebleau School Name given to artists associated with the French court of Francis I in the 16th century, mainly Italian Mannerist painters like Giovanni Battista Rosso and Francesco Primaticcio. See also **Mannerism.**

foreshortening Perspective applied to an object – for example, an arm is foreshortened when it is painted pointing directly out of the picture so that only the hand can be seen.

folk art Art based on the traditional designs of a particular country.

fresco (Italian: fresh) Wall-painting using water-based paint on lime plaster. For the true or *buon fresco* method, perfected in Italy in the 16th century, the wall is first rough plastered, then a coat, known as the *arriciato,* is applied on which the outlines of the design or cartoon are drawn. Fresh plaster mixed with lime covers one day's work area and then the painting is done with pigments mixed with plain water, while this layer, the *intonaco,* is still damp. Frescoes are more suited to dry than to damp climates.

Futurism Movement founded in Italy in 1909 by the poet Marinetti, concerned with fusing modern technology with art. The first exhibition in Milan in 1911 was followed by a tour through northern Europe. It contemptuously rejected 'museum' art. Boccioni was a notable Futurist. See also **Dada.**

genre In general terms, any type of art – landscape, portraits, etc. – but normally applied to paintings of everyday life. Most notable examples occur in 17th-century Dutch art.

gesso The bright white ground used in **tempera** and **oil** paintings.

gilding Method of applying precious metals such as gold and silver to another material. The precious metal is held in place with **size.**

Golden Mean or Golden Section Near mystical definition of a line divided in such a way that the smaller part is to the larger as the larger is to the whole, in practice on the ratio 8:13.

Gothic Style of architecture and painting that dominated Europe from the mid-12th to the 16th century. Characterized by pointed arches in architecture, in other arts by its rejection of Renaissance humanism, as in the work of Grünewald and Notke. See also **Classic** and **Renaissance.**

gouache Opaque, fast-drying **watercolour** paint, once widely used by manuscript illuminators and French watercolourists.

Grand Manner In **Academic Art,** the only way to portray themes from the Bible or ancient history was this elevated, heroic style of **history painting.** Sir Joshua Reynolds was a notable exponent.

graphic art Art which depends less on colour than on line, such as engraving.

grisaille Painting executed entirely in monochrome shades of grey.

grotesque A form of fanciful decoration dominated by linked festoons and decorative frames containing **figurative** or floral ornaments. In the 16th century, Raphael and his followers were inspired by the recently discovered 'grotta', meaning caves, of the Emperor Nero's Golden House in Rome. Only later did the term come to mean bizarre or abnormal.

ground The surface on which a design or painting is made.

hatching Shading carried out in parallel lines, a series of fine lines being laid close together.

herm Sculpted head or bust on top of a tapering, rectangular column. Also known as term.

High Renaissance The period from approximately 1495 to 1520 when **Renaissance** art attained a perfect balance between the ideal and the real in the works of Leonardo, Michelangelo and above all Raphael. See also **Mannerism, Renaissance.**

History painting Pictures of real or imaginary ancient historical scenes. In **Academic Art,** the first in the hierarchy of types of subject.

hot colour tone Colours and tones at the red end of the spectrum.

Hudson River School Group of mid-19th century American landscape painters, including Thomas Cole and Asher B. Durand.

icon Image of saint or other religious figure particularly applied to Russian and Greek Orthodox images.

iconography Branch of art history dealing with the subject matter of **Figurative Art.**

illumination Decoration of manuscripts, with borders or ornamental letters, especially common in medieval Europe.

illusionism Use of virtuoso techniques such as **perspective** and **foreshortening** to make a painted object seem three-dimensional; as in the paintings of the **Baroque** era. See also **trompe l'oeil.**

imago pietatis (Latin: image of pity). Depiction of the dead Christ standing in the tomb.

impasto (Italian: paste) Describes the thickness of paint on a canvas or panel, suitable only to oil paints or acrylics.

Impressionism The most important artistic movement of the 19th century, originating in the 1860s. Influenced by scientific findings that colour was not inherent in an object, but the outcome of the way light reflects from it, the Impressionists reacted against **Academic** doctrines and **Romantic** ideas alike, trying to depict life in an objective manner. Monet, Renoir, Sisley, Pissaro, Cézanne and others held the first of eight Impressionist Exhibitions in 1874. At first generally attacked and mocked for the flickering touches with which they applied paint in small brightly coloured dabs, they caused painters everywhere to lighten their palettes.

intaglio Concave 'relief' formed by cutting areas out of a surface.

International Gothic Essentially a courtly style of painting and sculpture that flourished in the late 14th and early 15th centuries, marked by a refined elegance and an interest in secular subjects, as in the works of the Limbourg brothers.

intimisme Domestic interior scenes rendered in **Impressionist** style.

intonaco See **fresco.**

Jugendstil German term for **Art Nouveau** derived from the review *Die Jugend* founded in Munich in 1896.

Junk Art Modern art forms using débris for artistic purposes.

Kinetic Art (Greek: moving) Art based on the idea that light and movement can create a work of art. Objects may be made to gyrate or create patterns of light and shadow.

limner See **miniature.**

linocut A **relief** printing process begun in the 20th century using thick linoleum, and allowing bold images to be cut in a negative form for printing.

lithography A method of surface printing in which a design is drawn or painted directly on to a limestone block or metal plate. It was invented in 1798 by Aloys Senefelder.

local colour The actual colour of an object, uninfluenced by reflected light or colour.

Luminists American landscape painters of the mid-19th century. Their concern with light and atmosphere connects them with the **Barbizon School** and **Impressionism.** Cole, Lane and Durand were all Luminists.

maestà (Italian: majesty) Describes a work of art portraying the Virgin and Child enthroned, surrounded by saints or angels.

Mannerism The dominant style in

European art from about 1520 to 1600. Characterized by elongated or otherwise unnatural figures, it was a self-conscious reaction against the serene **Classicism** of the **High Renaissance.** See also **Renaissance.**

masses The fundamental shapes to which paintings, sculptures or buildings can be reduced.

Master of Term used to label anonymous artists who seem to have a distinct style; the name usually refers to their most famous work.

masterpiece Work of generally acknowledged greatness, or the greatest work of a particular artist.

mastic Resin from trees, used to make varnish and paint **media.**

medium The physical material of which a work of art is made: oil paint, clay, ink, wood, etc.

Metaphysical Art The movement founded by Giorgio de Chirico in 1918, now seen as a bridge between a certain type of **Romanticism** and **Surrealism.**

miniature Very small painting, usually a portrait. The artist is called a limner.

Minimal Art Type of **Abstract Art** that uses only very basic, strictly geometric shapes and flat colours, free of personal overtones.

montage (French: mounting) Picture made by arranging images from newsprint or photography. Main reason for the choice of images is the subject matter. See also **collage.**

mosaic Picture or decorative pattern made by setting small fragments of marble, glass or ceramic materials into cement or plaster.

mural A painting or decoration on a wall. See also **fresco.**

Naive Art Painting in a style that looks untrained or child-like, often rejecting perspective and tending to use bright colours, as with Rousseau.

Naturalism The representation of objects in an accurate, objective and unstylized way. See also **Realism.**

Nazarenes A group of German painters

active in Rome in the early 19th century who advocated an art based on the inspiration of primitive Christianity, led by Overbeck and Pforr. See also **Pre-Raphaelite Brotherhood.**

Neo-Classicism The dominant style in the late 18th and early 19th centuries, notable for its severely **classical** forms and high moral ideas, in reaction against **Rococo.** It was initially inspired by archaeological discoveries at Pompeii.

Neo-Impressionism A development of **Impressionism,** also called **Divisionism** or **Pointillism,** pioneered by Seurat and employing small touches of pure colour so that they mix not on the canvas but in the viewer's eye. See also **Impressionism.**

Neo-Plasticism An extension of **Cubism,** also called *De Stijl,* founded by Mondrian, in which the action of colour and forms was reduced to utter simplicity by adherence to geometric forms. See also **Cubism.**

Neue Sachlichkeit (German: new objectivity) A group of German painters active in the 1920s and 1930s, whose work made strong social comments. Dix and Grosz were among its leaders.

New York School Group of artists based in New York in the mid-20th century, who wanted to discover a uniquely American form of artistic expression. Members of the school include Pollock, Rothko and Still.

Nocturne A night scene – a term first used by James McNeill Whistler for his paintings.

ochre Name of **pigments** made from natural earths.

oil paint Paint produced by mixing **pigment** and a medium of drying oils; the dominant **medium** in Western painting from the late **Renaissance** to the present day.

Op Art Painting, particularly that of the 1960s, which depends on dazzling optical effects to create visual illusions. Vasarely and Riley were among its leading exponents.

Orphism Term coined by Apollinaire in 1912 to describe a development of **Cubism** pioneered by Robert Delauney. It was mainly concerned with the primacy of colour over form.

painterly Technical term meaning the opposite of linear – Botticelli was a linear painter, Titian a painterly one.

palette The surface on which an artist sets out his paint, and so the range of colours used by an artist.

papier collé (French: glued paper) Type of **collage,** invented by Braque and Picasso, which is formed from layers of paper glued to a **ground.**

pastel A picture executed with crayon sticks made of coloured powder that has been mixed with gum and moulded into finger shapes.

pastiche Imitation or forgery which combines sections of various works of one artist to produce a supposedly original work by that artist.

Pastoral Idealized landscape painting, often influenced by pastoral poetry and populated with mythological beings.

pendant paintings Companion paintings meant to be hung together.

pentimento (Italian: repent) An alteration made by the artist while painting which later shows through the new work.

perspective Means of representing three-dimensional forms on a flat two-dimensional surface, invented in the 15th century. See also **vanishing point.**

Picturesque Aesthetic attitude, common in 18th-century Britain, which found delight in ruined buildings, wild or irregular landscape. Only later did it come to mean 'pretty'.

pietà (Italian: pity) Sculpture or painting of the Virgin Mary supporting the dead Christ on her lap.

pigment Mineral or organic, coloured material which is mixed with a **medium** – for example, oil – to produce paint.

plein-air (French: open air) Paintings done outside rather than in the studio. A central feature of **Impressionism.**

Pointillism See **Neo-Impressionism.**

polyptich See **diptych.**

Pop Art Art movement originating in the 1950s and drawing its imagery from popular culture and commercial art. Andy Warhol's famous paintings of soup cans are typical images.

portrait Likeness of a person or animal, worked in any **medium.**

Post-Impressionism Term referring to the art of Cézanne, Van Gogh, Seurat and Gauguin and first used by Roger Fry, the English critic, in 1910. See also **Impressionism.**

Post-Painterly Abstraction Group of abstract artists working in the 1960s who reacted against the extreme subjectivity of **Abstract Expressionism** to create more objective paintings. Members of this **School** include Noland, Stella, Kelly and Olitski.

Precisionism American style of painting of the 1920s, in which urban and industrial scenes were painted in a precise, simplified way. Precisionist artists include Demuth and Spencer.

Pre-Raphaelite Brotherhood (PRB) Short-lived (1848-54) group of young British painters formed with the aim of reviving what they considered the high moral tone of painting before Raphael. Millais, Collinson Stephens and Rossetti were among the founder-members. The movement proved very influential. See also **Nazarenes.**

primary colours Red, yellow and blue; by mixing them, all the other colours can be made.

priming A layer, or layers, of material applied to a canvas or other painting **support** in preparation for painting.

Primitive (1) Netherlandish and Italian painters working before about 1500. (2) Unsophisticated, **naive art** produced by amateur, self-taught painters – for example, Edward Hicks and John Kane.

Prix de Rome (French: Rome prize) Four-year scholarship for study in Rome awarded by the French Academy. Notable winners were David and Ingres.

props Objects or costumes that identify the characters portrayed in a painting.

putto (Italian: little boy) Plump, naked, cupid-like children often featured in Italian art of the 15th and 16th centuries. The plural is putti.

Quattrocento (Italian: four hundred) The 15th century, used especially when referring to that century's Italian art and literature. See also **Renaissance.**

Realism Fidelity to natural, sometimes depressing, appearances dating back to Gustave Courbet in the 1850s. See also **Naturalism** and **Impressionism.**

Regionalism Movement in American art during the 1930s. The style was often conservative and aimed to celebrate small-town, rural America. Members of the school included Thomas Hart Benton and Grant Wood.

relief Carving or moulding in which the design projects from, or is sunk into, the surface, the degree of projection varying from low relief to high relief.

Renaissance Art (French: rebirth) Art of the period from 1400 to 1520 but sometimes traced back to Giotto (c.1267-1337). During the 14th century, Italian art moved towards greater realism. Spurred in the 15th century by the rediscovery of ancient **classical** art, it reached its climax from 1500 to 1520 with Raphael, Leonardo da Vinci and Michelangelo. It then spread outwards to Northern Europe, where it is called the Northern Renaissance. See also **Gothic** and **Mannerism.**

Representational Art See **Figurative Art.**

Rocky Mountain School American artists of the 19th century who painted the mountains. Leading artists were Bierstadt and Moran.

Rococo Frothy, elegant style developed out of **Baroque** early in the 18th century, Boucher and Fragonard being typical Rococo artists. See also **Baroque** and **Neo-Classicism.**

Romanesque Art Style of art and especially of architecture prevailing in the 11th and 12th centuries in Europe, characterized by its massive stone vaults. See also **Gothic.**

Romanticism Intellectual and artistic movement flourishing from about 1780 to 1840, in which the imagination and intuition predominated. Fired by the writings of men like Rousseau, Byron and Goethe, painters turned with new enthusiasm and vision to nature and to historical scenes. Turner, Friedrich and Delacroix were typical painters of the Romantic period. See also **Academic Art, Classicism.**

sacra conversazione (Italian: holy conversation). Representation of the Madonna and Child with angels, painted as a group united by some common action in a single scene.

Salon The annual art exhibition held in the Louvre of the French academy, which originated in the 17th century. The *Salon des Réfusés* was established by Emperor Napoleon III after protests at the number of paintings rejected by the increasingly conservative jury.

sanguine Red chalk, one of the most common materials used by drawing.

School Group of painters connected by style, period or a specific town or country – for example **Rocky Mountain School, Ashcan School.** Also used to describe artists working with a master – for example, School of Titian.

Secession or Sezession Name taken by several groups of artists in Germany and Austria at the end of the 19th century who broke away from traditional **academic** institutions. Klimt was a leader in Vienna.

sfumato (Italian: smoke) Tones blended with imperceptibly subtle transitions, as in the works of Leonardo da Vinci.

size A form of glue used to **prime** canvases or panels.

Social Realism Painting in **Realist** style in which the subject has overtly political or social meanings, not to be confused with Socialist Realism: official Soviet state art.

staffage Inessential figures in landscape. Sometimes painted by another, specialist artist.

stippling Technique of shading in drawing and painting, using closely spaced dots rather than lines.

still-life Painting of inanimate objects, such as fruit or flowers.

stucco Light plaster, mixed with powdered marble, used as decoration on buildings. Used to its fullest extent during the **Mannerist, Baroque** and **Rococo** periods.

Superrealism British and American style of sculpture and painting of the 1960s in which the subject matter was reproduced very exactly with a smooth, featureless surface. Because these works of art resemble photography, the style is sometimes known as Photorealism. Chuck Close and Duane Hanson are members of this school.

support The untreated surface to which paint is applied.

Surrealism Originally a literary movement, inaugurated in 1924, it sought to reveal the reality behind appearances, especially in dreams. Hence the use of bizarre dream imagery, automatism and **symbolism,** under the influence of Freudian ideas. Magritte, Dali, Ernst and Miró were prominent surrealists. See also **Dada, Metaphysical Art** and **Symbolism.**

symbolism The representation of something immaterial by a material object – ripe fruit representing sensual pleasure.

Symbolism It started as a French literary movement of the 1880s inspired by writers like Baudelaire and his 'Fleurs du Mal', in reaction against **Impressionism** and **Realism.** Literary painters such as Moreau and Puvis de Chavennes used the striking imagery of the Symbolists – the severed head and the *femme fatale.* Painters like Gauguin and Van Gogh took a more formal, stylized aproach. See also **Surrealism.**

tempera Paint using egg as the **medium,** superseded for the most part by **oil paint** during the **Renaissance.**

Tenebrists Caravaggio and his 17th-

century Dutch, Neapolitan and Spanish followers, and La Tour in France, who painted interior scenes dramatically lit by candles or torches.

term See **herm.**

tondo (Italian: round) Circular painting or sculpture.

tone Term describing the degree of darkness or lightness of a colour.

tooth The degree of roughness of canvas or other support.

Trecento (Italian: three hundred) the 14th century in Italian art.

triptych See **diptych.**

trompe l'oeil (French: deceive the eye) The skill used to make a painted object appear to be a real, three-dimensional one. See also **Illusionism.**

underpainting Early stage in oil painting when the design and colour tones are worked out on the canvas.

value The gradations in **tone** seen on any solid object under light.

vanishing point The point on the horizon at which receding parallel lines seem to meet and disappear. See also **perspective.**

vanitas work (Italian: vanity) Still-life of a collection of objects meant to symbolize the brief span and uncertainty of human life – for example, skulls, clocks, smoking candles, petals falling from flowers. Vanitas elements can also be found as details in other paintings.

viewpoint Position from which a scene is depicted by an artist.

wash A thin, usually broadly applied, layer of transparent **pigment** such as **watercolour** or ink.

watercolour A pigment bound with gum and diluted with water, used to create translucent effects.